# From Saint-Domingue to New Orleans

Southern Dissent

UNIVERSITY PRESS OF FLORIDA

Florida A&M University, Tallahassee
Florida Atlantic University, Boca Raton
Florida Gulf Coast University, Ft. Myers
Florida International University, Miami
Florida State University, Tallahassee
New College of Florida, Sarasota
University of Central Florida, Orlando
University of Florida, Gainesville
University of North Florida, Jacksonville
University of South Florida, Tampa
University of West Florida, Pensacola

Southern Dissent
Edited by Stanley Harrold and Randall M. Miller

*The Other South: Southern Dissenters in the Nineteenth Century*, by Carl N. Degler, with a new preface (2000)
*Crowds and Soldiers in Revolutionary North Carolina: The Culture of Violence in Riot and War*, by Wayne E. Lee (2001)
*"Lord, We're Just Trying to Save Your Water": Environmental Activism and Dissent in the Appalachian South*, by Suzanne Marshall (2002)
*The Changing South of Gene Patterson: Journalism and Civil Rights, 1960-1968*, edited by Roy Peter Clark and Raymond Arsenault (2002)
*Gendered Freedoms: Race, Rights, and the Politics of Household in the Delta, 1861-1875*, by Nancy D. Bercaw (2003)
*Civil War on Race Street: The Civil Rights Movement in Cambridge, Maryland*, by Peter B. Levy (2003)
*South of the South: Jewish Activists and the Civil Rights Movement in Miami, 1945-1960*, by Raymond A. Mohl, with contributions by Matilda "Bobbi" Graff and Shirley M. Zoloth (2004)
*Throwing Off the Cloak of Privilege: White Southern Women Activists in the Civil Rights Era*, edited by Gail S. Murray (2004)
*The Atlanta Riot: Race, Class, and Violence in a New South City*, by Gregory Mixon (2004)
*Slavery and the Peculiar Solution: A History of the American Colonization Society*, by Eric Burin (2005; first paperback edition, 2008)
*"I Tremble for My Country": Thomas Jefferson and the Virginia Gentry*, by Ronald L. Hatzenbuehler (2006)
*From Saint-Domingue to New Orleans: Migration and Influences*, by Nathalie Dessens (2007; first paperback edition, 2010)
*Higher Education and the Civil Rights Movement: White Supremacy, Black Southerners, and College Campuses*, edited by Peter Wallenstein (2007)
*Burning Faith: Church Arson in the American South*, by Christopher B. Strain (2008)
*Black Power in Dixie: A Political History of African Americans in Atlanta*, by Alton Hornsby Jr. (2009)
*Looking South: Race, Gender, and the Transformation of Labor from Reconstruction to Globalization*, Mary E. Frederickson (2011)
*Southern Character: Essays in Honor of Bertram Wyatt-Brown*, edited by Lisa Tendrich Frank and Daniel Kilbride (2011)
*The Challenge of Blackness: The Institute of the Black World and Political Activism in the 1970s*, by Derrick E. White (2011)

# From Saint-Domingue to New Orleans

## MIGRATION AND INFLUENCES

Nathalie Dessens

Foreword by Stanley Harrold and Randall M. Miller

University Press of Florida
Gainesville/Tallahassee/Tampa/Boca Raton
Pensacola/Orlando/Miami/Jacksonville/Ft. Myers/Sarasota

First cloth printing, 2007
First paperback printing, 2010

Library of Congress Cataloging-in-Publication Data
Dessens, Nathalie, 1963–
From Saint-Domingue to New Orleans: migration and influences / Nathalie Dessens;
foreword by Stanley Harrold and Randall M. Miller.
p. cm.—(Southern dissent)
Includes bibliographical references and index.
ISBN-13: 978-0-8130-3037-1 (cloth); 978-0-8130-3567-3 (pbk.)
1. Haitian Americans—Louisiana—New Orleans—History—18th century.
2. Haitian Americans—Louisiana—New Orleans—History—19th century.
3. Immigrants—Louisiana—New Orleans—History. 4. Refugees—Louisiana—
New Orleans—History. 5. Refugees—Haiti—History. 6. Haitians—Migrations—
History. 7. Haiti—History—Revolution, 1791–1804—Refugees. 8. Haiti—
Emigration and immigration—History. 9. New Orleans (La.)—Emigration and
immigration—History. 10. New Orleans (La.)—Social conditions. I. Title.
F379.N59H273 2007
976.3'350496972949–dc22 2006022836

The University Press of Florida is the scholarly publishing agency for the State
University System of Florida, comprising Florida A&M University, Florida Atlantic
University, Florida Gulf Coast University, Florida International University, Florida
State University, New College of Florida, University of Central Florida, University of
Florida, University of North Florida, University of South Florida, and University of
West Florida.

University Press of Florida
15 Northwest 15th Street
Gainesville, FL 32611-2079
http://www.upf.com

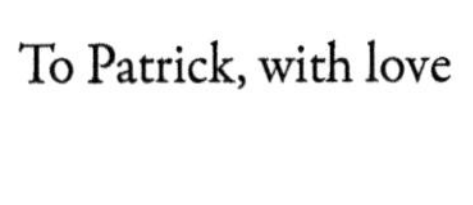

To Patrick, with love

# Contents

# Illustrations

## Maps



## Figures

# Foreword

For generations historians have sought to understand the American South. In his famous *Life and Labor in the Old South,* Ulrich B. Phillips began with the weather. Novelist Margaret Mitchell wrote that it was only the land that mattered. Others have insisted that God counted most in making Dixie. Even before there was a *South,* anyone who grew up below the Mason-Dixon Line knew that race made all the difference. Americans who lived after the American Revolution knew that slavery, the "peculiar institution," set the South apart from the rest of the United States, and many came to appreciate that slavery could destroy the Union. Neoconfederates insist that the South was born in defeat and will rise again.

French historian Nathalie Dessens, in *From Saint-Domingue to New Orleans: Migration and Influences,* does not dispute the aforementioned claims. Instead, she asks us to be more particular—to get down to cases. She wants us to begin with the people. In her case, the people are the white and black refugees from Haiti (then known as Saint-Domingue) who came to the lower Mississippi region, especially New Orleans, to escape the revolution that began in 1791 and raged for a decade. Dessens's purpose is not to contest prior readings of southern history so much as it is to ask us to consider the variety and particularity of places and people. By studying the perspective of Gallic creoles and by focusing on lower Louisiana, Dessens gives the South a more variegated character.

In Dessens's interpretation, the Haitian revolution was a transcultural event that profoundly affected the character of New Orleans and lower Louisiana. It made that subregion less *southern* than those places where cotton and slavery defined all. The free Haitian refugees were intent on holding onto as much of the world they left behind as their numbers, education, and wealth would allow. The enslaved refugees were as intent on asserting their own claims to freedom in Louisiana as their brethren were in Saint-Domingue.

As Dessens demonstrates, the Haitian migration to lower Louisiana reinvigorated Gallic culture there and strengthened the region's Creole identity, institutions, and interests. Through an interaction of family relations, cultural and educational institutions, social exchanges, newspapers and other publications, and economic development, the refugees cultivated a group consciousness. In doing so, they resisted assimilation and muted the impact of the American political, social, and cultural forces that came to Louisiana after 1803. In several important ways they dissented from emerging southern norms. To be sure, refugee slaveholders were no less demanding and brutal than other southerners in driving their slaves. The rigors of the sugar production the refugees brought to Louisiana pushed slaves especially hard. The slaves, for their part, used their Afro-Caribbean culture to resist the masters' demands whenever possible, and they bred in the Louisiana sugar parishes a violence that burst forth in rebellion on several occasions. Yet, in their acceptance of a tripartite racial order that recognized a special place of *gens de couleur libre,* the "white" refugees stood apart from a racial regime that in most of the South saw little in free African Americans but a threat to white supremacy. In their Catholic religion and urban orientation, among several factors, they also departed from major southern patterns.

By studying Haitian refugees in Louisiana, Dessens achieves a new understanding of the cultural diversity that underlay what has at times appeared to be a monolithic South. In considering the impact of Afro-Caribbean and Gallic cultures on the North American mainland, she expands the canvass of the black Atlantic revolutionary ethos. She suggests that, social and caste differences notwithstanding, the refugees' common cultural roots in Saint-Domingue and initial estrangement from the Louisiana power structure encouraged intricate interlacings of identity and interest among them. By examining the white, free black, and enslaved black Haitians, she offers a new approach to studying community formation and a new appreciation for the exceptionalism of Louisiana.

# Preface and Acknowledgments

This book is designed as a small contribution to the boundless field of Louisiana history. My hope is to add to the developing reflection on the large multiracial migration that eventually reached Louisiana at the turn of the nineteenth century, bringing several thousand whites, free people of color, and slaves from the lost French colony of Saint-Domingue. The idea for this research sprang from my discovery of this large refugee influx and my subsequent difficulty in finding information on the topic, despite the proportion it represented of the Louisiana population at the time.

Of course, much still remains to be done, although the importance and legacy of this migration has started to be properly assessed. In this research, I am heavily indebted to the pioneers on the topic, Gabriel Debien and René Le Gardeur, and to those few who followed in their footsteps, including Thomas Fiehrer and Paul Lachance for Louisiana, as well as the historians of the refugee diaspora in the Caribbean, Alain Yacou, Jacques de Cauna, and Carlos Esteban Deive.

This work is the result of many encounters with extraordinarily helpful people. I want to express my gratitude to the staffs of many archives and libraries for their availability and efficiency. I was heartily welcomed at the Special Collections of Louisiana State University at Baton Rouge, Tulane University and Xavier University at New Orleans, the Amistad Research Center of Tulane University, the New Orleans Public Library, the Historic New Orleans Williams Research Center, the Archives of the Archdiocese of New Orleans, the Notarial Archives Research Center of New Orleans, the Archivo General de la Nacion in Santo Domingo, and the Instituto Cultural Dominico-Americano in the Dominican Republic. My thanks go especially to Pamela Arceneaux, John Magill, Wilbur Meneray, Charles E. Nolan, Sally Reeves, Brenda Square, and Lester Sullivan for their invaluable suggestions.

During this research I met many scholars who helped and encouraged me. My deep thanks go to Virginia Meecham Gould for the challenging discussions we had over many a fine dinner in New Orleans, for the information we shared, and for her unwavering hospitality. I also thank Caryn Cossé Bell and Paul Lachance for their suggestions and interest, as well as Elizabeth Sullivan-Holleman and Isabel Hillery Cobb, who offered me their book at the end of the presentation I gave at a symposium celebrating the three hundredth anniversary of the French presence in the lower Mississippi basin (Biloxi, March 1999). I owe a great debt to Sylvia Frey for giving me the right contacts for easier access to the sources and to the Deep South Regional Humanities Research Center of Tulane University for granting me a Georges Lurcy Postdoctoral Fellowship, which offered me the best conditions for summer research, and for making my life in New Orleans so much easier.

I am also very grateful to my friends Sheryl Rahal and James Bolner for their patient revision of my manuscript and to Meredith Morris-Babb and the University Press of Florida for their trust in me. I also want to express my gratitude to the two anonymous readers and to the editors of the Southern Dissent series, Stanley Harrold and Randall M. Miller, for the time they spent on my manuscript and for their extraordinarily helpful suggestions. Finally, I want to thank my husband, Patrick Besse, for his understanding and support, and for being my faithful research assistant during so many summer stays in the archives.

Studying the demographic facts of a migration is a painstaking task. Trying to assess the influence of a refugee movement is still more difficult. Many people will find fault with my interpretative conclusions. Their remarks will help me move forward, since criticism is the fuel of research.

# Introduction

Some 200 years ago, a large refugee group settled in Louisiana after fleeing the turmoil of the slave revolution that occurred in Saint-Domingue. The revolution ended in the creation of Haiti, the second republic of the Americas and its first black republic, in 1804. Between 1791 and 1815, at least 15,000 (and possibly close to 20,000) refugees from Saint-Domingue settled in the lower Mississippi region, 80 to 90 percent in New Orleans and vicinity.[1] Considering the population of New Orleans at the time (the censuses give the figures of 5,028 in 1785, 8,056 in 1799, and 17,242 in 1810), the multiracial influx was enormous and more than doubled the size of the New Orleans free population of color. This migration could not help but have a deep impact on Louisiana's social, economic, political, and cultural context. It eventually reinforced Louisiana's cultural exception in the United States as well as Louisianans' conscious efforts to dissent from the rest of the American South.

Despite the importance of the migration, it attracted little attention from historians. A survey of nineteenth-century historiography reveals either a relatively brief mention of arrivals or a total silence.[2] It is true that, until the nineteenth century, migrations were studied in the general transatlantic context rather than in an intracontinental perspective. It is most probable that the incorporation of Louisiana into the United States in 1803, exactly in the middle of the refugee flow, also overshadowed the importance of this migration. The new national destiny of this colonial territory brought many changes in the society, economy, politics, and culture of Louisiana and became a topic of major concern for historians. Ironically, the refugee community, which contributed so much to the persistence of a Gallic Creole culture despite the ongoing Americanization of Louisiana, attracted little interest from scholars. Various reasons might account for this neglect, including the three-tiered racial composition of the refugee population that was at odds with the ideology distilled in the antebellum and post-Reconstruction Anglo-American South. Finally, acknowledging the importance of the refugee flow in the socioeconomic and cultural development of Louisiana might have implied recognizing the indebtedness of the United States to Haiti at a time when the political elite of the country were trying to downplay the importance of this newly independent republic.[3]

Early-twentieth-century historians of Louisiana seemed to discover this migration, as reflected in a few superficial articles that simply state the existence of the refugees.[4] The existence of the refugees seemed, by then, to have entered the Louisianan collective unconscious.[5] Interest in the topic had not yet arisen, however, and only the pioneering works of René Le Gardeur and Gabriel Debien, as well as Winston C. Babb in the mid-twentieth century (although his dissertation has remained unpublished), brought new light to this important event in Louisiana history.[6] These historians kept writing that there was still much to do to grant fair recognition to the migration.[7]

Some historians settled down to this task in the last two decades of the twentieth century, using Debien and Le Gardeur's work as a basis. Both Thomas Fiehrer and Paul Lachance, for instance, made invaluable contributions to the understanding of the "unfathomed legacy" of the refugee movement.[8] At that point, realizing the importance of this scholarly work, Carl A. Brasseaux and Glenn R. Conrad edited *The Road to Louisiana*, a collection of the main articles written by Debien, Le Gardeur, Fiehrer, and Lachance, with the aim of attempting to "fill comprehensively one of the most enduring lacunae in Louisiana historiography."[9] Gathering the scattered articles into a volume was the best way to draw attention to this forgotten aspect of Louisiana history. It was also a good incentive for other researchers to follow the trail of the refugees.

Today almost everyone in Louisiana has heard about this refugee movement which, according to Fiehrer, had "remained buried until recently in the recesses of the collective unconscious,"[10] and even most travel guides mention its influence on Louisiana society. Moreover, Louisianans now seem conscious of this impact, and all responded favorably to the author's assumption that the refugees had influenced Louisiana in more than one way. Most inhabitants of New Orleans with (real or supposed) Saint-Domingan ancestry are proud of their origins, and several individuals and genealogical societies have been working on the topic. Articles are regularly published in the *New Orleans Genesis*, and New Orleans boasts a Saint-Domingue Special Interest Group.[11] The refugees are even often surrounded by a mythical aura.[12] Now that the refugees' true contribution is being assessed, all kinds of legends circulate on their contribution.[13] A more precise assessment of their legacy—which will probably strengthen some beliefs and damage some legends—seems necessary.[14] It will undoubtedly enable a better understanding of Louisiana's dissenting tradition in the American South and in the United States more generally.

Although the present work will use extensively the first findings of the pioneers and will present a summarized view of the migration itself, its ultimate goal will be to pave the way for assessing the "unfathomed legacy," which may well prove to be unfathomable. This is an arduous task that necessarily implies interpretative conclusions with which other historians might disagree. Indeed, it goes far beyond studying the facts, figures, and conditions of the migration. It even goes beyond considering the refugees' reception by the Louisiana population and conditions of insertion into this population, although this will have to be included in the study. It is an attempt to determine what impact they had on the social, economic, and political life of Louisiana and to what extent they influenced Louisiana culture. Probably the most difficult task is to draw the line between mere visibility, due to the great number of immigrants, and real influence that might derive from the dynamism fostered by their previous experience in Saint-Domingue and by the trauma of flight and relocation in an unknown society.

This will require some reflection on a number of notions involved in the migration processes, in terms of ethnicity, integration, assimilation, amalgamation, acculturation, and creolization (or rather re-creolization here).[15] These notions will not be treated theoretically, however, but will be systematically applied to the case of the Saint-Domingan refugees in Louisiana. This will imply a reflection on the existence of a symbolically ethnic community.[16] In this respect, the conditions of this forced migration play an important part. Studying a migration necessitated by revolution calls for totally different concepts than when studying a voluntary migration, whatever proportion of push (rather than pull) factors may have caused the latter.

Moreover, both the similarities and differences between the society they knew before their migration and the one they found upon arrival are essential to understanding their easy integration and potential influence on their new homeland. The reflection on the legacy of the refugees—especially their cultural legacy—requires an intimate knowledge of both their original society and the society that they discovered upon reaching their new abode. The task is made especially difficult by the multiracial character of the refugee population as well as the various social statuses found among the migrants. The migrant group not only included white people and black slaves, but also free people of color with various proportions of African ancestry. The present study will thus have to focus on the three groups, which obviously had very different statuses. Because of the long neglect of people of African descent, free and enslaved, by the dominant historiography and the later attempt by historians to compensate for this omission, the various groups have often been studied separately. Within the scope of the present historical rehabilitation of the entire refugee community, dividing the refugee population—which included people from all three groups in almost equal numbers—was inappropriate.

If these people, either of African, European, or mixed ancestry, had been influenced only by their original birthplace or that of their ancestors, such an association would have proved overly complex. The initial hypothesis of the present work, however, is that they all came to the Americas with definite social and cultural patterns but that they gained an identity, a kind of common cultural blend, through their stay in Saint-Domingue. This implies a creolization due to their coexistence (whether chosen or unwanted) as well as the specific character of the place in which they lived and the society that emerged from it. This will to treat the community without separating the groups does not, by any means, run counter to any study of the specific African contributions to Louisiana or the French, Spanish, or American influences. This study is aimed to be complementary, since its main focus bears on the specific traits developed in Saint-Domingue by French colonists, African slaves, and their offspring of mixed ancestry who came to the Gulf Coast and to New Orleans at the turn of the nineteenth century.

The present work is deeply indebted to the historians who have started exploring this migration, which occurred at a crucial point in Louisiana history. The sources also include much archival material, from the sacramental records to the notarial acts of the period. It also draws from public and private correspondence, from the letters of the officials who ruled Louisiana to the private papers of several families, either from Saint-Domingue or from the Louisiana Creole society, thus bearing witness to the refugees' intimate experience and how they were perceived by the Louisiana Creoles. Finally, the present study relies on many secondary sources dealing with specific aspects of the Saint-Domingan society, the revolution, and subsequent events, as well as on the abundant literature concerning the Louisiana society. Those works on Saint-Domingue and Louisiana were read with the constant purpose of tracing influences and determining the legacy of the refugees in their new homeland. Some influences were easily traceable, for the authors of the pioneer studies had—at least partially—identified them. Others, however, had not been associated with the Saint-Domingan group, and tracing them was sometimes an arduous task. Articles have been written on newspapermen, printers, authors, and many other professionals who were refugees or descendants of refugees, although their authors were unaware of those origins.[17] They simply thought they were writing about Louisiana Creoles of European or mixed African ancestry, which may be a good indicator of the perfect assimilation of the refugees into nineteenth-century Louisiana Creole society.

The present overview of the migration and of its legacy to the history of Louisiana will be a novel attempt at understanding this specific population movement. I hope it will launch other scholars on the path of the refugees, especially on the "road to Louisiana." It will also be a new attempt at understanding Louisiana's difference and dissenting tradition (both in the South and in the United States), a characteristic that has persisted even into the twenty-first century.

The present study will open with a brief historical survey of Saint-Domingue in the eighteenth century, including some references to the revolution itself, with special focus on the various waves of departures from the island. It will also briefly examine the way in which the migration occurred, as well as the various destinations of the refugee diaspora. The second chapter will study more specifically the Louisiana destination, the reason why the refugees chose to go (and stay) there, the society the newcomers found in this new homeland, as well as their reception by the Louisiana population and authorities. The study will then focus on the refugee population, the links between its various members, the sense of community it developed, and the kind of "symbolic ethnicity" it built. The last four chapters will assess the refugees' legacy in the economic, social, political, and cultural fields.

1

# The Saint-Domingue Epic

Before assessing the weight of the migration on Louisiana society and determining the migrants' areas of influence, it is necessary to survey the territory they migrated from and the circumstances of their migration as well as the experiences they carried with them in exile. In the case of the Saint-Domingue refugees, it is essential because the conditions under which the migration occurred may indeed be considered an "epic" that modeled their resettlement pattern and shaped their subsequent influencing of the Louisiana society.[1] This opening chapter will describe the French colony prior to the revolution before examining the migration that brought several thousand refugees to New Orleans within two decades at the turn of the nineteenth century. This is essential because it may account for a number of distinct features that the refugees carried in their flight.

## French Colonial Saint-Domingue

From the beginning, the island of Hispaniola had an unusual fate. Among the first "discoveries" of Columbus in December 1492, and as the seat of the first attempted Spanish settlement, Navidad, as early as 1493, Hispaniola harbored the first successful Spanish colony in the Americas and was the strategic base from which Hispanic settlement spread to the rest of the Caribbean and even to the mainland. It was thus the cradle of European expansion in the Western Hemisphere. Through Hispaniola, slavery became an institution of the Americas.

The French presence in the western part of the island began in the seventeenth century. By 1670, almost thirty years before France had established a beachhead at Biloxi, the French plantation colony of Saint-Domingue was already thriving, although its possession by France was not formally acknowledged until the Treaty of Ryswick in 1697.[2] By 1714, while Louisiana was still a sparsely settled colony, the development of Saint-Domingue was such that it no longer depended on the colonial government of Martinique and it had its own general government, called that of the Leeward Islands (Gouvernement des Iles sous le Vent).[3] While the Lesser Antilles shifted back and forth between France and England and Louisiana itself went from France to Spain at

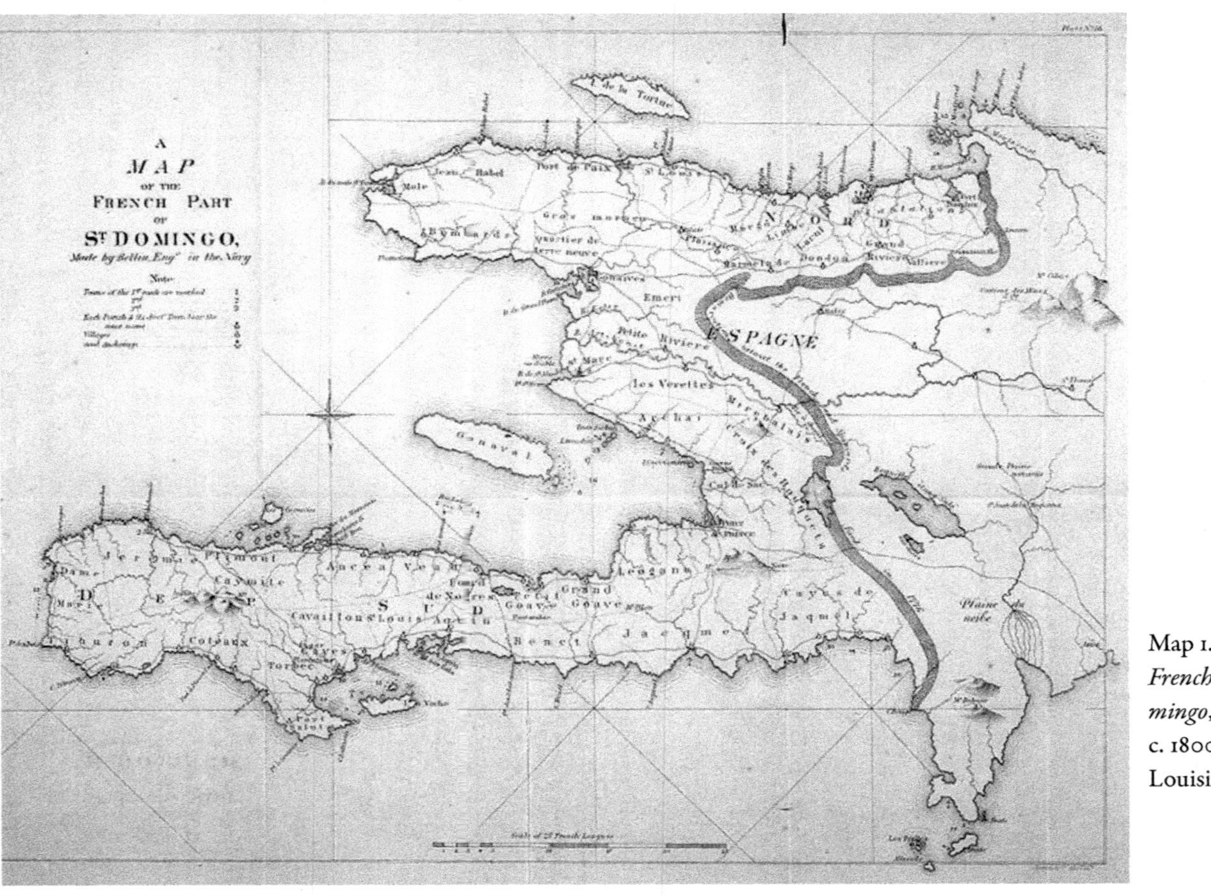


Map 1. *A Map of the French Part of St. Domingo*, by Jacques Bellin, c. 1800. Courtesy of the Louisiana State Museum.

the end of the Seven Years' War, the French colonization of Saint-Domingue continued unimpeded until 1790.[4] The eighteenth century may even be called the heyday of Saint-Domingue. As the largest West Indian French colony, it was totally undisturbed by the Seven Years' War. It grew so rapidly that, after less than a century, it was the richest of the Antillean colonies.

Many differences may be noted between Louisiana and the French Caribbean colony. Louisiana's population stagnated throughout the eighteenth century while Saint-Domingue's grew steadily from 77,000 inhabitants in 1687 to 523,800 in 1789. The ratio of blacks to whites grew from a slight majority of whites in 1687 (4,400 for 3,358 slaves) to a large majority of slaves on the eve of the French Revolution. As for Louisiana, although it undoubtedly developed into a slave society, it received low contingents of African slaves during the French period and never matched Saint-Domingue in this respect. The census of 1789 in Saint-Domingue counts 30,831 whites, 24,848 free people of color, and 434,429 slaves.[5] Despite slight variations in the figures, it is thus admitted that 90 percent of inhabitants were slaves, a proportion unequaled anywhere in the West Indies or in any North American colony.[6] For comparison's sake, the 1788 census gives a total population for lower Louisiana—including Natchez—of 20,673 slaves and 18,737 free people (white and black), which is a very slight majority of slaves.[7]

If its demographical pattern was one of the most distinctive characteristics of French Saint-Domingue, the vitality of its economy was another, a vitality that has to be opposed to the situation of the colony of Louisiana, which had to be heavily subsidized by the colonial powers for much of its first century.[8] The economic development of Saint-Domingue was extremely rapid: the growth was permanent throughout the eighteenth century, and the colony was already well established by midcentury.[9] It increasingly traded with foreign nations, especially after the American Revolution terminated the monopoly that the British government had instituted for its North American colonies. The importance of Saint-Domingue within the French traffic with its Caribbean colonies also grew rapidly.[10] While its next-door neighbor, Santo Domingo, had stopped exporting and was producing essentially tobacco and food crops for local consumption, Saint-Domingue had become a highly developed agricultural exporting center. This was never the case of eighteenth-century Louisiana. The Caribbean colony even started devising real agro-industrial structures for its sugar and indigo production; cotton and coffee production also created the need for incipient mechanization. While Louisiana hardly managed to support itself, Saint-Domingue became, in the last years before the French Revolution, the main driving force of France's commercial capitalism.

This prosperity had undeniable effects on the society of the colony, attracting many young members of aristocratic French families who became less and less anxious to return to France, thus causing a reduction in the absentee planter class and the emergence of a local social life. This, in turn, fostered numerous calls for autonomy among the economic elites of the island, which was not the case in colonial Louisiana. In Saint-Domingue, the social stratification stabilized after midcentury, whereas Louisiana remained in many respects a frontier society. Like the other French and Spanish slave societies of the Americas, the society of Saint-Domingue divided into three subgroups. At the top of the hierarchy was the white population, which occupied a leading social, economic, cultural, and political position. Next came the free people of African descent, composed of an increasing number of offspring of white men and slave women but also of freed slaves of unmixed African ancestry. Although the free population of color was anything but socially homogeneous, the group was economically powerful, much more so than in Louisiana, although the group existed. In Saint-Domingue, they possessed one-third of the cultivated land on the eve of the French Revolution.[11] Many members of the group were slave owners who apparently sanctioned the system. The free people of color benefited from numerous privileges, although these were significantly reduced in the second half of the eighteenth century.[12] Slaves composed the largest group. They were proportionately more numerous than elsewhere but shared the same statutory inexistence with all their counterparts in the Western Hemisphere.[13] The economic prosperity of the colony and its uncommon demographical proportions were thus two obvious features that set Saint-Domingue apart from the rest of the colonies.

Another specific trait was the social and intellectual dynamism of the colony compared with the rest of the French colonial possessions, including Louisiana, which according to all accounts had remained, in the late eighteenth century, a frontier colony, still not highly developed socially and culturally. Although Saint-Domingue first had a very limited social life, a definite cultural development occurred there in the eighteenth century. There were also many attempts at urban modernization, although the early conditions had often been described as rudimentary by visitors to the colony.[14] For instance, hospitals were opened (as early as 1692 at Le Cap and Port-au-Prince, then at Léogane, Fort-Dauphin, Petit Goave, Saint-Louis, and Les Cayes). The inhabitants of the colony felt the need to open places for cultural exchanges. By 1789, six theaters had been built, and colonists staged the latest plays performed in Paris. The theater of Le Cap Français offered 1,500 seats for three performances a week, including seats reserved for all three categories of the population. Printers also opened businesses, newspapers started appearing, including *La Gazette de Saint-Domingue* in 1764 (which boasted 1,500 subscribers in 1788) and *La Gazette du Jour* in 1790 (later renamed *Le Moniteur Colonial*). Two almanacs were printed from 1773 on. A bookstore (with a library) was opened in 1765 at Le Cap, a second one in 1775, and three more between 1777 and 1788. In 1784, the cultural elite also founded the Société Royale des Sciences et des Arts at Cap Français. By 1789, the Society had twelve permanent members, forty resident associates, and forty nonresident associates, including Benjamin Franklin. Saint-Domingue also became a dynamic center for Freemasonry, the first lodge being founded as early as 1740. Among the most famous freemasons of Saint-Domingue was Moreau de Saint-Méry.[15] The island thus displayed uncommon features and an unusual dynamism especially when compared with Louisiana, where no such cultural life was organized until the 1790s.

The political scene also featured many discrepancies. Contrary to what was the case in Louisiana, the Creoles of Saint-Domingue developed a clear tendency toward contestation and autonomy early in the history of the colony. While the exercise of government was always strongly centralized in Louisiana under French and Spanish rule, Saint-Domingue enjoyed greater self-government, which gave the residents both the taste for political power and the notion of its limitation. This increased their frustration, created in them a real thirst for autonomy, and led them to protest more openly against the metropolitan power than any of their counterparts in the other French dependencies, including, of course, Louisiana. Similarly, the free population of color, endowed with a tremendous socioeconomic role, was progressively deprived of its most basic civil rights. This created a wide-scale current of discontent among those who saw a potential solution to their problems in the French Revolution.

From its very creation, the colony had always displayed a tradition of contestation linked with the conditions of its birth and development. Between 1670 and 1789, several rebellious waves occurred. Although there were always precise reasons for these outbursts, they were often a pretext for demanding more autonomy. This was generally granted to the colonists, at least to a certain degree. The superior councils, for instance, were given judicial functions as well as the power to defer the implementation of a law that ran counter to the interests of the colony, a right that colonial Louisianans never had. This made the Saint-Domingan colonists still more intent on requesting economic freedom and political authority. Because those two privileges were denied to them, they persistently refused to accept their subjection to the metropolitan power.[16]

While the Louisiana colonists never openly rejected their colonial status, the inhabitants of Saint-Domingue, encouraged by the island's economic vitality, gradually developed the political philosophy of the contract theory. Because the settlement of Saint-Domingue had been the result of the individual enterprise of some freebooters and buccaneers, they refused to acknowledge French domination over them. They argued that they had never officially been given the mission to colonize and that their dependence on France was the result of a contract willingly entered into. The philosophical consequence of this theory was that, as their counterparts of the British North American colonies later argued, they felt they could dissolve any such contract as soon as they perceived that the other side no longer respected its terms. They closely followed the example of the British colonists, envying their right to self-government as well as the representation of the British West Indians in Parliament. They also wished they could freely trade with them without any limitation set by the motherland for the protection of its own economic privileges and benefits. Thus they shared with their British counterparts a tendency to rebel. This tendency was reinforced by the example of the American colonists and their fight for autonomy and freedom during the Revolutionary War. After 1776, Saint-Domingue colonists considered the North American colonies to be a successful example and, from 1783 on, the model to emulate.

## Revolution and Departures

The rebellions that shook the island in the late 1780s were anything but surprising. What was really unexpected was their outcome, which deprived the French colonists of all privileges, including the most basic one of residing safely in the colony. The triggering of the Haitian Revolution was one more example of the colonists' rebellious mind-set, even though other movements soon submerged them. A detailed presentation of the revolutionary events would be useless here.[17] It is sufficient to say that the revolution was a complex mixture of local, national, and international factors. The Haitian Revolution was the result of several movements resulting from the various interpretations that each of the three groups in Saint-Domingue had of the values of the French Revolution.[18] The situation was made still more complex by the permanently shifting alliances between the three groups and the authorities, be they French or foreign. The government sometimes tried to use the free people of color to contain the whites fighting for colonial autonomy. Or it decided to ally with the insurgent slaves against white sedition. The whole situation was further complicated by the interventions of Britain and Spain, which were attempting to capture the island under the pretext of defending the interests of the colonists or of the colony. While England relied on the white colonists, Spain enrolled the rebellious slaves, giving Jean-François the title of general of the Spanish army and Toussaint-Louverture that of colonel.[19]

Although the first two years of revolutionary agitation were marked by political actions launched successively by the white separatists and the free group of color attempting to regain their lost privileges and more, the rebellion that is of interest to the present discussion is that of the slaves from August 1791 onwards. It is indeed this large-scale revolution which triggered the departures of the many refugees who eventually settled in New Orleans in the two decades that followed. It started in August 1791 in the northern part of the colony. Within four days, one-third of the northern plain was admittedly reduced to ashes and all the plantations were destroyed. By late September, over 1,000 people had been slaughtered and 161 sugar plantations and 1,200 coffee plantations had been destroyed. The damage reportedly amounted to about 600 million Livres.[20] The rebellion was partly repressed but never totally suppressed. Although the free population—that is, the whites and free people of color—allied to try to contain the insurrection, it lasted for about two years. In March 1792, more than 15,000 slaves were involved in the insurrection. The authorities managed to regain some control in the summer, but the insurrection spread in early 1793.[21] Throughout those first two years, individuals fled from the colony. Later, the population movements became more massive. In June 1793, for instance, Léger Félicité Sonthonax, French commissioner, tried to use slave support against the whites, an alliance that obliged General Galbaud, governor of Saint-Domingue, and some 10,000 people to evacuate Cap-Français. Thousands of refugees set out to sea, mostly toward North America. The French government was in a relatively uncomfortable position. It feared that a massive repression might entail the loss of the colony to England, which was then at war with France. They attempted to gain the support of the black insurgents against the British, who, they said, had come to rescue the slave owners. Following the decision made by Sonthonax, the representative of the Republic in the northern province, to abolish slavery in the region under his authority in August 1793, the French eventually extended abolition to the whole of Saint-Domingue (and to all the French colonies) in February 1794. All the inhabitants of the French colonies, of whatever color, were immediately granted all the rights contained in the new French constitution.[22]

This sent more colonists away from the island and marked the beginning of the era of Toussaint-Louverture. Toussaint was first a member of the group commanded by Georges Biassou, leader of the 1791 slave rebellion and general of the rebel army. Toussaint and Biassou had allied with the Spanish in their fight against the French authorities. Toussaint had then rallied the French revolutionaries in April 1794, an alliance that permitted his unchecked ascension to the head of the colony. After 1795, he managed to rid himself of his adversaries and past allies (including slave leader Jean-François) and ship Sonthonax back to France in August 1797. At the same time, the English decided to abandon the island (after losing more than 12,000 men to yellow fever). Toussaint remained at the head of the colony and devised a policy of autonomy, if not independence. He endowed the island with a constitution, a central assembly of ten members representing the various regions of the colony (all of them whites and people of mixed African and European ancestry), appointed himself governor for life, and announced that he would appoint his own successor. The constitution of 8 July 1801, however, acknowledged the dependence of the territory on the French Empire. Paradoxically, it declared the island's allegiance to France and its total independence in law.[23]

In his attempt to redress the economy of the colony, Toussaint encouraged the whites to stay, conscious as he was that the island needed their expertise. Although the evacuation of the English troops in 1798 occasioned new departures (among those who had supported the English attempt to gain control of the island), the whites stopped leaving the island during Toussaint's rule. Several of those who had fled even came back to the island, while Toussaint sequestered the property of the others and leased it to his officers. Most of the owners who had left the island (temporarily, they thought) requested the restoration of order and of French authority over the island, as well as the recovery of their sequestrated property.

In February 1802, after confirming Toussaint in his command of the colony, Napoleon sent an expeditionary force to recapture the island under the lead of his brother-in-law, General Leclerc. Much later, he acknowledged that this had been a mistake, since it would have been more effective diplomatically to maintain French control over the colony through Toussaint. The expeditionary corps seemed successful at first, and within a few days it recaptured Le Cap, Port-au-Prince, and Port-de-Paix. The black army of Toussaint capitulated and receded, imprisoning and killing all the whites they met along the way and burning whatever remained standing. Yellow fever, however, rapidly decimated the French corps, and the blacks' resistance resumed. Toussaint was deceitfully captured and deported to France, where he died in prison. The resistance became easier because the French army fell to yellow fever. Within a few months, over 20,000 of the 43,000 men sent to the colony had perished, including Leclerc himself.[24] By October 1803, Toussaint's lieutenant, African-born Dessalines, had regained control of the island. On 9 October, the French army evacuated the colony. This was the beginning of an absolute antiwhite policy ordered by Dessalines. All the plantations were burnt.[25] This set off a final wave of departures from the island, and all the whites who had not managed to flee were exterminated. On 1 January 1804, Dessalines proclaimed the independence of the island and renamed it Haiti, from its first native name, although this independence was only belatedly acknowledged by the French king Charles X in the ordinance of 17 April 1825.[26]

Throughout the decade of violent slave insurrection, the fate of most of the island's inhabitants had been far from enviable, especially if they were white or property owners, a category which also included many free people of color, especially those of mixed African ancestry. As soon as the slaves started revolting, their rebellion became a racial war that did not spare free people of color. Except during the short leadership of Toussaint, terror reigned on the island.[27] Between 1793 and 1803, many inhabitants, of white or mixed ancestry, decided to flee the island, if only temporarily, hoping for a return to normalcy. Departures occurred from the early years of the Revolution until Toussaint's rule, when not only did people generally cease to leave the island but some of those who had fled returned. The English evacuation triggered a second main wave of departures. The third main migratory wave was occasioned by the terror that followed the capitulation of the French expeditionary corps and proclamation of the independence of Haiti by Dessalines. This time, it essentially concerned the whites who had been so imprudent as to stay. Dessalines launched campaigns of pillage and slaughter. In March 1804, he openly called for a complete destruction of the white race. For three days and nights in April, men, women, and children were relentlessly slaughtered.[28] The accession to power of Dessalines thus precipitated the final departure of those who managed to find a way out.[29]

Altogether, white people who managed to escape death in Saint-Domingue fled from the colony, together with free people of color, especially those of mixed ancestry who either had family ties with the white colonists or had been politically allied with them. They could not remain, for they epitomized the old economic order, which the slaves understandably resented and wanted to end.[30] Many slaves, whether of their own free will or under constraint, followed their masters in their flight. This large-scale population movement sets the background to the migration of several thousands of refugees to Louisiana.

## Away from the Island

A very precise study of the migration from Saint-Domingue is still impossible, for lack of records and because, until 1804, refugees moved back and forth, to and from the island.[31] Although it is not possible to give either exact figures, with accurate dates and detailed information about the way people departed from the island, or a list of the precise destinations in all cases, a general schema may be drawn of who left the island, how, when, and for what destination. Despite these difficulties, it is possible to indicate some important waves of departures, thanks to eyewitnesses or through deduction from the refugees' arrivals at their various destinations. The first slave revolt of 1791 in the northern part of the island provoked a first wave of displacements, either within the colony (toward the southern and western provinces and toward Cap Français) or elsewhere in the Americas, essentially to Jamaica, Cuba (Santiago de Cuba and Baracoa), and seaport cities along the Atlantic coast of the United States.[32] The second main wave occurred in 1793, as a consequence of the burning of Cap Français by rebellious slaves. The Atlantic coast of the United States was the main destination of those migrants.[33] The withdrawal of the English troops in 1798 triggered a third wave, partly to Jamaica (for those who followed the British soldiers) and partly to the eastern United States.[34] The surrender of the French Expeditionary Corps in 1803, followed by the proclamation of Haiti's independence and massacres ordered by Dessalines, brought still more refugees to Cuba and the Atlantic and Gulf coasts of the United States.[35] Up to this point Louisiana was not a primary destination. The reason is that this summary only mentions the main waves, which sometimes involved thousands of people at a time (such as the 10,000 people who fled Cap Français after the 1793 burning), none of which had Louisiana as a main direct destination. Between 1791 and 1803, however, people left individually for Louisiana, and many of those who had reached other destinations during the Haitian revolution eventually made their way to Louisiana in the first decade of the nineteenth century.

Some refugees went back to metropolitan France, especially those who had not been long in Saint-Domingue, those absentees who had repatriated part of their fortunes or had family interests in France, or those who were somehow connected with the French army and administration.[36] Most of those who left Saint-Domingue, however, found refuge in the Caribbean or on the North American continent. For most refugees, indeed, the absence of ties with the motherland after so many years or even so many generations in the Caribbean colony rendered a migration to a totally unknown destination, with so little in common with their recent residence, unimaginable. The other Caribbean or North American colonies, as well as the United States, were geographically, climatically, socially, and culturally much closer to their present environment. This trend may also be accounted for by the fact that those who had slaves could hardly take them back to France and thus looked for destinations where they would be more readily accepted.[37] Finally, for most of the refugees, the stay away from their only home was to be temporary. For a relatively long period after the beginning of troubles, they thought they should stay close to Saint-Domingue, for they would undoubtedly regain possession of their property and return to their homes. This lasted at least until Napoleon's failed attempt to recapture the island and subsequent proclamation of the independence of the Haitian Republic. In the refugees' collective unconscious, the hope for a return home probably lasted until the compensation granted by Charles X to the refugees in the early 1830s.[38] Among the reasons that led the refugees to avoid the metropolitan destination is also the fact that restricting their movement to an inter-Caribbean migration was much more affordable than a transatlantic one, especially because most of them had left their former residence with practically nothing. White planters usually had little more than a handful of slaves, whom they could rent out for revenue, which obliged them to relocate in a slave society and excluded a return to metropolitan France.

Although Louisiana was eventually the main destination of many refugees, the Caribbean basin was one of their first destinations.[39] Considering the issue of geographical proximity, the first obvious destination, also the easiest and cheapest in terms of transportation, was the Spanish part of the island, Santo Domingo. If it was the easiest, it was by no means the safest or the most permanent, as it remained prey to struggles and/or exchanges. Many inhabitants of Saint-Domingue crossed the border and remained along it. Montecristi, for instance, was a few miles away from Fort-Dauphin or Ouanaminthe and thus welcomed many residents from these areas.[40] Some refugees were hosted temporarily by the Spanish colony and mostly lived on subsidies granted by the

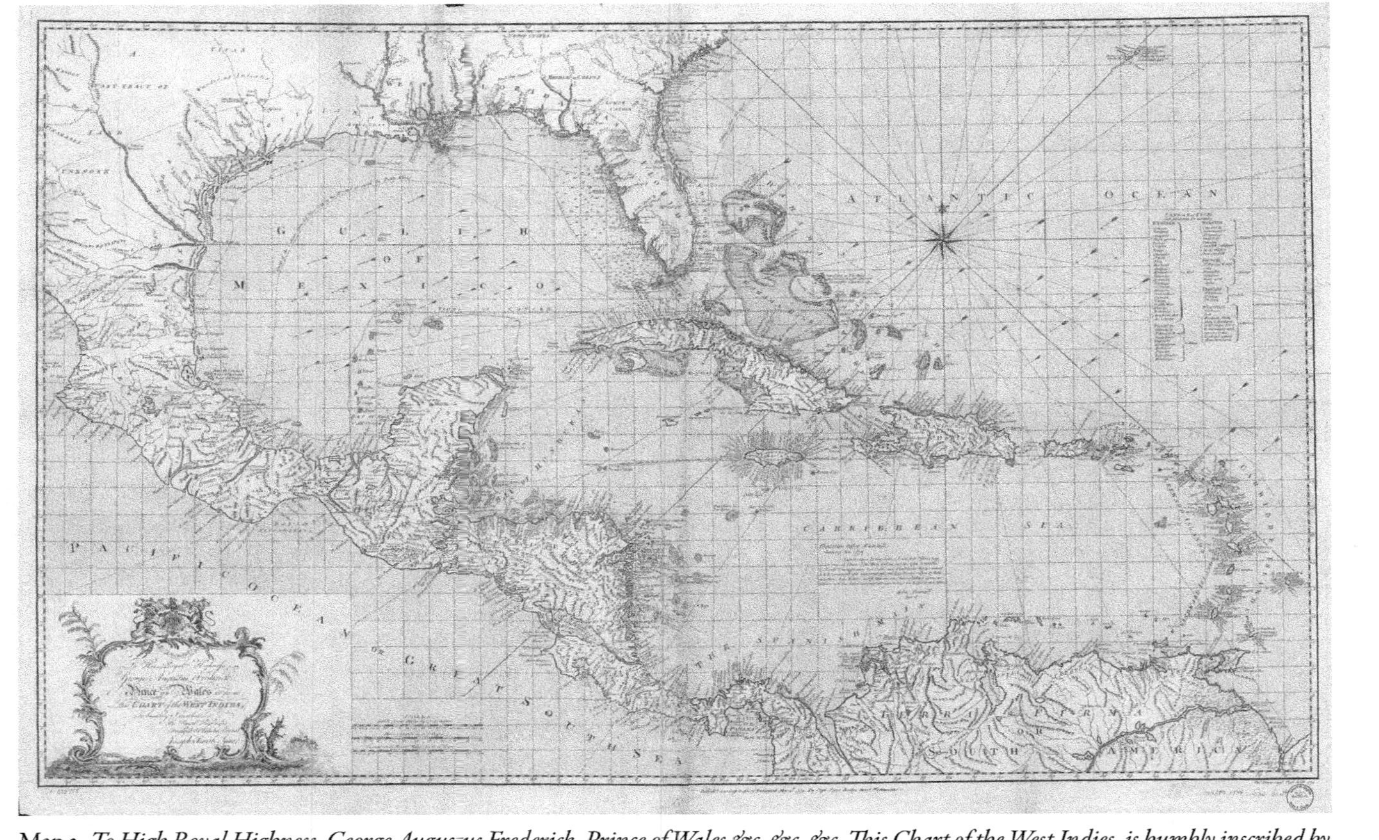


Map 2. *To High Royal Highness. George Augustus Frederick. Prince of Wales &c. &c. &c. This Chart of the West Indies, is humbly inscribed by His Royal Highness faithful and obedient servant Joseph Smith Speer. Thos. Bowen, sculp*. Westminster, 1774. LC Maps of North America, 1750–89, 1699. Library of Congress Geography and Map Division, Washington, D.C.

authorities.[41] Members of the auxiliary troops, often referred to as "auxiliary negroes," were also taken in charge by the Spanish authorities, together with their leaders Jean-François and Biassou. These blacks from Saint-Domingue, who had joined the Spanish troops, left when the Spanish authorities departed at the turn of 1796. Many of those refugees remained on the island only for a short time.[42] Some did stay in Santo Domingo, where they mixed with Santo Domingo Creoles or Spaniards, and many Dominican families still bear names inherited from those refugees.[43]

Next in distance came Cuba, located a few dozen nautical miles from the northeastern coast of Saint-Domingue. Cuba was close to Gonaïves, Môle St. Nicolas, or Port-de-Paix. Quite logically, the refugees crowded in the regions of Baracoa and Santiago de Cuba that were the closest to Saint-Domingue.[44] Some also settled in (and around) Havana. Arrivals staggered throughout the 1791–1809 period, although many refugees came in 1803 after Leclerc's defeat. Most figures revolve around 25,000, although some go up to 30,000.[45] For Santiago alone, the figure of over 6,000 is given.[46] The refugees generally received a heartier welcome in this island than in most other places generally cited.[47] Many of those Cuban refugees are of interest to the present study because they eventually made their way to Louisiana.

Slightly farther from the Saint-Domingan coasts, but still within easy reach, lay Jamaica. It was a destination made easier by the fact that many colonists followed the English troops upon evacuation. Independently from this military involvement, Jamaica was always an obvious destination for all those who fled from the south of the island, from Les Cayes or Jérémie, or even Léogane and Port-au-Prince.[48] The first refugees had reached Jamaica in 1792 and had found it difficult to prosper, especially as the population welcomed them quite coldly, fearing a spread of revolutionary ideals through them. In 1793, when France and England went to war, all the refugees in Jamaica had to pledge allegiance to the British king before the court of justice of Kingston.[49] More refugees came in 1798, essentially from the southern area of Saint-Domingue, from Les Cayes and Jérémie, including those who had served in the colonial corps recruited by the English and those who had remained in their official administrative positions or had accepted those newly created by the English. Some planters feared that Toussaint's rule might give renewed strength to insurrections and massacres. Several thousand refugees found shelter in Jamaica, although it is difficult to give precise figures, for their stay on the island was sometimes transient.[50] When trouble expanded between France and England in the first years of the nineteenth century, indeed, many refugees had to seek other refuges, particularly in Cuba and Louisiana.[51] Those three European colonies were thus the main Caribbean destinations of the refugees.[52]

The second pole of attraction was the northern continent. From Georgia to Massachusetts, all the Atlantic harbors received refugees. Among the favorite destinations were Savannah, Charleston, Norfolk, Baltimore, Philadelphia, New York, and Boston, where large refugee communities settled, sometimes for long periods, sometimes permanently.[53] In small numbers first, then in larger crowds, the former inhabitants of Saint-Domingue also reached the Gulf South, from Panama City to Gulfport, Bay St. Louis, and New Orleans. The links between Saint-Domingue and the United States had always been strong. When French islanders had come to assist the American revolutionaries, for instance, Saint-Domingue had been the main base for military and naval assistance.[54] The number of refugees in the United States was high. Some estimates give figures around 20,000 before 1797.[55] The new nation generally welcomed those refugees.[56] The refugees settled both in the south and in the north. Virginia was one important southern destination.[57] As Moreau de Saint-Méry explains it, the convoy that left Cap Français in 1793 reached the American coasts at Hampton, and many migrants settled at Norfolk. They tended to remain there for want of means to move elsewhere, but also because of the pleasant climate, legal existence of slavery, and generally warm welcome of the inhabitants.[58] Among the common destinations were Savannah and Charleston. Several thousand refugees settled in Charleston, possibly attracted by the existence of an important Huguenot community and by the alluring prospect of a French-speaking group.[59] The pattern witnessed from South Carolina to Maryland was partly reproduced in New York, Philadelphia, and Boston. Exact numbers of refugees are difficult to assess, for lack of record of their arrivals.[60] The estimates, however, revolve around several tens of thousands.[61] Refugees usually arrived in a state of utter destitution, were granted a generally warm welcome, and benefited, as elsewhere, from the financial aids provided by the federal and local governments.

Although their main destinations are easily listed, the refugees were very mobile, and many of them moved from one to the next. They also often went back and forth between Saint-Domingue and their places of exile. They sometimes followed members of their family who had met a better fortune elsewhere. There were even some large-scale migratory movements from one place to another. Many refugees in Santo Domingo left for neighboring Caribbean colonies when the territory was transferred from Spain to France after the Treaty of Basle, because this transfer meant that the 1794 abolition of slavery would also affect the colony. Napoleon's aggressive international policies also led to a large migration from Jamaica to the northern continent in 1803 and from Cuba to Louisiana in 1809–10.[62] In the United States, some refugees remained where they had first settled, but there were movements between the different refugee centers of the United States, and there were some departures for metropolitan France as well.[63] Many of those refugees in the United States eventually moved to Louisiana.

Throughout the twenty years that followed the revolution in Saint-Domingue, refugees traveled around the Caribbean and tried to find their place in the Western Hemisphere.[64] Their experiences were many, since the societies they found in their various American destinations were diverse. In all these areas, however, they displayed a real dynamism and exhibited a will not only to survive but also to thrive. Although they became highly involved in their new homes, they also remained in contact with each other, building a real diaspora with a convergence zone: Louisiana.

## The Saint-Domingue Diaspora

The sources (narratives written by refugees, published correspondences, and family papers, among others) give the impression of a real Saint-Domingan diaspora, that is, of people with shared experience who settled in various territories, sometimes moved from one territory to another, but always maintained close contacts within and between these various host countries.[65] The Lambert family papers, for example, which include abundant correspondence sent to Pierre-Antoine Lambert, ultimately a New Orleans refugee, by various friends and relatives, show that there were many exchanges between Lambert and friends who had settled in various American refuges. There are letters from Philadelphia, Charleston, Annapolis, Santiago de Cuba, and Kingston, addressed to Lambert, wherever he was (Saint-Domingue, Santiago de Cuba, or New Orleans).[66] The exchanges did not cease as time went on, since the various letters cover about three decades, from 1803 until Lambert's death in the early 1830s. Lambert even spent a few months visiting friends who had remained in Cuba, showing the persistence of links between them, since this trip occurred in 1821, more than twelve years after his settlement in New Orleans. His correspondence with his wife during his stay in Cuba shows the many contacts he had maintained in the colony. Throughout his stay, he moved from one address to another, staying with various friends at Santiago, San Antonio, San Diego, Havana, giving news of the ones to the others, also mentioning other friends he visited or heard from.

There were obvious contacts between friends or mere acquaintances, but there were also close ties between members of a same family who had settled in various American refuges. The memoirs of Eliza Williams (Chotard Gould) mention her living in Georgia, while her aunts had found refuge first in Cuba, then in New Orleans, and her sisters lived in Natchez.[67] She clearly shows that they are in constant contact, since she discusses their settlement in their various residences, and she comments on their feelings and successes. In her *Souvenirs d'Amérique et de France par une Créole*, Hélène d'Aquin describes the fate of her family, her grandparents having found shelter in Jamaica while her grandfather's brothers had found shelter in the United States. The family ended up in Louisiana, as many others did.

The Saint-Domingue diaspora in the Americas thus displayed common reactions to the refugee situation, an important vitality despite (or because of) the vicissitudes of life. Be they in Santo Domingo, Santiago de Cuba, Kingston, Charleston, Baltimore, New York, Philadelphia, Boston, or elsewhere, they remained in contact. Families spread into these various refuges and moved from one refuge to another, but ultimately many of them rebuilt their shattered lives in Louisiana.

Louisiana was an essential pole of attraction to the Saint-Domingan refugees, but its case is very different from that of the main destinations already cited. If, ultimately, many refugees settled there, the direct migrations to the territory were slow and scarce at first. When several tens of thousands settled in the United States and in Cuba, only a few hundred were numbered in Louisiana. It was only later—after the turn of the nineteenth century—that refugees came flowing to Louisiana, mostly as a second destination after a few years spent elsewhere in the Caribbean or in the United States. Moreover, it was in Louisiana that the community flourished. It was also in Louisiana that large numbers of refugee families definitively settled and left enduring marks upon society. It is this migration which remains to be examined, that is, to paraphrase the title of the most complete contribution to the history of the refugee movement, "The Road to Louisiana."

2

# Louisiana, Land of Welcome

Louisiana was not the primary destination of the refugees, which is relatively easy to understand. Proximity, both geographical and socioeconomic, made other Caribbean territories more attractive. The principles put forward by the Founding Fathers and the easy access the United States' harbors offered to the boats hurriedly leaving Saint-Domingue made the young republic another obvious pole of attraction, as did the presence of slavery in its institutions and its image as a land of opportunity. Louisiana, with its midway position—both geographically and metaphorically—between the European Caribbean colonies and the United States, only became the main asylum for thousands of refugees later. The political turmoil it experienced at the turn of the nineteenth century largely accounts for its new image as the Promised Land in the refugees' eyes.

Both the timing of the migration, which spread over the last decade of the colonial period and the first decade of the American era, and the peculiar character of the host society, which shared important similarities with the Saint-Domingan society but also displayed many differences with it, are essential to understanding the importance of the migration in shaping nineteenth-century Louisiana. The timing of the refugees' arrival—because the new American fate of Louisiana overshadowed this significant migration—ironically downplayed, in the eyes of the observers and later historians of Louisiana, the role of the refugee community in shaping the local response to Americanization. The new national fate of Louisiana indeed led observers immediately to identify the refugees as members of the Gallic population, regardless of their origins and recent arrival. This largely contributed to the silence that surrounded the community's role in early American Louisiana. The new national fate, however, was also what gave them increased opportunities to participate more fully in the Creoles' resistance against cultural assimilation and was thus a major factor that eased their integration into the Louisiana fabric and facilitated their influencing Louisiana society.

Their integration into Louisiana society and strong influences on it may thus be explained by the size of the migratory wave, the motives for this geographical choice, the nature of the Louisiana society, and the timeliness of the migration, which shaped the reaction of the Louisianans to this massive migration.

## Louisiana-Bound

As the nineteenth century moved closer, Louisiana—successively Spanish and French colony, then territory and state of the Union during the era of migration and settlement of the refugees—progressively became the main destination of the Saint-Domingan refugees. There were already some movements between Saint-Domingue and Louisiana during the first years of the slave rebellion. Refugees settled in the Gulf South during the late colonial period, although these arrivals were individual experiences rather than mass movements.[1] The number of refugees that reached Louisiana between 1791 and 1803 is relatively difficult to assess, all the more so because Louisiana was generally a second destination for refugees who had migrated to the United States. Moreover, it appears that some records of those early migrations only concern the white—or at any rate the free—migrants.[2]

Very low figures of direct arrivals to Louisiana during the colonial period are generally given, and Debien and Le Gardeur believe there were "fewer than 100 refugees who disembarked at Louisiana between 1792 and 1794."[3] They were mainly whites of modest social background, although some already well established families (with relatives in Louisiana) are to be found among them. From 1794 to 1796, arrivals became more numerous and often took the form of group migrations. Louisiana received political deportees and survivors from the massacres perpetrated in the South of the French colony (Les Cayes, Sale-Trou, and Jacmel) by the followers of Faubert, a racially mixed San Domingan.[4] The 1798–1803 period, following the withdrawal of British troops from Saint-Domingue, seems to have brought slightly more numerous refugees to Louisiana, at least several hundred, but possibly in the thousands.[5] Although accurate assessment is still impossible, the St. Louis Cathedral sacramental records confirm a relative increase in the number of refugees reaching Louisiana in the three years immediately preceding the transfer of the colony to the United States. Only one entry had concerned Saint-Domingan refugees between 1791 and 1795, and only two entries between 1796 and 1799; the figures go up to 23 for 1800–1803.[6]

Few migrants reached Louisiana directly during those early years, but many came indirectly through the United States and even some Caribbean colonies, as confirmed by various primary sources. Before 1803, several hundred refugees came to Louisiana from the Atlantic ports of the United States.[7] Movements from Jamaica to Louisiana may be found between 1793 and 1800, to the point that the arrivals could be described as "an incessant flow."[8] What is certain is that many inhabitants of Saint-Domingue, who did not enroll in the British expeditionary corps occupying Saint-Domingue in those early years, left the island for Cuba or Louisiana. Moreover, among the migrants who left the former French colony with the British troops in 1798, some were taken to Jamaica against their will by English Corsairs but later managed to leave for Louisiana. Among them, for example, were Joseph Villars Dubreuil and his children, the Louis d'Aquin family, Dr. A. Rolin, and Jean-Baptiste Piedmont.[9] The first ten years of migration from Saint-Domingue to Louisiana are thus characterized by constant direct or indirect arrivals, generally the migration of individual families. Because there were both sea arrivals—directly to the Gulf Coast ports either from Saint- Domingue or from neighboring West Indian colonies such as Jamaica—and many arrivals by land from the United States, and because these movements were never mass migrations, they are almost impossible to count precisely. No boat passenger lists can be used extensively, and the censuses of the Spanish era are insufficiently accurate. Only sacramental records and individual accounts may be used concerning the first decade of Louisianan migration. From the numbers of such accounts, it is apparently not exaggerated to estimate at several thousand the total number of arrivals.[10] Some of these refugees did not stay in Louisiana, however, making the counting still more difficult.[11]

It becomes easier to find more precise accounts on the massive waves after 1803. Many refugees came directly from Saint-Domingue at the time of the final French evacuation of 1803. A large colony was thus formed in New Orleans from Les Cayes by those who hurriedly managed to flee the massacres ordered by Dessalines when he took control of Saint-Domingue and turned the colony into the republic of Haiti. There are hints at the fact that they did not choose their destination but took whatever available boat to wherever it was bound (or ended up), Louisiana for instance. A very famous example of this, which attests to the numbers of refugees who reached Louisiana from Saint-Domingue at that time, is that of the American ship *L'Express*, whose commander was a Frenchman and which left Môle St. Nicolas for France in October 1803 with 450 soldiers, women, and children on board. The frigate never made it to France. Instead, navigating against contrary winds to Santiago de Cuba, then Havana (where it could not go ashore), again to Santiago, then to Charleston (without being able to reach shore again), it finally made its way to Louisiana, although this precise example does not account for the increase of the refugee community in Louisiana, due to the high death rate among the passengers.[12] There are also several examples of refugees who would have preferred to go to Charleston but were deterred from this original intention by restrictions imposed there on the importation of slaves. A petition was even sent to President Madison by refugees requesting a boat to sail back to France, although they remained in Louisiana, since their names are found in later Louisiana population censuses.[13]

At the same time as the wave brought over to Louisiana by the ultimate fall of the colony, a large wave reached the territory in 1803–4 from Jamaica. The resumption of hostilities between France and England led the Jamaican authorities to expel the French refugees who had not been naturalized.[14] Many of them found refuge in Louisiana. At least 1,000 of them reached the newly acquired American territory, but the numbers could well be higher than this.[15] On 26 February 1804, indeed, Governor Claiborne wrote that there were "now on the Mississippi River Several hundred French Emigrants from Jamaica, and two or three other Vessels filled with Passengers (were) daily expected." On 13 April 1804, Claiborne also mentioned a boat on the Mississippi, with 150 French passengers from Jamaica.[16] More arrivals were registered in the following months. The figures should probably be upgraded, since some refugees came over with their slaves, who are probably not counted as refugees, as shown by the example of the Danish schooner *Nancy*, which came from Jamaica carrying more refugees and slaves.[17] It is very easy to trace those migrants in the sacramental records, for instance, the baptismal records of the St. Louis Cathedral in New Orleans, which mention children born in New Orleans in 1804 or 1805, whose brothers and sisters had been born in Jamaica between 1798 and 1803.[18] The later marriage records also give many examples of brides and grooms born in Jamaica at the turn of the century of refugee parents.[19] Several personal narrations also confirm this, for instance, that of Hélène d'Aquin whose family escaped first to Jamaica and then to New Orleans. Altogether, the flow (both direct and indirect through Jamaica) of 1803–4 was more important than during any previous period: 1804–6 reveals over 50 entries in the St. Louis Cathedral sacramental records, which already shows a sharp increase from the periods previously studied.[20] Unfortunately, this cannot be confirmed by the official records (contrary to the case of the 1809–10 wave from Cuba), probably because the period was a historical turning point for Louisiana, and because the transfer of the French colony to the

United States was the main focus of the authorities.[21] Both official sources and the press—despite the high degree of involvement of the refugees in the creation and development of the Louisiana press—display mostly documents and articles focusing on the integration of the territory into the Union and reveals very little concern for the refugees who flocked to New Orleans at the time.[22]

For the next five years, refugees continued arriving in New Orleans, but the flow had returned to small numbers of individuals or families coming from other refuges of the Americas. Some refugees, for instance, came from Cuba or Santo Domingo.[23] The number of refugees reaching New Orleans from Cuba was roughly in the same proportion as those coming from Jamaica, except that they did not come in massive waves, which made them less visible.[24] Among the most famous refugees reaching Louisiana from Cuba in the early years of the century is Louis-Marie-Elisabeth Moreau-Lislet, who had gone from Saint-Domingue to Philadelphia (in 1794), then back to his native island (in 1802–3), then to Santiago de Cuba with his family (in 1804), and finally to New Orleans, where his first appointment to an official position occurred in 1805.

Other refugees reached New Orleans from the Atlantic United States. Among them was Father Louis-Guillaume-Valentin Dubourg, future bishop of New Orleans. Born in Saint-Domingue, he was in metropolitan France when the revolution started. He first went to Spain, then to Cuba, Baltimore, and finally New Orleans. Many other refugees reaching New Orleans in the early nineteenth century came from the United States, such as Jean-Pierre Morgan (from Baltimore in 1804), Paul Lanusse (from Philadelphia in 1801), Claudin de Béleurgey (from Charleston in the late 1790s), Joseph Faulic and Joséphine Dalban (from Baltimore at the turn of the century), Barthélémy Simon, Anne-Augustine Morgan, Jean-Antoine Dacqueny, and Joseph Belzans (all from Charleston, before 1806), and many others from Baltimore, New York, or Philadelphia.[25] The preface to *My Odyssey*, a narrative written by an unnamed young refugee, also indicates that the author of the narrative died in New York before his family moved to Louisiana.[26] This slow influx is difficult to assess precisely, but the total figure of several hundred from Philadelphia, Baltimore, and other Atlantic ports is realistic.[27] Although this assessment lacks accuracy, it gives a general impression of the permanent migration to Louisiana throughout the period and allows an approximation of the total number of refugees. The existence of this permanent flow is largely confirmed by the many entries involving refugees in the St. Louis Cathedral sacramental records. It becomes difficult to list the precise entries, for they become far too numerous, especially since they start recording the baptisms, marriages, and deaths of refugees' children, as well as the sacraments given to the refugees themselves. The first 100 pages of the published volume concerning 1807–9 (which did not yet concern the large Cuban wave that was still to come or at least only concerned it peripherally in the year 1809) list over 70 entries, attesting to an important increase in percentage compared with the previous periods.[28]

The next important migratory wave, the largest and most massive of all but also the best documented, came from Cuba in 1809 and 1810. It followed Napoleon's attempt to invade Spain and place his brother Joseph upon the Spanish throne. The Cuban authorities declared the French refugees settled in Cuba personae non gratae and decided, through a proclamation issued on 12 March 1809, to expel all those who did not have Spanish spouses or who had not requested naturalization. The first boat carrying refugees reached Louisiana on 12 May. By January 1810, at least 9,059 recorded persons had reached Louisiana from Cuba, especially from Santiago and Baracoa, with only one boat leaving from Havana.[29] There were people belonging to the three categories of population composing the societies of Saint-Domingue, Cuba, and Louisiana. Each group amounted roughly to one-third of the migratory wave: 2,731 whites, 3,102 free people of color, and 3,226 slaves, according to the mayor.[30] Some more arrived in Louisiana in January, bringing the total to roughly 10,000 within nine months.[31] These being official figures, this wave is clearly the best documented of all, and historical sources confirm the importance of this migration, which "doubled the number of French-speakers in New Orleans."[32] Added to the accuracy of the figures, the documentation of this Cuban wave presents the advantage of dividing accurately the numbers along the color line, suppressing questions of whether or not the slaves were counted among the refugees. It is interesting to compare these figures with those of each category of the New Orleans Parish population, which amounted, before the arrival, to a total of 17,001, with 6,311 whites, 2,312 free people of color, and 8,378 slaves.[33] The new influx thus represented an increase of 43 percent in the white population, 134 percent in the free population of color, and 38 percent in the slave population. To these impressive percentages must be added the fact that the New Orleans population already comprised a significant proportion of refugees from previous waves. The family papers of Pierre-Antoine Lambert give an insight into the way this migration occurred. They show, first of all, that some people did not flee precipitately, since Lambert first purchased a pharmacy in New Orleans in June (the sale record indicates 8 June) while still residing in Cuba. It also shows that he kept interests in Cuba while living in New Orleans, since there is an abundant correspondence sent to him from Santiago concerning coffee yields and slaves rented out to work. This correspondence seems to indicate that Lambert had sworn allegiance to Carlos IV and to Ferdinand and was, by then, requesting naturalization to try to recover his sequestrated property.[34]

Although there was no later flow of this importance, refugees went on arriving in Louisiana in small numbers in the 1810s, essentially from the seaboard states. They mostly were people whose family had settled in Louisiana and who came to join their relatives. Apparently, "with the end of maritime hostilities in 1815," there were some returns from metropolitan France of "Creole families who . . . were still unadapted to life and the winters there" and who "found in Louisiana an atmosphere analogous to the one they knew in happier times."[35] Finally, a number of families who had found refuge in Jamaica and had remained there at the time of the large migration to New Orleans in the early years of the nineteenth century kept arriving as late as the second half of the century. These individual arrivals are not recorded precisely, although proof may be found attesting to their relative importance. For instance, among the descendants of the Rossignol des Dunes family, there are several examples of such late movements especially from Jamaica, and in the mid-1850s, "most of the last remaining French came to New Orleans."[36] Mme Daron, for instance, who was still in Jamaica in 1834, later arrived at New Orleans; Jeanne Lagourgue, who was still in Jamaica in 1817, died in New Orleans in 1840; the Charest de Lauzon family had members who are known to have arrived around 1830; Father Duquesnay, the first Jamaican-born Catholic priest, left his island of birth for New Orleans in 1845.[37] There are proofs of even later arrivals of descendants of Saint-Domingan refugees, as indicated by the example of Constance Marie Le Mercier Duquesnay, born at Kingston in 1841, whose five-month-old child died at New Orleans in 1866.[38] Although extrapolating from a reduced sample is not evidence, it may be estimated that if the study of one family lineage gives so many individual examples, the late movements from Jamaica to Louisiana must not have been entirely marginal.

In short, between 1791 and the late 1850s, Louisiana was a land of welcome for many former residents of Saint-Domingue. It is difficult to give a precise total, which would require resorting to sacramental and notarial records, indemnification requests, boat passenger lists, personal accounts, and censuses. The sacramental records are helpful in this respect, as shown by the huge increase in the number of entries concerning refugee families in the 1810–12 volume published by the New Orleans Archdiocese Archives.[39] The indemnification requests of the turn of the 1830s also give a snapshot of where people had settled at that time. A precise counting is not, however, the purpose of the present study. What may be concluded is that the total number of arrivals is well over 12,000.[40] If the accurately recorded 1,000 refugees from Jamaica in 1803–4 are added to the also accurately recorded 10,000 from Cuba in 1809–10, as well as to the several hundred direct arrivals of the 1791–98 period and the several hundred refugees from the U.S. East Coast, the figure is already above 12,000. Considering that individual arrivals have been mentioned from Cuba before and after the 1809–10 wave, as well as arrivals from Jamaica between 1804 and 1860 and returns from metropolitan France after 1815, the figure is probably much larger than this. It must also be remembered that, except in the case of the 1809–10 wave from Cuba, it is difficult to ascertain that the figures given include the slaves brought over by their masters. In many cases, the recorded migrants most certainly include only those who came of their own free will.

The assessment of the number of refugees is also disturbed by the fact that some people did not stay in Louisiana—as proved by the example of Henri de Sainte-Gême, who returned to France in 18169–and that many migrants died shortly after reaching Louisiana, as the sacramental records of Louisiana's Catholic churches indicate. There were also incessant movements to and from Louisiana, which makes the tracking of the refugees difficult and often inaccurate.[41] After some time, the number of refugees in New Orleans was thus probably much lower than the estimate given above. Nevertheless, while many refugees died in the months or years following their deportation, many children were born to these refugees in the decades that followed their settlement in Louisiana, which is of great significance to the present work. Indeed, the cultural dilution of the refugees' community within the Louisiana society did not occur immediately, and subsequent discussions will show that direct Saint-Domingan influences did not cease with the migrants' generation but, rather, persisted for at least the next two generations, most certainly well into the 1850s. Since the aim here is to determine the influences brought to Louisiana from Saint-Domingue, refugees' children are essential vehicles of those influences, which explains why the population considered here is well above the 15,000 that probably set foot in Louisiana.

Progressively, Louisiana became the main pole of attraction of the refugees in the first decade of the nineteenth century. Although, at first, New Orleans did not appear as the chosen destination, it later came to host thousands coming from other refuges, and the diaspora finally tended to gather in what became their ideal port of call. Once it was perfectly clear that a return to their island had become highly improbable, the refugees converged to Louisiana and settled there for good. The question as to why this concentration occurred requires close examination, and appears as a sum of contingences and objective reasons.

## Louisiana, the Meeting Place for the Diaspora

The first effect of the migration had been to break family units. In many cases, the members of a same family found their way to various host territories as a result of circumstances rather than as a deliberate choice. The urgency of the flight often took refugees from a same family to distant shores. When they could willingly choose a destination, they tended to converge on one single territory. Most refugee families whose members had spread out in the circum-Caribbean area were reunited in Louisiana. Louis-Joseph Le Gardeur, for instance, remained in Saint-Domingue for a few months after the 1798 evacuation of the British troops in which he had enrolled. He then left for New Orleans, where he was joined by his eldest brother, who had found refuge on "the American continent," and finally, in 1809, by his parents, who had left Saint-Domingue for Cuba in 1803. In some cases, whole families were reunited. In other cases, individuals finally stopped where many of their relatives had found shelter, as is the case of Joseph Villars-Dubreuil, born in Louisiana but living in Saint-Domingue at the time of the troubles. While he had initially boarded a ship bound for Philadelphia, he was in fact transported to Jamaica, but he finally headed for Louisiana to meet the rest of his family.[42]

The relative geographical proximity of the territory was one incentive for those refugees who persisted in their hope that the plantations they had abandoned would be returned to them. Among the main reasons was also the old link between Saint-Domingue and the Gulf Coast. When French colonization first started there, under the lead of Pierre Lemoyne d'Iberville, the regular base of colonization was Saint-Domingue, and the garrison stationed at Biloxi heavily depended on the island for resupply. Later in the colonization process, there were many family ties between settlers of the two French colonies.[43]

As exemplified by the case of Villars-Dubreuil, who was born in Louisiana and then settled in Saint-Domingue, there were many population movements during the parallel colonization of the two locations. For example, the Charbonnets went from Louisiana to Jérémie in the 1770s, then back to Louisiana in 1799, and the d'Aquins moved from Biloxi to Artibonite, then back to New Orleans through Jamaica.[44] Even among Acadians who had sought refuge in Saint-Domingue at the time of the Grand Dérangement, family connections tied the two colonies. About half of them later moved to Louisiana.[45] Others who went to Saint-Domingue and then to Louisiana may be quoted, for instance, Julien Poydras, who became one of the wealthiest planters of the Pointe Coupée area.[46] Some men were even deported from Louisiana by the Spanish authorities after the abortive coup d'état of 1868. They were pardoned but declared personae non gratae in Louisiana and they finally settled in Saint-Domingue before returning to Louisiana. This was the case of Jean Milhet, whose two daughters later married Moreau de Saint-Méry and Baudry des Lauzières before settling with their husbands in their father's homeland.[47] A small migration from Louisiana to Saint-Domingue also occurred in the three or four years that followed this rebellion by the Louisiana planters against the Spanish authorities.[48] Not scarce were thus the inhabitants of Saint-Domingue who had relatives in Louisiana. Added to those kinship ties, good commercial relationships and a tradition of assistance bound the two colonies together.[49] It is not surprising that Saint-Domingan refugees were (either directly or secondarily) attracted to Louisiana. The diaspora—born from the decadelong exodus—had indeed maintained permanent connections and was already starting to build up a community identity. They tended to feel a strong urge to regroup.

The next reason that accelerated the convergence to Louisiana was its purchase by the United States in 1803. Many refugees saw this territory—about to be transferred—as a great land for opportunity. The transfer seemed to open new possibilities for them, and they started imagining the possibility of re-creating Saint-Domingue there. There were vast expanses of land available, and the incipient territorial stage seemed to offer many opportunities. One refugee even clearly expressed his waiting for the transfer to be completed before contemplating the possibility of settling in Louisiana. He explained that, until then, he disliked the idea of a Spanish influence imprinted on the territory and feared that the return of the territory to French dominion might imply the progression of revolutionary ideals there.[50]

Finally, and this was probably the most powerful reason of all, Louisiana appeared as an oasis of French colonial culture in the United States, a place where refugees thus could contemplate a successful planting of new roots. As Laussat, colonial prefect at New Orleans in 1803–4, noted, there was a real cultural continuum between the two colonial entities. According to him, "Saint-Domingue was the (colony) from which Louisiana has borrowed the most customs and ideas."[51] common colonial entrepreneurial spirit had been shared by San Domingans and Louisianans, as well as a similar Creole spirit and a very close vision of society. In order to better understand this colonial parallelism and the attraction it exerted on the refugees, it is essential here to describe this land of welcome.

## The Louisianan Asylum at the Turn of the Nineteenth Century

Although the following depiction of Louisiana will include generalities about the history and organization of the colony, its main focus will be on New Orleans and vicinity, for this is where the vast majority of the refugees settled. Some of them did move to rural parts of the territory. Poydras, for instance, became a man of influence and wealth in Pointe Coupée Parish. Other cases are found in the various sources, for instance, that of a white refugee who settled at Plaquemine,[52] of free families of mixed African descent who settled in the Cane River colony,[53] or of families reaching Louisiana with the 1809–10 wave from Cuba and settling as far as Natchitoches. Several dozen families also settled on the Gulf Coast, and Saint-Domingan surnames are distributed rather evenly over Louisiana.[54] Those cases, however, represent a very small number, and refugees overwhelmingly chose New Orleans as their new home.[55]

Louisiana presented, in many respects, close similarities with the colony of Saint-Domingue, which explains the attraction it had for the refugees. It also displayed several differences that will serve as a basis for further reflection on the influence these refugees had on their host society. Both the similarities and the differences explain the easy integration of the refugees, since they had no strong feeling of strangeness upon arrival and, on the other hand, there were several areas of Louisiana society that offered them interesting prospects. Several specific aspects of New Orleans society at the turn of the nineteenth century indeed account for the mode of integration of the refugees.

First, the French colony of Louisiana had undergone a slightly less linear evolution than Saint-Domingue. French settlement had started later there than in the Caribbean—after 1699—and expanded very slowly compared with its Caribbean counterpart. The reasons that led the French to start a colony in Louisiana were strategic rather than economic; they wanted to check Spanish and English progress in the imperial race and hoped to set up an outpost to defend their West Indian colonies. Due to these political and strategic priorities, the colony never thrived under French dominion. At the end of the Seven Years' War, weary of financing this costly and slowly developing colony, France gave it away to Spain, as a repayment for Spain's alliance with France against England during the war. Spain accepted the present, for strategic reasons, including the advantage of thus setting a buffer area between Mexico and the British eastern colonies, but also because holding the mouth of the Mississippi River meant ensuring a real Spanish supremacy over the western Gulf of Mexico. Although the formal Spanish possession started only on 20 January 1767, La Louisiane had already, by then, become Luisiana. This lasted only until 1800, when Napoleon started elaborating dreams of a strong French empire in the Americas. Because France had regained power on the European scene and because Spain was then weak and almost bankrupt, it did not cling to this colony and France easily obtained the retrocession of the old colony, sanctioned by the October 1800 Treaty of San Ildefonso. Luisiana thus became La Louisiane again, although not officially for fear of attempted invasions at a time when the defense of the colony could hardly be insured by its new owners. The rebirth of French Louisiana was short-lived, however, since it became a territory of the United States in 1803.

These events are common knowledge. Their consequences within the framework of the present study, however, are several. The French background and historical conditions partly explain the attraction of Louisiana for the Saint-Domingan refugees, as well as their relatively easy relocation there. The transfer to Spain before the crucial period of the French Revolution accounts for the relative exclusion of Louisiana from the turmoil, as well as for the attraction the colony thus had for some of the early migrants.[56] Settling in a Spanish territory indeed meant staying clear of revolutionary upheaval and not risking the expansion to their new refuge of the 1794 act which emancipated the slaves throughout the French colonies. The later transfer to the United States obviously meant for the refugees avoiding both Spanish and French domination. It was probably essential to the refugee waves of the early 1800s to be rid of the French rule that had piled upon them all the misfortunes they had gone through. It was as essential to the later wave from Cuba to reach a territory totally neutral in the French-Spanish feud that had caused their expulsion from their new refuge. Obviously, American rule was also considered as a guarantee that they would remain in a slave society close, at least to some respect, to the model they were familiar with, especially since the Louisiana Purchase Treaty had promised the new citizens they would keep the rights and prerogatives they had upon becoming American. The refugees' arrival in Louisiana within a time frame—less than two decades—exactly centered on its transfer to the United States also meant that they were among the actors of the most crucial turning point in the history of Louisiana. The arrival of the last wave from Cuba even more or less coincided with the end of the territorial phase, occurring right before the accession to statehood of Louisiana (in 1812). By strengthening the Francophone community at the time of the Louisiana Purchase, then again when Louisiana became a state of the Union, in 1812, the migrants reinforced the Creole community and delayed the Americanization of the territory. The new political situation also made their welcome by the Creole society much warmer. Finally, as the next chapters will show, the renewed cultural diversity of Louisiana's population at the time of the transfer doubtlessly made way for a reinforced influence of the refugees.

The historical background is thus of primeval interest in trying to assess the integration of the refugees in Louisiana and their subsequent influence on it. The organization of Louisiana society is another essential feature that requires thorough examination. This survey is again aimed at describing the general situation in terms of social, economic, and cultural common features and differences to better understand the fitting of the refugees within Louisiana society.[57]

To understand the impact of the migration, it is indispensable to give an assessment of the total figures and of the racial and ethnic composition of the population they found upon their arrival. During the first period of the French colonial era, population increase had been very low and very slow for the white and slave populations. In 1763, when Spain took over, the population was still relatively sparse, and New Orleans contained less than 2,500 inhabitants.[58] Although French immigration to early Spanish Louisiana was almost nonexistent, Spanish liberal immigration policies launched a series of new migrations, bringing together several thousand Acadians and Canary Islanders, a few hundred Malagans and, toward the end of the Spanish colonial era, a large flow of Anglo-Americans, after Governor Miró's promulgation of a new land grant policy.[59] This population increase went along with a reopening of the slave trade and thus a re-Africanization of the colony. The population increase was steady throughout the Spanish era, giving on the eve of the first arrivals from Saint-Domingue a total population of 39,410 in lower Louisiana (20,673 slaves and 18,737 free persons).[60] By the time the main 1803 wave came, there was a total population of almost 50,000, over half being slave, and in 1810, the population of the Territory of Orleans had reached 76,476, half being slave.[61]

Although this already gives a good measure of the ratio of refugees to this population, a closer look at the city of New Orleans shows it to be the main pole of attraction of this migration. In 1791, before the first migrants started arriving, New Orleans had a total population of slightly over 5,000 (2,386 whites, 862 free persons of color, and 1,789 slaves). By 1805, before the large final wave from Cuba, it was up to over 8,000 (3,551 whites, 1,566 free people of color, and 3,105 slaves).[62] The arrival of the last wave from Cuba doubled the population of New Orleans. Considering the composition of this last wave, it is already clear that it represented a large part of the free population of color of New Orleans and quite a good proportion of the slaves of the city (about one third of the slave population of New Orleans and precincts and 10 percent of the slaves of the Orleans Territory).[63] Since there were already many refugees among the inhabitants of New Orleans, the figures suggest the impact of these refugees on the host population.

The demographical features of the Louisiana population hint at a number of similarities and differences between Saint-Domingue and the refugees' new homeland. To assess the role they played in Louisiana, it is essential to understand those features. Both shared a French colonial past. Although French colonial rule had been much shorter in Louisiana than in Saint-Domingue (about 65 years altogether versus almost a century and a half), the two colonies had been subjected to the same colonial policies and legislation. The transfer of Louisiana to Spain did slightly modify the situation, however. French institutions were replaced by Spanish ones, in particular the French Superior Council which gave way to a *Cabildo*, thus depriving its members from the policymaking and judicial powers they had previously exerted. French law was progressively replaced by the Spanish Laws of the Indies—also known as the O'Reilly Code—and the military was organized around the Fixed Regiment of Louisiana, mostly composed of Spanish speakers. Spanish rule, however, barely lasted 35 years, and did not totally overrule many of the institutional landmarks of French colonial rule (the *Code Noir*, for instance was superseded by Spanish legislation but the latter did not really alter the spirit of the original code). Even though, superficially, the Spanish authorities did implement an "aggressive restructuring of Louisiana's military, judicial, and civil government," the Hispanicization of the territory was relatively superficial.[64] Public offices were granted to French-speaking locals, as well as positions in the militia and even in the Fixed Regiment of Louisiana. Throughout the Spanish period, facts confirm that Gallic cultural and social patterns persisted.[65] The refugees from Saint-Domingue (at least before the Purchase) thus came into contact with a colonial organization that was not very far from the one they had experienced on their island.

Moreover, the society they found largely revolved around French cultural traits, despite the Spanish takeover of the last three decades of the eighteenth century. The new colonial situation did not really trigger any large-scale Spanish population movement. The potential Hispanic influence from the Canary Islanders and Malagans was largely counterbalanced by the more massive arrival of Acadians, and only the ruling governmental officers and the military were Spanish. For instance, Antonio Ulloa came to take official possession of the colony in March 1766 with only 75 men, and in 1769 a new contingent of only 2,000 came with General Alejandro O'Reilly.[66] This means that Spaniards formed a cultural minority that never deeply influenced Louisiana society. The Spanish language was used for official documents (at least a translation into Spanish was indispensable), but it was confined to this use. Spanish officials spoke French and frequently intermarried with women belonging to the Francophone society of New Orleans.[67] French culture prevailed by the force of majority but also through tradition and because no forced acculturation was ever attempted by the Spaniards.[68] The Francophone population was ready to resist any attempt at forcing a foreign culture on them.[69] This means that the Saint-Domingan refugees found, upon arrival, a culture that was similar to theirs, especially since the dominant religion had remained Catholic, the Spanish takeover having only reinforced the religious background by sending Spanish clergy to Louisiana and by adding Spanish nuns to the predominantly French female clergy of the Ursulines. Anecdotally, only the architecture underwent real Spanish influence, but merely by accident, since large-scale reconstruction was made necessary by the destruction of most of the buildings of New Orleans by the big fires of 1788 and 1794. In short, when the first refugees started flocking in, "Louisiana was a Spanish colony with a French population and a merchant class with close ties to France," even though the Spanish presence was slightly more perceptible in New Orleans than in the rest of the colony.[70]

When the refugees reached New Orleans, the structure of the economy was not very far from what they had left behind, since Louisiana was mostly an agricultural plantation society. After very harsh beginnings, when the Louisiana production could not meet even local needs, the colony had finally become self-sufficient under Spanish rule, even starting to turn from subsistence to cash-crop agriculture. Although the Louisiana economy was inferior to that of Saint-Domingue, the colony produced tobacco and indigo and then cotton in the late eighteenth century. The Louisiana economy and society also relied on slavery, even though with fluctuations in the importance of the trade and never in the same proportions as Saint-Domingue. Slavery and the slave trade remained limited throughout the French period but underwent a real surge under Spanish rule, with a return to large-scale importation of African slaves. Even if the Louisiana slave population was always about equal to the white population, the colony was doubtlessly a slave society when it welcomed the Saint-Domingan migrants. Spanish rule never notably altered the Louisiana social fabric based upon the institution of slavery. On the contrary, it reinforced the power of the slaveholding class, more in keeping with what could be found in colonial Saint-Domingue.[71]

Finally, the basic hierarchy of the Louisiana society followed the same model as that in Saint-Domingue with, at both ends of the ladder, a large substratum of slaves and a white society that comprised both nonslaveholding and slaveholding categories. Moreover, although in very different proportions as in Saint-Domingue, the Louisiana society was also a "three-tiered" society.[72] Although this population did not equal its Saint-Domingan counterpart either in numbers or in power and influence, it existed when the refugees came to Louisiana. In short, the main basis of Louisiana society in the late eighteenth century had nothing really unusual for the newcomers from the Caribbean island. There was even a real proximity "in ethos and class structure" between the two societies.[73] This explains both the attraction of Louisiana for the refugees and their relatively easy relocation in this new homeland. This was also true, of course, for the later migratory waves since, upon reaching the territory, they found other refugees who had settled before them.

Despite this close proximity between the original and host societies, however, there were differences that also contributed to the easy relocation of the refugees by giving them a number of opportunities in the host society and by leaving whole spheres for them to occupy and in which to exert some influence. Any comparative study of the two societies proves, without the slightest doubt, that the advantage goes to Saint-Domingue when considering the financial prospects the colony offered to its inhabitants. This explains the island's attraction throughout its colonial period. The economy of the Louisiana colony lagged far behind, even during the Spanish era. While

Saint-Domingue was the uncontested economic leader of the French colonial world, Louisiana, constantly propped up by subsidies from the mother countries, was still trying to launch an exportation economy. The main goal of either France or Spain in founding or taking over the colony had always been political and strategic, never economic. Despite the surge of the cotton production in the last decade of the eighteenth century, Louisianans were still seeking their prosperity. There was still much available space for agriculture, as opposed to Saint-Domingue, which was "overcrowded" and where land was "over-subdivided."[74] This undoubtedly left room for enterprising and skilled newcomers.

Although the social hierarchy of Louisiana closely followed that of Saint-Domingue, there were also major differences which may explain that the refugees found space for insertion relatively easily. How the refugees, whatever their racial status, fit into this social structure is a revealing feature. The slave population, although it had increased in the last decades of the eighteenth century when the slave trade had resumed under Spanish rule, was never a large majority in Louisiana. It was slightly more numerous than the white population when the Saint-Domingan refugees started arriving in the colony, but far behind the proportion found on the Caribbean island, where the slaves had outnumbered the white population by a ratio of fourteen to one. Slave labor was always necessary, and despite the Louisianans' suspicion of slaves potentially perverted by revolutionary ideals, any additional help was welcome. Moreover, Saint-Domingan slaves very often had special skills that most Louisiana slaves lacked, as shown by the participation of Saint-Domingan slaves in the sugar venture at the turn of the nineteenth century.

As for the free people of color, they existed in both colonial societies, but again in very different proportions. According to the figures available on prerevolutionary Saint-Domingue, the number of free people of African descent was almost equivalent to the white population, or at least of the same order of magnitude. Not so in Louisiana, although Spanish rule had been slightly more favorable to that class than the earlier French rule. When Spain took over, their number was apparently very low, although that class had existed for a very long time.[75] Under Spanish rule, their number in New Orleans rose drastically.[76] By the time of the Louisiana Purchase, the New Orleans free black population had reached over 1,800, representing 37 percent of the black population and over one-fifth of the total city population, this total number already including the Saint-Domingan free blacks of the first migration waves.[77]

Compared to Saint-Domingue, Louisiana's free population of color was thus relatively small. In Saint-Domingue—where the relative scarcity of white women in the early colonial period had largely favored interracial unions—the degree of blood mixture had been very high among free blacks. In New Orleans, the free population of color was largely of mixed African descent, but it also included people of pure African descent, who had always entertained close relationships with the slaves, especially in this urban environment, although by the early nineteenth century, the two categories were less close than previously.[78] Whatever the degree of racial mixture in Louisiana compared with Saint-Domingue's free population of color, the free refugees of color were mostly racially mixed and thus reinforced this group of the Louisiana free population of color. The status of the group in New Orleans was also much lower than that of their Saint-Domingan counterparts. They had much less economic, social, and political power. They were less affluent than the Saint-Domingan free people of color, although their future was apparently promising.[79] Their very existence, however, meant that the refugees of that class could find their place in the New Orleans society. Their small number implied that a numerical reinforcement of the class would probably be beneficial to their claim for a better position within society. Finally, although they were relatively poor, they were also dynamic and could only be further stimulated by representatives of the same class who had known better economic, social, and political prospects in their original society.

As for the white population, it also differed from that of Saint-Domingue in many respects. There were comparatively fewer differences and more social cohesion among the Louisiana white class in general. While in Saint-Domingue the division between *Grands Blancs* and *Petit Blancs* had been important, representing an impenetrable barrier, intermarriage was frequent among the various categories of the New Orleans white population.[80] This social fluidity had been stronger during French rule, but in the late colonial period, it still marked Louisiana society which remained very close to a frontier society, thus leaving many opportunities to those who were part of it.[81] This undoubtedly left sufficient fluidity for newcomers to integrate within this social fabric, especially since the arrival of the refugees coincided with the growth of the Anglo-American population (even before the takeover by the United States), which started dividing the white society along cultural lines, making new inclusions on either side easier.

The consequences of this lingering frontier-type society and of its renewed diversity were easily perceptible in the cultural field as well. The cultural life was less developed than it had been in Saint-Domingue. Schooling was limited, despite Spanish attempts at creating a public school in 1771. When the first refugees started arriving, New Orleans counted eight French-speaking academies that had no more than 400 students.[82] There was no newspaper, no scientific society, no theater, no opera, very little cultural and artistic life. This relative cultural bareness left much room for dynamic migrants. At the same time, the wide cultural diversity of the population made it relatively more permeable to new influences. French, Spanish, African, and Anglo-American cultural features were already mingling quite closely, each group tending to slowly acculturate the others, with more or less success according to the group, and the Louisiana culture had already reached a high degree of creolization.[83] It is thus not surprising that the refugees could participate in their own way in the development of a unique culture.

Finally, among the differences between Louisiana and Saint-Domingue relevant to this discussion, political awareness and activism must be mentioned. While the situation in Saint-Domingue had strengthened the political dynamism of its colonists, both among whites and free people of color, the Louisiana locals had very little political power once the first French colonial period was over. The Spanish administration was overpowering, and little could be done at the local level. The attempted rebellion of the Louisiana planters was rapidly crushed by O'Reilly in 1769, thus ridding the colony of its most active elements.[84] Creoles were members of the *Cabildo*, but this structure had no policymaking or judicial powers. Rather than a real political effectiveness, it conferred a symbolic "corporate identity" on the slaveholding class.[85] The Spanish administrators, who were obviously skilled diplomatically, thus limited the political ambitions of the Louisianans. This was the situation when the first refugees arrived, and there is little doubt that the inclusion in the Louisiana society of these politically active immigrants, together with the turning point of the American takeover, had a real impact on the politics of Louisiana.

In short, the refugees found in Louisiana a structure that was close to the one they had known before their migration. It was a slave society, based on an agricultural economy, with a "trilevel" social organization and a background of French colonial history and culture. Their uprooting thus did not take them to a strange land the functioning of which they could not grasp, which made their integration far easier. At the same time, the Saint-Domingan colony had been much more advanced socially, economically, politically, and culturally, which left room for the immigrants to exert an influence in many sectors.

Another factor at play in the later integration of the refugees is the reaction of the Louisiana population to their arrival.

## The Louisianans and the Refugees

As in the other North American refuges, Saint-Domingan immigrants to Louisiana met a twofold response from the local population.[86] The first reaction was that of spontaneous assistance toward a community ravaged by a rebellious slave movement. Many North Americans, especially in those areas with developing slave societies, pitied these white refugees sent to a strange land, totally destitute, and often desperate after losing their home, their family (either through hopefully temporary separation or through death), and their property. The populations of these refuges helped them through public financial aid and private charity, sometimes quartered them in private houses, sometimes dedicated public buildings for their lodging, fed them, tended the sick and wounded, and offered to assist them if they wanted to migrate to another destination.[87] There was also a second response, one of fear and distrust, especially concerning the populations of color, both free and enslaved.[88] Their contact with revolutionary ideas and their closeness to rebellious and violent actions made the North Americans—as well as the other West Indians who welcomed them—fearful of a contamination of their own populations of color. Moreover, the Revolution was raging in France, and Americans feared the arrival of these Frenchmen, even if they were colonials. They feared both the introduction of royalist elements and the violence of some of the revolutionary ideals, especially after the French Revolution had started displaying a clear tendency toward acts of violence and mob rule.[89]

The situation in Louisiana followed a similar pattern, although with variations in time and with adaptations to the specific local situation. The reactions were exacerbated by the general importance of the migration wave (in particular in 1810) and by the local political situation, especially after the Louisiana Purchase, because of the dual—Creole v. Anglo—composition of the population. The response of the locals needs to be examined in detail, for it really depended on the period (colonial or American), on the local group considered (authorities or population), and on the race and status of the immigrants (white, free people of color, or slaves). The fears mostly had to do with disruption of public order, introduction of revolutionary ideas (a fear especially voiced by Spanish authorities), excessive increase of the free population of color (a concern especially expressed by Americans), or introduction of slaves contaminated by rebellious tendencies. In general, however, the fears were ultimately hushed, and all those who desired could come to New Orleans, if with some delay.

The problems of whether to accept the refugees or not and how to help them were certainly less acute during the Spanish era, since arrivals were few and spread over the last decade of Spanish rule. The welcome was apparently not uniformly enthusiastic, if some testimonies (by Berquin-Duvallon or Dr Alliot, for instance) are to be believed.[90] Whether these testimonies are exaggerated or not, they suggest that all the refugees did not feel welcome. Moreover, the Spanish authorities did forbid the entrance of slaves from the French islands, unofficially as early as 1790, officially after 1793.[91] This legislation condemned those who brought their slaves into the colony to a fine of 400 piasters per slave as well as payment of the deportation fees. This meant not only excluding the slaves themselves but also their masters unless they agreed to come to Louisiana without their slaves. The slaves who traveled with their masters were generally the most faithful slaves who, according to many accounts, had often prompted their masters' flight by warning them of danger, sometimes even saving their lives. They were also often the only fortune the refugees had brought with them. It is valid to conclude that, without this ban, many more refugees would have chosen Louisiana rather than the Atlantic Coast of the United States for their first asylum.[92] The prohibition was finally removed by the Spanish government and announced in Louisiana in November 1800, which coincided with the secret return to French rule. Even though this ban probably reduced the size of the first migration to Spanish Louisiana, it was mostly overlooked by those who settled in the colony with their slaves, and its implementation was apparently never a priority for the local authorities, probably because of a feeling of solidarity for these fellow colonials banished from their homes. Moreover, considering that those who came mostly stayed, they probably felt that the Louisianans' behavior was much less hostile than what either Berquin-Duvallon or Alliot described.

The reactions of Louisiana to the later waves, once the colony had become a territory of the United States, were similar despite the increased magnitude of the migration. They could be summarized as a charitable welcome to suffering human beings, together with a fearful reaction to the consequences—due to the personality of those refugees and to their past—followed by an ultimate acceptance of the refugees' presence and integration into Louisiana social fabric. The first reactions were often negative, several ships being prevented from entering the harbor of New Orleans either for fear of diseases (as was the case of the frigate *L'Express* in 1803) or to prevent black people of either status from being brought in (as was the case at the time of the wave from Cuba, when ships had to remain stationed at Fort-Plaquemine for a while).[93] Some details, however, can be added on each of the population categories (which came in several waves in the territorial era), especially concerning the last wave from Cuba, in which the three categories of population were almost equally represented. The response of white residents to the arrival of the refugees obviously differed according to the racial group the refugees belonged to.

The slaves were systematically the objects of all fears from the authorities, although they were eventually allowed to enter the territory as a special favor to their unfortunate masters. As in the Spanish era, their contamination by revolutionary ideals made them less than welcome. In 1804, the Federal Act of territorial organization had banned the importation of slaves from outside the United States, under the penalty of $300 and the forfeit of illegally imported slaves for anyone who broke the law. In June 1804, however, the Congress had allowed the president to remit the penalties for those refugees originating from Saint-Domingue. Similarly, the 1808 ban of the slave trade later forbade the entry of foreign slaves on the territory of the United States. The residents of New Orleans pressured Governor Claiborne, who forwarded their petitions to the federal government. In June 1809, Congress passed an act that remitted penalties concerning the slaves belonging to the refugees from Cuba. The arguments behind this exceptional rule were humanitarian, both for the sake of the slaves themselves and for that of their masters who often had no other means of survival than hiring their slaves out upon reaching their new home.[94] There is thus evidence that, despite the fears of the authorities, the Louisianans dissented from the general feeling and favored admission of these slaves, on behalf of the white refugees.

Free people of color were considered with almost as much distrust, and the Louisiana authorities did not exactly welcome the massive migration from Cuba, which had the immediate effect of doubling the free population of color in New Orleans.[95] Legally, free men of color over age 15 were not allowed to enter Louisiana. No law was ever passed to authorize their entry, as had been the case for the slaves. They were tacitly accepted, however, on humanitarian grounds, and were taken care of by their own class, upon request of the mayor.[96] Here again, there seems to have been a relative divergence between the American authorities and the locals as to whether or not the free group of color should be admitted.

As for the white refugees, they were warmly welcomed by the already present Saint-Domingans as well as by the Creole population of New Orleans, as a reinforcement of the Gallic community, at a time when they felt highly threatened by the new Americanization of the territory. There was a permanent flow of Anglo-American migrants, who were according to George W. Cable "few in number, but potent in energies and advantages," which made the Creoles consider them "with hot jalousy."[97] To these Creoles, who strongly dissented with the new American owners of Louisiana, the arrival of the white refugees was an incredibly beneficial addition. For the same reason, the refugees were considered as a negative influx of French-speaking population by the American authorities who hoped for a quick Americanization of Louisiana.[98] The new rulers especially feared the propagation of too extreme revolutionary ideals and were displeased with the refugees who sometimes came to be identified with the pirating community of the Baratarians.[99] On humanitarian grounds, however, the city council passed a resolution in May 1809, offering temporary relief to the refugees, and several actions were organized by a Welfare Committee.[100] For the Creoles, favoring the admission of those refugees was a clear act of cultural and political resistance which the American authorities did not manage to successfully oppose.

In general, all those who wanted to come were eventually accepted within the Louisiana territory.[101] They all received the necessary aid to settle (through public help, private charity, and the organization of social events, for instance at the Théâtre Saint-Pierre)[102] and their requests for work or lodging were advertised by the main two newspapers of New Orleans, the *Moniteur de la Louisiane*, and the *Courrier de la Louisiane*. The already present refugees, together with the Louisiana Creoles, made every effort to provide help and ensure that the refugees' relocation might be as easy as possible. Since the refugees generally obeyed the law and did not create any public disorder, no official measure was ever attempted against them after their relocation in Louisiana, despite the initial reluctance of the authorities.[103] In general, the strong opposition of the Louisiana Creoles to the American efforts to prevent the refugees' settlement was thus victorious, and the refugees remained, for the most part. Their massive settlement proved that, however mixed the welcome may have been in the first moments, Louisiana was no place of torment to those homeless (twice homeless for the last waves from Jamaica and Cuba) fellows of French colonial background who, as Cable puts it, "came to their better cousins with the ties of a common religion, a common tongue, much common sentiment, misfortunes that may have had some resemblance and with the poetry of exile."[104]

This large refugee flow composed of people belonging to the three subgroups of population—slaves, free people of color, and whites—was thus absorbed into the Louisiana society. Louisiana was sufficiently close to what the refugees had left behind to give them a sense of familiarity but presented enough differences to offer them space for insertion and influence. However mixed the first reactions, once the migrants were in Louisiana, very few voices rose against them, and their presence went officially unnoticed. Before focusing on their contribution to their new homeland, it is essential to survey their own reaction to this relocation and assess their degree of integration into the Louisiana society.

# 3

# The Refugee Community

Due to the diversity of the refugee group in terms of race, status, and class as well as the staggering of the arrivals over twenty-odd years—although with peak periods—into a host territory marked by radical political changes, it is indispensable, before assessing the group's influences, to examine the degree of cohesion among its members. In other words, it is essential to determine whether or not the refugees built a community and how long that sense of community lasted. To this purpose, the notions of identity and integration, applied to a racially disparate refugee group, will be set in perspective.

## Building an Identity

To tentatively answer the question of the existence of a refugee community, it is essential to dwell first on a number of considerations not usually included in discussions on ethnicity. Thinking in terms of identity is easier in the case of an ethnically unified alien immigrant group. In the present case, the group was anything but homogeneous and was far from being totally alien, since it shared with the majority of the host population identical roots, history, language, and even religion. It is, however, possible to determine its cohesiveness by first examining the links the refugees established among them. A sense of identity developed among the forced migrants for a number of obvious reasons. The conditions of their departure from their island had been horrendous, as had often been the conditions of their transportation to their new homeland. Estrangement had been a characteristic of their arrival, no matter how warmly they had been welcome. Most of them, whatever their previous degree of affluence, were destitute or at least had left their wealth and property in Saint-Domingue. For most immigrants, the journey to Louisiana and subsequent reconstruction of their shattered lives was a second try, the first attempts, whether in Jamaica or Cuba, having proved permeable to international politics and eventually unsuccessful. Although to various degrees, dependent on the social and racial status of the various refugees, this was true of all of them in different forms. Be they free or slave, be they of mixed or pure ancestry, they had met the same conditions of flight and migration, and the same feeling of estrangement had affected them upon resettlement. Facing such adversity developed instinctive feelings of solidarity among the various members of a same group and also among members of the different racial categories.

This solidarity is perceptible in all the testimonies left by the refugees. It is easier to pinpoint among the white refugees, who left most of these testimonies, but it is also to be found in the few memoirs written by people of African descent.[1] Those of the refugees already settled, for instance, organized for the later waves of immigrants charity events that they advertised in the local papers. An article of the *Louisiana Gazette* of 21 March 1810, for example, mentions the organization of a concert and ball for the benefit of Mr. Valois and the committee of benevolence founded to help the refugees.[2] When it was not financial, the refugees' assistance to their fellow refugees was, at the very least, psychological. One of them, Eliza Williams Chotard Gould, even though she was in Georgia herself, describes the migration of her sisters to Louisiana, adding, "In New Orleans, [they were] cheered by the society of their companions of misfortune."[3] This solidarity is clearly felt in the contacts they maintained, whether their refuges were geographically close or not. An example of this faithfulness to each other, although probably extreme, is that of the enormous correspondence of Jean Boze to his companion of exile, friend and benefactor Henri de Sainte-Gême.[4] Between Sainte-Gême's departure for France, in 1818, and Boze's death in 1842, the latter wrote monthly letters to his friend. Rather than simple letters, these messages, which easily covered ten pages, were chronicles of the life on Sainte-Gême's Louisiana plantation of Gentilly written as the events occurred. For over twenty years and through hundreds of letters, Boze told his friend about life on his plantation, the condition of the illegitimate family he had left to his care in New Orleans, and events in Louisiana at large and in the refugee community more precisely. Boze's letters create the impression of a real community whose members were in close contact. The news he gives concerning the other refugees is often as abundant and precise as that given to Sainte-Gême about his racially mixed children. Boze gives Sainte-Gême personal information on some refugees, keeping him informed about marriages, deaths, and births but also about financial problems and successes, political fates, and anything that pertains to daily life.

The refugees remained in epistolary contact, but they also looked after each other's interests. Sainte-Gême helped Boze when they both found shelter in New Orleans in 1809 and let him live on his plantation for over twenty years after he departed from New Orleans. Proof that Sainte-Gême's generosity was not unique is given by Boze, who at one point wrote that he was contemplating the possibility of moving back to Cuba to reside with one of his friends there.[5] In exchange for his friend's long-lasting hospitality, Boze looked after Sainte-Gême's financial and personal interests. He assisted Sainte-Gême's illegitimate family after Sainte-Gême's final departure from Louisiana with his white family in 1818. He took care of the Gentilly plantation, the slaves working on it, and the properties in downtown New Orleans. He even traveled to Cuba to settle the question of his friend's sequestered property there as well as debts still unpaid to Sainte-Gême, both in Cuba and Jamaica. From June 1820 until at least June 1828, he remained in "St. Yago" (Santiago de Cuba), struggling to save his friend's assets there.[6] This example was not exceptional, as the Lambert Family Papers show. Letters sent from Cuba reveal that several friends were trying to settle the interests of Pierre Lambert, native of Cap Français, who had moved to New Orleans, where he was an apothecary.[7] There existed among the refugees a strong sense of solidarity reinforced by the necessity to face adversity together. It is unfortunately easier to prove for the white refugees. It is obvious, however, that members of the free group of color heavily relied on each other to survive and thrive in this new homeland and that the refugees' slaves must have felt, in the beginning at least, a strong bond of solidarity due to their common fate and common cultural bond. The rare testimonies also prove that they manifested solidarity with other refugees.[8]

Solidarity thus reigned among them, and they displayed an obvious wish to communicate and socialize with one another. The profuse correspondence among refugees witnessed between their various asylums of the Americas is also true concerning the New Orleans refugees. Examination of the various exchanges shows that they did not lose touch, even when their correspondents were in distant refuges.[9] They obviously needed information about people they had left behind.[10] Correspondence also served to maintain contacts, in the hope of a future reunion, especially since they clearly refused to think that the loss of their island and property was to be final. For some years, they believed in the eventuality of a return. Napoleon's failed attempt to recapture the island doubtless shattered this prospect. Only the compensations distributed by the French government in the late 1820s terminated forever the faint hopes that still lingered. Several of the early accounts and items of correspondence clearly reveal this strong wish to return to the island.[11] There seems to have been an imperious need for these refugees to meet, share their hopes, imagine the future, and devise plans for revenge and for the recovery of what they had lost.[12] This favored the development of strong links between them, the longing for private occasions to meet, and the existence of public places for socializing.[13]

The most famous public place for socializing in New Orleans was probably the Café des Réfugiés, which was located at 514 St. Philip Street before it was moved in 1833 to 287 Old Levee (now 921 Decatur).[14] The place was made eternally famous by Cable's *Old Creole Days*, although he differentiates his "Café des Exilés" from the Café des Réfugiés, where he says there was much more political talk. Whether real or mythologized by Cable, the place seemed to respond to a real need among the refugees to be together and share their experience of estrangement, because they are "homeless in a land of homes [and] see windows gleaming and doors ajar, but not for them." This social place is depicted by the famous New Orleans author as a place of welcome because "if any poor exile, from any island where guavas or mangoes or plantains grow, wants a draught which will make him see his home among the cocoa-palms, behold the Café des Exilés ready to take the poor child up and give him breast." All can find assistance there and even support, since the customer "will pay when he can." The Café is essentially shown as a place for togetherness, for shared memories: "there, lolling back in their rocking-chairs, they would pass the evening hours with oft-repeated tales of home," a place of hopes and solace, even if the moon is the only link with their homeland "because from her soaring height she looked down at the same moment upon them and upon their homes in the far Antilles." Cable's Café sometimes seems to take people through a cathartic experience: "some old man would tell his tale of fire and blood and capture and escape," and "the heads would lean forward from the chair-backs and a great stillness would follow the ending of the story."[15]

*The Creoles of Louisiana* takes on a more historical and less mythologized form than the previously quoted collection. Cable, referring to the refugees' apparent need to assemble, also mentions the West Indians' leadership "in licentiousness, gambling and dueling," adding that "the number of billiard-rooms, gambling-houses, and lottery offices was immense" (218). He also depicts them gathering, together with the Creoles, "at those open-air African dances, carousals, and debaucheries in the rear of the town that have left their monument in the name of 'Congo' Square" (219). Although most entertainment places served as gathering places, it is probably at Congo Square that the whole refugee community, slaves, free people of color, and whites met more often.[16] Surrounded by white refugees, Louisiana Creoles, and free people of color (Creole or refugee), slaves gathered in celebrations that either surprised or shocked most Americans. Congo Square became one of the places where the refugees' identity manifested.

In a less entertaining mode, their sense of solidarity is also expressed in the fact that they were witnesses to each other's notarial acts (wills, for instance) and weddings, and served as godparents, a trend which may be found among both whites and free people of color. Both groups of refugees were also godparents to slaves. Most of the events noted in the sacramental records of the Archdiocese of New Orleans bear the mention "all refugees in this city from Santo Domingo" with slight variations in the form of the expression.[17] This trend was also described among the refugees in most of their asylums, for instance in Jamaica, and was attributed to the "fact that they were all companions in distress" and that they were tied by a "community of interests."[18] The very same feeling of solidarity led the refugees to appeal to each other professionally whenever possible. It was either from a will to help their pairs in their professional activity or out of a special trust that the community of experience created. When comparing the files of several notaries of New Orleans, the proportion of cases involving refugees dealt by Marc Lafitte, himself a refugee, is evidence of this trend.[19] A closer study of the refugees' occupational trends also demonstrates that they worked together in their journalistic or educational ventures.[20]

Solidarity, appeals to one another for help, and social gatherings were part of the construction of the community. A clear tendency to endogamy, in the early years, also reinforced the ties between the refugees. When examining the marriage contracts and church records, the trend is obvious.[21] Refugees tended to marry other refugees. Although there was a reversal in the trend after a decade or two, the first years tended to link those expatriates according to cross-class patterns that would probably not have been possible in their homeland. This was true among whites as well as free people of color.[22] Solidarity and a tendency to intermarry (endogamy) are not necessarily sufficient to create a sense of ethnicity. Many other features of the refugee community, however, attest to this ethnic reaction. A sense of ethnicity, at least a "symbolic" one, is conveyed by the specific way in which they turned their origins into some kind of intrinsic characteristic. All official documents, be they notarial or sacramental records, bear witness to this. Studying the phrasing of these documents gives the measure of the importance, in the eyes of the refugees, of their Saint-Domingan origins. Many marriage contracts, for instance, reveal this trend. When examining the Marc Lafitte files, it is noticeable that the origins of the parents were not often mentioned when the contracts con-

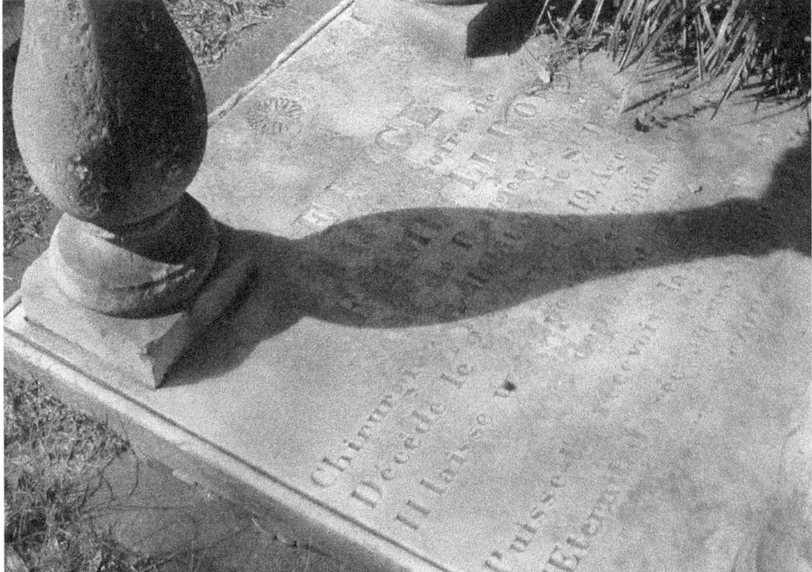

Figure 1. Tomb of Firmin Leroy, Church of St. Mary of the Annunciation, Charleston, S.C. Photo courtesy of Hilda Kenner.

cerned nonrefugees. In the case of the refugees, they were indicated, most of the time, as exemplified by the contract of Jeanne Elisabeth Berquin, born in Charleston, whose parents were from Cap Français, Saint-Domingue.[23] Another example is that of Jean-Baptiste Marie Funel de Seranon, who was born in France to Pierre Joseph Jean-Baptiste Antoine Funel de Seranon and Marie Margueritte Margest of Saint-Domingue.[24]

Often the phrasing used in the entries concerning the refugees is not typical of the rest of the files and clearly indicates their wish to proclaim those Saint-Domingan origins as a kind of personal mark, as essential as name, date, and place of birth. The sacramental records reveal several examples worth citing. Some entries of the 1810–12 period refer to refugees as natives of Saint-Domingue, "residents of this parish," and "landowners at St. Marc."[25] Others insist on the former residence in Saint-Domingue, although the individuals were born in metropolitan France.[26] A still more interesting formulation links a new bride, Magdaleine Beuron, born in Metropolitan France and resident of the Faubourg St. Marie, to the refugee group by indicating that she is the widow of Claude Marie, "resident and deceased at Comily, a quarter of St. Louis Parish in Jérémie on Santo Domingo" (10:37). Be they recorded as "native," "resident," "house-owner," "landowner," or "refugee," their relationship to Saint-Domingue is systematically emphasized. Indication of their origins is sometimes in the form of a marginal note. Francisco Carlon, born in metropolitan France, is thus included in the refugee group through the marginal indication "family from Santo Domingo" (10:72). Other entries involve more personal notes, with unusual formulations, compared with the rest of the records. Joseph Carmagnol's mother's name is indicated as "not known because all his papers were lost in the disasters which took place on the unhappy island of Santo Domingo" (10:73). In some cases, the mention of "resident" is all the more interesting because it was highly improbable that they still resided on the island. For instance, the baptism of François and Jean-François Bonnemaison, whose father is said to be a "resident of Cap Français," while the mother is referred to as a "native of Croix des Bouquets" (10:46). Many more examples could be cited from this volume (confirmed by the other volumes of the early nineteenth century), which includes a large proportion of entries involving Saint-Domingan refugees. Those already mentioned, however, clearly show that, whatever their birthplace or previous condition, the Saint-Domingan refugees bore their link with the island as a distinctive mark, a trend that was equally witnessed among whites and free people of color.[27]

It is possible that these indications may have been motivated by the sole wish of recovering their property or being compensated for the loss of it. This theory could be sustained after a close examination of the marriage contracts between Saint-Domingan refugees (or involving at least one refugee) and the wills written by members of the group. When listing their property, they systematically mentioned property left in Saint-Domingue or indicated the inheritance rights they had on the property of their family there.[28] This interpretation cannot, however, account for all the cases mentioned. For instance, there were inscriptions of residence in Saint-Domingue on the tombstones of persons born in metropolitan France, in which case it can hardly be interpreted as a will to recover lost property or to be indemnified.[29] This kind of epitaph is a clear sign that the identification with the Saint-Domingan group remained essential. The New Orleans sacramental records also contain several such examples where the birthplace is apparently insufficient as an indication and where the residence in Saint-Domingue is mentioned. Among many other examples is that of Juanna Bacque, who died in 1809 and is cited as "native of [P/V]aillet in the Diocese of Bordeaux in Guienne, resident of St. Marc on the island of Santo Domingo" (10:15). Use of the French language may also be considered part of this very strong feeling of identity. In

Figure 2. Tomb of Adélaïde Remoussin, St. Louis cemetery #1, New Orleans.

New Orleans, the wills of the refugees were still written in French long after the Louisiana Creoles and migrants from France had turned to the English language.[30] Confirmation of this resilience of the use of the French language may be found among the Charleston refugee community, despite the Anglophone Protestant environment. In contrast with the Huguenot community, which had Anglicized rapidly, the Saint-Domingan refugees retained their Francophone identity, as suggested by the tombstones in the St. Mary of the Annunciation cemetery. Inscriptions made as late as 1875 are still written in French.[31]

Considering the need displayed by the refugees to remain in contact (either physically or through correspondence), to bring assistance to each other, to be present at all important events of their pairs' lives (serving as witnesses in marriages or wills, godparenting for children born to other refugees), the clear trend toward endogamy among them in the first decades after the migration, as well as the imperious need they had to proclaim their link with the lost island (whether they were natives or had only resided there), there is little doubt that the refugees were united by a feeling of identity or rather of

Figure 3. Café des Réfugiés (second location), St. Philip Street, New Orleans.

"separate identity."[32] The phenomenon is slightly easier to evidence for the whites and for the free group of color than for the slaves, for obvious reasons including the absence of testimonies by slaves. The few available black sources, however, confirm that there was some kind of solidarity that ignored the racial barriers. This was probably encouraged by the fact that the slaves belonged to the domestic class, were most often the faithful slaves, including nurses and maids, and that their implantation in Louisiana most often did not separate them from their refugee masters. It is thus not incongruous to include them in this community.

This very peculiar ethnicity, be it symbolical or not, made the refugees, whatever their status and degree of racial mixture, a distinct group in the larger Louisiana community or "a visible subgroup of the New Orleans population," a phenomenon which seems to have lasted more than a decade but "something less than three decades."[33] This remark on the duration of their visible difference is essential to the understanding of the other main aspect of the refugees' interaction with the New Orleans society. Even as they constituted so obviously a subgroup in the New Orleans community, united around a common history, common sufferings, and a common present experience, they mingled with the Creole population of the Crescent City to the point that they seemed to dissolve within it.

## Dissolving within the New Orleans Creole Society

When dealing with the potential influences of a migratory group upon the host society, the existence of an ethnic identity is, of course, essential. The means of diffusion of these influences, however, largely depend upon the inclusion of the refugee community within the larger host community. In the years following resettlement in Louisiana, the refugee group remained closely knit. Among factors explaining this kind of survival reaction is the long-cherished hope of returning to their homeland. After one generation, they started mingling with the New Orleans Creole society, as well as with the new group of "foreign" French that continued to enter Louisiana. This probably explains why most historians place between one and three generations the duration of the visibility of the refugees as a distinct community. Many factors tend to confirm this dissolution, including the disappearance of such institutions as the Café des Réfugiés after the 1830s.

After the first decade, a strong exogamous trend started developing. Between 1800 and 1839, frequent intermarriages may be observed, with a strong tendency of white female refugees to marry "foreign" French—46 percent compared with 14 percent marrying Louisiana Creoles—while white male refugees married more often into the Louisiana Creole society—45 percent as opposed to 4 percent contracting unions with "foreign" French brides.[34] The 1850 census indicates that "only eight percent of all refugees remaining in Louisiana had a refugee spouse."[35] Beyond famous individual examples of intermarriage, such as that of Jean-Baptiste Donatien Augustin to Elizabeth Mélanie Labranche,[36] the notarial files of Marc Lafitte attest to this trend. Among the twenty marriage contracts of the 1814–18 period concerning Louisianans connected to the refugee group, only three involve two refugees. The notarial files of Michel de Armas covering 1810–17 display a similar trend. Among the twelve contracts involving Saint-Domingan refugees, only four can be classified as homogamous unions. Quite often, when indications are given concerning the origin of the nonrefugee spouse, he/she is found to be a "foreign" French rather than a Creole New Orleans resident, although unions with Creoles also existed.[37] This is exactly the same phenomenon as that found among the refugees in Cuba, where this trend "caused the amalgamation of the French community into the island's Cuban population, forming a Franco-Cuban blend."[38]

Going further down the generations, the marriage patterns of the refugees' children confirm the creolization of the group. More and more second-generation St. Domingans intermarried with Louisiana Creoles, which Paul Lachance says "may be interpreted as evidence of integration into the Creole side of the Gallic community." This lesser tendency to marry into the refugee group may be interpreted as "confirming a loss of identity by the 1830s."[39] The same type of study conducted for the free group of color leads to the same conclusion that there was, in this subgroup as well, an increasing trend to marry into the free Creole population of color, with clear signs that, among them, "St. Domingue refugees remained a distinct subgroup longer . . . than among whites in the Gallic community."[40] Even the whites' exogamous tendency, that is to say, amalgamation with the host community, may be interpreted as a clear sign, a posteriori, that the refugees were, upon arrival, a distinctly cohesive group. Indeed, it "reveals the extent to which the refugees formed a distinct subgroup within the Gallic community," and "reflects the distinct identity of the group on arrival in New Orleans."[41] In short, despite the refugees' effort "to retain separate identity," there are obvious proofs that "the fusion between the two groups was quite easy."[42]

This dissolution into the Louisiana Gallic fabric was favored by several factors that had to do either with the refugee community itself or with the broader situation in Louisiana. The first reason for easy integration was the proximity "in ethos and class structure" of the refugees to the host society.[43] The community of culture, language, and religion erased any difficulty usually met by migrants upon reaching a new society, as did the overall common points between the social and economic organizational patterns of the original and host societies. The general situation of Louisiana also favored this inclusion, in particular the strong cultural resistance of the Gallic community to the Anglo-American invasion that tended to weld the two groups together in this resistance. External aggressions also favored the blending of the refugees into the larger Louisianan—or even, later, southern—fabric. When English troops threatened New Orleans in 1814–15, Saint-Domingan refugees joined the Creoles and Americans in the battle. Cable picturesquely declares that "Creoles, Americans, and San Domingans, swords and muskets in hand, poured in upon the Place d'Armes from every direction and sought their places in the ranks."[44] White refugees accounted for at least 28 percent of the Battalion of New Orleans. The second battalion of free men of color (counting 256 men) was also made up of refugees, and many among the Baratarians (Jean Laffite's pirates) who came to defend New Orleans were connected to the refugee community as well.[45] Throughout the nineteenth century, foreign migrations to Louisiana tended to solidify the French-speaking community. Against Anglo-Saxon invasion from other states of the Union, but also faced with migrations from Ireland and Germany, Creoles, Saint-Domingan refugees, and "foreign" French tended to unite against common competitors, which eased the insertion of the Saint-Domingan community within the Louisiana fabric. During the Civil War, the necessity of opposing Union troops further reinforced the cohesion among Louisianans, whatever their origins.[46]

The refugee community also displayed specific traits that favored this easy integration. They were intent on rebuilding their shattered lives and showed strong dynamism in their efforts at economic resettlement. This will be examined in detail in the next chapter, but their sustained efforts at managing without resorting to charity must be acknowledged. The integration of the refugees is often described as a "blending" or a "dissolution" into the Louisiana fabric, metaphors that are perfectly adapted to summarizing their fitting pattern.[47] This attitude was further reinforced by the fact that the refugees who had come to Louisiana had generally chosen their destination (they could have settled elsewhere in the United States, as others did), which suppressed the resistance to integration generally attributable to forced settlement. Moreover, their final disappearance into the Louisiana society—if the limit of the 1830s, often set to their loss of identity, is considered—coincided with the payment of the indemnities by the French government to compensate for the refugees' loss of property.[48] This marked the final destruction of their hopes to return to their homeland and recuperate their property. At that moment, they decided to remain in Louisiana, which undoubtedly reinforced their wish to blend into the New Orleans society.[49] This decision, which might be equated to a loss of illusions, most certainly entailed the wish for a long-lasting insertion.[50]

The refugees' integration into the Louisiana fabric may be considered final when all later mentions of the refugees are under the identification either with the Gallic community or with the Creole society of New Orleans, although it is almost impossible to ascertain that they themselves had the feeling that this fusion was total. Mentions can be found, for example, of Edward Livingston's wife, Louise Moreau de Lassy, from a notorious Saint-Domingan family (she was Auguste Davezac's sister), evoking the receptions she gave (where Jules Davezac, the president of the Collège d'Orléans, read his poetry) without a single mention of her origins, and with the additional remark that her "family became closely identified with the French society of New Orleans."[51] Similarly, Jean-Baptiste Donatien Augustin, the famous New Orleans judge, born in Saint-Domingue, naturalized in 1835,[52] is celebrated in his 1876 obituary as "one of the representatives of that class of our old Creole population, to eulogize which words have ever been found inadequate."[53] Along the same line, there are many references to descendants of refugees—whose Saint-Domingan origins are certain—under the title of Creoles. Cable, mentioning Gottschalk in "Creole Slave Songs," says that he was "himself a New Orleans Creole of pure blood," thus laying a peculiarly strong emphasis on the identification of the composer with this category of the New Orleans population. Similarly, in *Creoles of Louisiana*, Cable describes Gottschalk as "a New Orleans Creole" and defines Jean-Jacques Audubon, another Louisianan with clear Saint-Domingan origins, as "a Creole of Louisiana."[54] Obviously, the dissolution was by then so complete, at least to those outside the refugee group itself, that they were granted choice position among the old Creole group.

The group of the free people of color displays a similar trend of inclusion. Rodolphe Lucien Desdunes, in his 1911 *Nos Hommes et Notre Histoire*, conducted a detailed survey of the famous Creoles of color who greatly contributed to the Louisiana society in various fields, such as literature, politics, or philanthropy.[55] As a descendant of Saint-Domingan refugees (his father was born in Saint-Domingue and his mother in Cuba), he includes himself among the Louisiana Creoles of color. He deals at large with members of this community, usually without mentioning their Saint-Domingan ancestry. Victor Séjour was the son of a "veteran of the War of 1812, Haitian émigré,"[56] but Desdunes refers to him as a "Creole writer," "born in New Orleans in 1819." Similarly, Camille Thierry, who was "regarded as one of our most outstanding Louisiana scholars" (32) was, in fact, "the offspring of a Haitian émigré, free woman of color Phélise Lahogue."[57] Finally, the "Haitian ancestry"[58] of Armand Lanusse leaves no doubt, although, according to Desdunes, for "this distinguished Louisianan" (13), the "pride in being Creole was more dear . . . than his being Louisianan, or than anything else pertaining to his origin" (20).[59] In some cases, Desdunes mentions the Saint-Domingan origins (as for Thomy Lafon, 92), but he clearly sets the individuals within the Creole group, thus showing the integration of most of the second generation into the Louisiana fabric. He goes as far as apologizing for integrating among Creoles of color Julien Déjour, who was "born at Cayes, Haiti, but we claim him as our own because he was reared by a Louisiana family" (94). This shows an interesting reversal, after one generation, of the original pride refugees professed in the refugees' Saint-Domingan origins. It is not, however, totally incompatible with a certain feeling of community, especially since many of these eminent Creoles of color shared the same background but were intent upon preserving their Louisianan identity to give more weight to their claims to equality and to ensure a better progression of their racial group within the Louisiana society.

The cohesive refugee community constituted in the first decades after the migration thus may appear to have progressively dissolved into the New Orleans society as time elapsed. The refugees seem to have identified with the Louisiana Creoles, whatever racial group they belonged to, in part because of their own wish to become integrated in their new host society, in part because the Gallic community tended to unite to resist the Anglo-Saxon cultural invasion. This close association in the eyes of most observers, however, did not toll the knell of a certain form of identity among the refugees.

## Between Symbolic Ethnicity and Mythic Influence

Even as this dissolution was occurring, a resurgence of ethnic reaction was manifested among the refugees. At the turn of the 1830s, a renewed ethnic consciousness apparently occurred, corresponding in part to the payment of the compensations, and probably reinforced by the aging of the original refugee community. The Will Books of New Orleans display a multiplication of wills made by Saint-Domingan refugees at that time, most certainly because they felt they were nearing death and because the declaration of their property left in Saint-Domingue could be used for their heirs' compensation claims, but also perhaps out of a sheer need to be identified as members of a group. A close examination of volume 4 of the Will Books (1824–33) leads to a number of deeply interesting conclusions. There was a clear increase in the proportion of wills by refugees between August 1825 and January 1832. The wills emanated from all categories of the free refugee community. Several concern free women of color and reveal their wish to ascertain that their property would be passed on to their natural children.[60] Others are from (apparently white) fathers who bequeath their belongings (or part of them) to their illegitimate children.[61] Still others are more commonly written by white persons who give their property to various members of their family. Some (although relatively few) mention property left in Saint-Domingue.[62] In some cases, the compensations had not yet been paid. Allard mentions his Saint-Domingan property (142); Anne Faunifs writes: "Tout ce que je puis posséder est dans l'isle de Saint Domingue" [All I do possess is on the island of Saint-Domingue]. She also accounts for her wish to write her will by the fact that she wants her daughter to be indemnified for part of the plantation.[63] In some cases, however, the refugees acknowledge that nothing more needs to be compensated.[64]

The motives for this recrudescence of wills are naturally difficult to assess precisely. In some cases, as expected, the reason seems to be the indemnification by the French government and the necessity to assess officially the property owned in Saint-Domingue. But those are rare. In other cases, an explanation might lie in the old age of the refugees and thus the feeling they had that they should settle their inheritance. Some testators, however, were very young.[65] The interpretation of a certain surge of ethnic consciousness also seems valid. Most of those refugees had their wills legally recorded by Marc Lafitte, a fellow refugee. In several cases, he was named the refugees' executor (for instance, Charles Dair, 69) and was even proclaimed the sole possessor of Thérèse Charles de Saint Rome's goods to be distributed after her death (185). Moreover, whereas several wills by "foreign" French were written in English, none of the refugees' wills were, as if they had remained untouched by the progression of the American language and culture, as if they wished to retain their Gallic cultural difference. Some wills show the community of sentiment shared by the refugees, beyond differences in race and status. Several wills are written specifically to emancipate slaves, especially, as mentioned in several occasions, slaves who had come from Saint-Domingue with their white masters or their descendants.[66] Finally, what seems interesting is the care with which the testators mention their Saint-Domingan origins or their connections to the lost island, as if they wished to bequeath these origins as well as their property to their children, legitimate or not.

Similarly, Boze's letters to Sainte-Gême between 1828 and 1836 contain more mentions than earlier letters of Saint-Domingan refugees, including the deaths of many older refugees, although not exclusively.[67] He also mentions the compensations,[68] gives news of other refugees,[69] transmits to Sainte-Gême the best wishes of many famous refugees like Moreau-Lilet or Fortier,[70] announces weddings,[71] and gossips about several inhabitants of New Orleans, refugees of Saint-Domingue or connected to refugees.[72] There are pages of mentions of the refugees, and many more can be found which do not bear explicit reference to Saint-Domingue, most certainly because Boze knew that Sainte-Gême was aware that the people mentioned were compatriots.[73] All in all, this correspondence is so rich concerning the Saint-Domingan refugees that it would justify a monograph in itself. The conclusion to be drawn from this is that, apparently, whatever the motive—be it the end of hopes of return, the compensation episode, or the extinction, from old age, of the first generation—the group felt a need to be united once more after more than forty years away from the island, which provoked a surge of ethnic feeling and a revival of the community spirit that had been so strong in the first years after the migration.

The consequence of all this is that a very strong resilience of West Indian cultural traits may be witnessed. The integration studied above was social and economic, without any doubt, but not necessarily cultural. Louisiana offered the refugees "opportunity to attain success as a group without having to assimilate into the dominant culture."[74] The New Orleans refugees may thus be described as "culturally and linguistically resilient," "their ethnic persistence" being partly accountable to the "social network that they appear to have established in the Crescent City's First and Third Municipalities," which made them form "homogeneous clusters in culturally, linguistically and racially heterogeneous neighborhoods." There are signs of "the smoldering embers of island identity in the New Orleans area," and "many early twentieth-century New Orleans Creoles of refugee ancestry still cherished portraits of refugee ancestors, still attended the French Opera, and still considered themselves a people set apart from their neighbors by culture, language and class."[75] This feeling is confirmed by many testimonies by descendants of Saint-Domingan refugees in Louisiana, always ready to proudly mention those origins.[76] The authors of *The Saint-Domingue Epic*, who descend from Saint-Domingan refugees, for instance, keep mentioning the "courage and industry" that the refugees displayed to survive in their various asylums, but also the fact that they "remained faithful to their cultural inheritance" (307). This obvious attempt to highlight their difference may also indicate that they were resisting more vigorously American cultural assimilation and thus expressing their dissenting position from the Louisiana Creole population, which displayed a lesser tendency to oppose it (as is suggested by the use of the English language in the wills written by Louisiana Creoles). This renewed feeling of ethnicity might thus be interpreted both as a dissent from the increasingly numerous American population as well as a dissent (although a less uncompromising and much more discreet one) from the New Orleans Creole population, which seemed readier to comply with the new Americanization of Louisiana.

The first three decades of the refugees' presence in Louisiana display three consecutive trends of ethnic reaction. After acting as a community in New Orleans, the refugees began mingling with the rest of the Gallic population. They disappeared into it, so to speak, all the more so because, by then, many original refugees had died and their descendants became more numerous than the refugees themselves. This is what generally sustains the thesis of their ethnic disappearance as a group after the 1830s. The present discussion, however, has proved that an ethnic revival, in the form of a new surge of community spirit, occurred in the 1830s. This ethnic revival, which might be considered some kind of symbolic ethnicity, gains significance because it occurred at a time when the original refugees were becoming much less numerous and when their direct descendants increasingly pervaded New Orleans society. Because they were present everywhere in New Orleans, the refugees and their descendants permeated society with their culture.

Fusion with Louisiana society may have been the best occasion for Saint-Domingan cultural features to spread. The notion of "symbolic identity" as defined by Herbert Gans in 1979 is pertinent to the Saint-Domingan refugees.[77] Indeed, all the essential elements highlighted by Gans are traceable among them. The ethnic revival of the 1830s went together with the refugees' assimilation into the Louisiana fabric. It was manifested through ethnic pride and through increased resurgence of memories of the past and of their homeland. This phenomenon was undoubtedly linked to the notion that they (or their parents) had shared an extraordinary experience on the island, but also an uncommonly traumatic experience during migration and resettlement. It was also a way to revive a number of features peculiar to the Saint-Domingans, even in a symbolical form. In this ethnic revival there may have been a wish to be identified as Saint-Domingan refugees at a time when their ethnic belonging was becoming increasingly less visible and thus to recover a specific identity through a return to their origins. Louisiana was then receiving new waves of immigration, and there must have been a need for the refugees' descendants to distinguish themselves from these new immigrants. The development of this "symbolic" identity did not necessarily require places or systems of socialization. It manifested, for instance, in the proud identification of the refugees to those among them who had succeeded. This may be seen, for instance, through already quoted mentions of many successful members of the Saint-Domingan group by Boze in his correspondence (notary Lafitte or such influential representatives of the refugees as Moreau-Lislet). This may also be seen in the fact that many persisted in mentioning their belonging to the group late into the nineteenth century and even in the twentieth century.

Their dissolution into the Louisiana fabric, either through social and economic integration or through amalgamation (which soared in the early 1830s), may be considered the best means to ensure the existence of persisting contacts between the refugee group and the rest of the population. Through those continuous contacts, acculturation could occur, involving both the adaptation of the Saint-Domingan group to local cultural traits and a pervasion of the Louisiana society by Saint-Domingan features.[78] In the context of multiethnic Louisiana, the notion of creolization might even be more appropriate, suggesting a syncretic culture emerging from the long coexistence of the several ethnic groups in Louisiana and favoring the interpenetration of the various cultures, together with an adaptation to the milieu in which this interpenetration occurred.[79]

Even though the refugee group diminished, due to the disappearance of individuals originally involved in the migration, the study of the way their specificities pervaded the Louisiana society is valid.[80] Their descendants, raised in the memories and "symbolic" ethnicity of the community, remained numerous in the New Orleans fabric and thus went on transmitting their pride and peculiarity to their children and to other Louisianans, still more easily when contacts became closer with other groups of different ethnic origins. The strong reduction in the number of original refugees, either through relocation or death, is thus unimportant as such, since Saint-Domingan influences did not cease with the disappearance of the first-generation refugees.

Moreover, because the question is more one of "symbolic" ethnicity, it is not necessary to systematically separate the three racial groups that composed the Saint-Domingan community, all the more so because there was among the three groups—despite the obvious differences due to the various statuses—a community of spirit originating from common background. They all had known life in Saint-Domingue, they had fled under the same conditions, and they all had found relocation relatively difficult, although it was more difficult for some than others. They also often cared for each other, as shown, for example, by the special interest Boze's correspondence betrays for the free refugees of color. Several of his letters mention members of this subgroup of the refugee community. He also strongly criticizes Louisiana politicians for supporting the bill excluding people of color, in particular Mr. A. B. Roman and Mr. Amédée Reggio—whose death he announces to Sainte-Gême—to whom, he says, the Saint-Domingan colonists bear implacable hatred, due to their political position against the free group of color.[81] Of course, he mentions several cases of white men who had children with refugee women of African descent (folder 182 among others) or even of a white man who married his racially mixed companion he had brought over from Saint-Domingue (folder 223), and he writes at length about Sainte-Gême's illegitimate family, giving him news of them. All in all, these examples show that there was proximity between St. Domingans of different racial statuses, or at least a definite interest displayed by the members of the refugee community, even when they belonged to different classes. They even lived in close proximity: "They congregated in the 'back of town' and in Faubourg Marigny, where their building traditions are everywhere in evidence. Households in those areas were frequently shared by all three castes, as several of the federal censuses illustrate."[82] This "symbolic" ethnicity thus ensured the cohesion of the group obviously for over one generation. Neither race, nor status, nor racial position seems to have broken the strong bond of common origins.

This group cohesion may even partly explain the sense observers had of the refugees' paramount importance within the society of New Orleans and even of Louisiana. Because they were seen as one entity, as a unified—and thus powerful—group, the refugees were visible in New Orleans. Most contemporary protagonists pinpointed areas in which they attributed new developments to the refugees. Even if their influence has sometimes been slightly downplayed by later writings on nineteenth-century Louisiana, the witnesses of early American Louisiana grant them an essential role in the development of the sugar industry.[83] Many cultural features of the slave community have also long been seen as being the St. Domingans' specific influence.[84] Several important slave rebellions were also described by contemporaries as having been triggered by Saint-Domingan refugees.[85] Whatever their direct involvement in those areas, it is interesting to note that most early-nineteenth-century Louisianans believed in their significant role and proclaimed their great influence. The attribution of slightly mythologized influences to the group is as interesting to the present study as any real influence it might have had, since it draws attention to their vitality and visibility in the Louisiana society. These exaggerated influences may also be the best sign of a group identity and of a "symbolic" ethnicity.

Throughout the nineteenth century, the refugees' visibility in New Orleans has often been stated without any attempt to prove the statement. Cable, for instance, speaks of "the prevalence of West Indian ideas in New Orleans" and mentions the "French West Indian tincture" perceptible in New Orleans.[86] It is thus easy to conclude that the group appeared to observers as a real community, a perception reinforced by the persistence of certain specific cultural traits. Because of their easy integration into the host society, however, these specificities eventually reached a relatively high degree of diffusion in Louisiana. Through their "unfathomed legacy" and "profound influence," it is obvious that they played a pivotal role in nineteenth-century New Orleans, particularly in the cultural resistance displayed by the Gallic Creole community to Americanization.[87]

If their role seems certain, the question remains whether it was more a matter of visibility than proportion. Their presence may have been more strongly felt because they were more particularly dynamic, because they were proportionately numerous in New Orleans, or because of a perfect conjunction between their arrival and the political turmoil of the early American era. Their role may have been exaggerated by the contemporaries because they reinforced the Gallic community at the crucial period of the Americanization of Louisiana. It may have been downplayed by later commentators of Louisiana for the same reason, which makes Cable declare that "it is easier to underestimate than to exaggerate the silent results of an event that gave the French-speaking Louisianans twice the numerical power with which they had begun to wage their long battle against American absorption."[88]

After an immediate acknowledgment of their importance by contemporary observers and posterior erasing of their presence in later epochs, the recent tendency has been to state that not only did they reinforce the Gallic community but they also endorsed the leadership of the reaction against the Anglo-Saxon invasion of Louisiana and thus had a profound influence on this American territory.[89] Interesting theses also develop the hypothesis that they became a "major force in their new community," first because they were more directly in competition with the American immigrants than with the long-settled Louisianans, in particular "for that mastery of the affairs of the state," and also because their situation had developed in them a strong will to succeed.[90] It is thus interesting to determine whether they were peculiarly dynamic (due to the pioneer spirit and efficiency acquired in Saint-Domingue, the traumatic experience of the revolution and migration, and/or because of the necessity to display more dynamism to fit into the host society) or whether they became more visible because of the very unusual political situation born from the dichotomy of the existence of an ancient colonial elite, confronted to the arrival of the new "proprietors" of Louisiana.[91]

The threefold conclusion here is that the refugees did build a community, at least in the early decades of their presence on the Louisiana soil, and that they progressively melted into the New Orleans fabric, while retaining a certain identity, at least "symbolic," due to their common origins and the conditions of their uprooting. It is also clear that, even if the historiography of the late nineteenth and early twentieth centuries has largely omitted their presence, the contemporary observers often granted them a visibility that is sometimes considered slightly mythologized. It is essential to examine the various fields in which their presence was felt to determine whether they did leave an everlasting imprint on Louisiana, as some of their descendants proudly proclaim. At times it is possible to consider the three categories of population (whites, free people of color, slaves) together in a kind of cultural continuum. At times it is indispensable to examine the three categories separately, particularly in the economic and social fields. The first challenge of a migrant is economic and social integration. Playing a political part in the new homeland and exerting cultural influences on it can only be a second step. The study of the refugees' influence will thus bear first on the markers of the refugee community's economic and social roles in early nineteenth-century Louisiana and on the more discreet marks they left on the economy and society of their host society.

# 4

# Influencing Louisiana's Economic Pattern

Whatever their new host country, the refugees seem to have left their imprint on the economy of their host societies. In Spanish Santo Domingo, they opened grocery stores, cafés, and gambling places.[1] They also began cultivating sugar cane and coffee.[2] Their agronomical expertise triggered a rocketing development of coffee production in Cuba and Puerto Rico.[3] In Cuba, they developed cocoa and cotton production as well and expanded the cultivation of citrus, tobacco, and indigo.[4] Cuba received immigrants from Santo Domingo as well as refugees from Saint-Domingue when the island became French in 1795 by the Treaty of Basle. Comparing the two sets of immigrants economically gives a good measure of the role of the refugees from the French part of the island. This comparison proves that their dynamism was much more marked, their economic success greater, and their contribution to the Cuban economy far more significant than those of the immigrants from the Spanish part of the island.[5] The French refugees also greatly influenced the island's urbanism by building a second city in Santiago with cafés, dance halls, and the very famous Ballroom gardens.[6] In Baracoa, they organized the water supply system and built a coconut oil plant as well as many houses with tiles imported from Marseilles.[7] They advanced the prosperity of the city and colony and introduced luxury and a certain idea of comfort by building beautiful houses and gardens and by importing elegant furniture. They also initiated the development of a much more dynamic social life and made for the intellectual development of the island. Their legacy to Cuba was that of a "civilized life and survival of a French culture, transplanted after a long period of colonial and Creole adaptation in Saint-Domingue."[8] In Jamaica, they triggered a coffee and sugar boom.[9] Their contribution to the island's agriculture was said to be both qualitative and quantitative.[10] They also greatly influenced the landscape of Jamaica, if we believe a visitor to Jamaica at the turn of the nineteenth century, who describes the beautiful gardens they had planted around Kingston, which abounded in fruits and vegetables.[11] They endowed the town of Kingston with gaming houses and shops, including dry goods stores, and strengthened the Catholic Church of Jamaica.[12] Several other Caribbean islands have long borne their mark, although in less obvious ways. In Trinidad, for instance, the introduction of the Creole language and of some forms of voodoo cult immediately followed their migration and was one of their most obvious legacies.[13]

The seaports of the eastern United States bear a similar testimony to their bequest. Be it in Charleston, Baltimore, Philadelphia, or New York, they were dynamic in certain fields. Agriculture was one of their favorite areas of influence. They introduced the use of chemical agents to increase South Carolina's indigo yield. Some more peripheral products also benefited from their agricultural expertise. James Achille de Caradeux, the son of a Saint-Domingan general, who settled on Cedar Hill Plantation, South Carolina, pioneered in the cultivation of grapes for the domestic wines of the Charleston area.[14] Other refugees cultivated roses in Maryland.[15] In 1818, James Madison gave them credit for the development of an irrigation system.[16] They vitalized several specific fields in all of these havens, launching newspapers and opening schools, theaters, and opera houses.[17] They became fencing masters, teachers, journalists, lawyers, and shopkeepers.[18] Considering the variety of their trades, they heavily influenced fashion and cooking.[19] They revitalized the Catholic Church, which was not very powerful in the Anglophone South. They also introduced dissent within it. In Charleston, for instance, the Church of St. Mary of the Annunciation, founded by Irish Catholics in 1789, received innumerable refugees in 1790s. They turned the church into a pocket of Gallic resistance in English-speaking Charleston. The registers were even kept in French until 1822, when newly appointed bishop John England directed that records be kept in English. From 1810 to 1821, a schism occurred due to struggles for influence and power between the Irish and refugee members of St. Mary.[20]

In New Orleans, their fields of activity were as varied as they were elsewhere. Due to the very specific nature of Louisiana's colonial history and cultural pattern and to the timeliness of their arrival, however, their economic influences were slightly different and much stronger than in the other refuges. This is partly due to the permanence of their settlement (contrary to most of their West Indian asylums) and to the closer proximity of the host culture to theirs, compared with the Anglo-Saxon United States. Their influence was bound to be stronger, considering that Louisiana was their new home and that the territory was swept up in the turmoil of a real political and institutional upheaval. Their integration was bound to occur differently there, since many features of the society and culture they found upon arrival shared a distinctly common tincture with what they had known prior to the migration. Despite the overall strong background similarities, however, the New Orleans society also displayed many weaknesses, compared with the Saint-Domingan one, which left huge undeveloped areas for them to occupy.

## Success Stories

The refugees' first immediate impact on the Louisiana economy was negative, especially when the Cuban wave arrived. This had not been the case with the refugees who had come earlier, due to the relative staggering of arrivals, which had given them time to be absorbed within the New Orleans fabric before more refugees came. Not so with the 1809 massive migration of mostly destitute people which instantaneously caused the prices of food and lodging to soar. This increase rapidly drained the few resources the newcomers had, and despite the welfare committees organized to relieve them, the number of poor, homeless people and even beggars increased tremendously. Many New Orleanians even contended that they induced a brutal lowering in the morals and that they "disturbed order."[21]

These negative effects were relatively short-lived, and the story of the refugees' integration within the Louisiana economy is one of fitting easily into the existing fabric. It is sometimes contended that the planters did not fit into the local society, rejected as they were by the Creole planters who were jealous of the superiority of those refugees "who had been greater planters than anyone in New Orleans, in some cases being the former owners of hundreds of slaves."[22] It seems, however, that things are far from being that simple. The Grands Blancs, according to the Saint-Domingan nomenclature, were a tiny minority among the refugees. Several successfully returned to their occupations, while others undertook new occupations. Most refugees, however, had not owned huge plantations, and they settled relatively easily in New Orleans. Their economic resettlement was not always immediate and differed according to the socioeconomic and racial backgrounds of the refugees.

The story of the refugee community as a whole, however, is a success story. After the first months, or even weeks, very few continued to apply for charity.[23] They were better skilled, in general, and more educated than New Orleanians, whatever the category of population considered.[24] "Out of the whole number of male grown persons, it must be admitted that two thirds of them possess some trade," Mayor James Mather wrote to Governor W.C.C. Claiborne on 7 August 1809.[25] The explanation has to be sought in Saint-Domingue, where both whites and Creoles of color were educated, where both categories could even benefit from a higher metropolitan education, and where all, including slaves who were experienced sugar workers, displayed some form of expertise.

All testimonies of the main protagonists of the period attest to the successful economic integration or conversion of most refugees.

In May 1809, Claiborne wrote: "They are said, for the most part, to be industrious planters and mechanics" (Rowland, 4:365). In August 1809, Mather, who had been required to make a report on the refugee community, summarized in a few words what he had heard about the three categories of population, indicating that the whites among them "appear to be an active, industrious people" (4:388). Insisting upon their respectful attitude toward the laws and government of Louisiana on several occasions, Mather praised their "industry and activity," which "must be astonishing indeed, since it has till now afforded the most part of those who had no slaves, the means of lawfully getting a livelihood, and that too, in spite of the increase of prices of house rent, and of many other difficulties" (4:405). He pursues, in one of the most direct testimonies to their versatility: "Several among them who once possessed estates, or belonged to wealthy families in the Island of Saint-Domingo, now follow the occupations of Cabinet Makers, Turners, Bakers, Glaziers, Upholsterers" (4:405). He concludes his enquiry on the refugees by advising the federal government to ease the process of land acquisition, adding that he has no doubt that the result would be "the settling of many new plantations, which would give in large crops of cotton and other produce before three years time" (4:407).

The real question is what, in the refugees' economic insertion, led all observers to admire their striving dynamism and versatility, or what led François Barbé-Marbois, the intendant of Saint-Domingue (1785–89), the French negotiator of the Louisiana Purchase, Napoleon's minister of the treasury, to contend that "Louisiana has been enriched by the disasters of St. Domingo, and the industry that formerly gave so much value to that island now fertilizes the Valley of the Mississippi."[26] Private correspondence, family papers, and public correspondence such as Claiborne's give insight into the refugees' occupational pattern. Newspapers (*Le Moniteur de la Louisiane* or the *Louisiana Gazette*) offer a wide range of examples of refugees advertising their trade or a new venture. The New Orleans directory also helps to pinpoint the refugees' trades, while marriage contracts and wills often indicate both their occupation and level of wealth. Finally, the Indenture and Apprenticeship contracts offer an accurate view of what trades the refugees adopted.[27]

The marriage contracts reveal the extent of the refugees' trades. Although the contracts involving refugees until 1835 reveal that for one generation after the migration they still had a lower average income than the native Louisianans, they found "easy employment" in many trades: they became "hotelier, baker, silversmith, cabinetmaker, hairdresser, fencing master, musician, barber, or actor." They were "physicians, lawyers, engineers, builders, surveyors, and public printers."[28] Some occupations might be added to the list (teachers, journalists, businessmen, planters, overseers, among others), but it faithfully suggests the wide range of the refugees' skills.[29]

Several individuals reached very prominent positions in New Orleans's economic landscape, although they were, of course, not the majority. Several of them were involved in the legal profession and reached a high level of political involvement. This was the case of Louis Casimir Elizabeth Moreau-Lislet, who was a lawyer, publisher, and attorney general of the state and was one of the authors of the Louisiana Civil Code. He was the author of "a prodigious quantity of the legal literature of Louisiana," and tried "more than twenty cases before the Louisiana Supreme Court."[30] Among these prominent refugees, Jean-François Canonge, who was first translator, then judge of the Criminal Court of New Orleans, may be cited. His offspring followed in his footsteps. Alphonse Canonge was an "eminent lawyer and prominent as the Superintendent of Public Schools," and Louis Placide Canonge was a famous lawyer who taught French at the University of New Orleans, edited *Le Propagateur Catholique* and *La Lorgnette*, wrote for *L'Abeille*, wrote plays, and even managed theatrical troupes.[31] Diego Morphy was a lawyer, a teacher, and the first Spanish consul at New Orleans. His son Diego became a justice on the Supreme Court of Louisiana and fathered Paul Morphy, one of the world's greatest chess players.[32] Paul Lanusse was a prominent subject under the Spanish regime. Although he came to Louisiana only in the 1790s, he was an attorney general of the *Cabildo* and became senior judge in 1803. In 1804, he became an administrator of the Louisiana Bank; in 1805, he was appointed justice of the Territory of Orleans by Governor Claiborne. He was a member of the first board of Marguilliers of the Saint-Louis Cathedral, and he was appointed captain of the Louisiana Militia in 1806, the year he also became the president of the Merchant Association of New Orleans. In 1812, when the Collège d'Orléans was founded, he unsurprisingly became one of the regents of the institution.[33] Among the great refugee figures of the legal profession in New Orleans, Jean-Baptiste Donatien Augustin should also be mentioned. He was a counselor at law and secretary of the city council of the first municipality. He owned property in New Orleans (Faubourg Trémé, at the corner of Esplanade and St. Claude) as well as a summer house at Pass Christian. He was elected brigadier general commanding the Louisiana Legion in 1845.[34]

Other refugees gained prominence in the fields of education, agriculture, or business. Henri de Sainte-Gême, who had been a planter in Cuba after leaving Saint-Domingue, obtained (through marriage) a sugar plantation at Gentilly. He was also a member of the Louisiana Militia and commander of the elite corps of the Dragons à Pied. He served as a major under Jackson during the Battle of New Orleans, probably made part of his fortune financing the privateering operations of the Laffite brothers, and was a wealthy property owner. Beside the Gentilly plantation (with its slave population), he had several houses in the Crescent City, one that he had given to his illegitimate children, and at least two that were rented out.[35] Augustin Dominique Tureaud was given Union Plantation when he married the daughter of Marius Pons Bringuier, the owner of White Hall plantation, in 1803. He lived off his plantation and became judge of the St. James Parish.[36] James (Jean-François originally) Pitot, who occupied high political functions, was famous for building the first cotton press in the city. His son Armand became a distinguished member of the Louisiana Bar.[37] Pierre Auguste Charles Derbigny, who became secretary of the Municipality of New Orleans, and who was Claiborne's official interpreter, was also a successful businessman. He operated the first steam ferry on the Mississippi River and managed the business interests of the land donated to Lafayette by the State of Louisiana.[38] In the Davezac family, all members reached the upper rungs of the New Orleans social ladder. The daughter married Edward Livingston, the famous lawyer who played an important part in the political and institutional history of New Orleans. The sons became renowned members of the community, Jules for being the French translator of Livingston's Penal Code, and Auguste for founding the Collège d'Orléans and serving as its first president. Auguste entered into partnership with Livingston and is sometimes considered "the best criminal lawyer in New Orleans." He was even sent by President Jackson, then by President Polk, on diplomatic missions to The Hague, where he was chargé d'affaires.[39] Finally, among those prominent refugees coming from diverse backgrounds, was Pierre Lambert, who had been a planter at Grand Rivière (Saint-Domingue), then at Santiago (Cuba), and who purchased a pharmacy from Doctor Blanquis in June 1809. He was a physician and apothecary on Bourbon Street and taught physics and mathematics at the Collège d'Orléans. His son, Pierre-Alexandre, became a physician and surgeon, was appointed administrator of the Charity Hospital in 1837, and became a member of the Eastern Medical Board in 1843.[40]

Those are a few among the many refugees who attained real prominence in New Orleans shortly after their arrival. Their dazzling successes and meteoric ascension occurred in varied fields. For many, success came within a few years after their reaching Louisiana. Most of the time, it came along with a dynamic role in the Louisiana political field and an easy social integration into the New Orleans fabric. Of course, the larger group of refugees never attained such prominence. Most of them, however, as testified by all official correspondences, did integrate the economic world of New Orleans through diverse fields of activity.

## Fitting into the New Orleans Occupational Pattern

The refugees were versatile, and they often managed to adapt to the New Orleans occupational pattern. They found positions to fill. The legal profession, as has been amply exemplified, counted many white refugees in its ranks. It was an area in which many of them had been employed in Saint-Domingue. Because of Louisiana's Latin colonial past, the legal principles were not far from those that had prevailed in the French Caribbean colony. Those who came found it easy to adapt to the Louisiana legal system, especially since it was, for the very same reason, an area in which the Americans could not compete with them, for lack of knowledge of the principles of Roman law. Countless were those who chose this field of activity. Beside the famous lawyers already mentioned, there were many others, slightly less famous or successful, like Etienne Mazureau or Thomas Patrice Dubourg, the archbishop's younger brother, who was judge in Plaquemine Parish and then at New Orleans.[41]

Agriculture was another area that attracted many refugees. Some became planters, like Sainte-Gême and Tureaud or, to give a single additional example, Docteur Lebeau, who owned a small plantation at Gentilly. Others became the managers of large plantations, like Antoine Morin on Etienne de Boré's plantation or Pierre Baron Boisfontaine on Daniel Clark's plantation at Cannes Brûlées.[42] Others still turned to business or industry, either on a large scale or by being mere shopkeepers. Pierre David Bidet Renoulleau established a tobacco mill and was a gauger, weigher, measurer, and merchant of dry goods. Pierre François Dubourg (another of Archbishop Dubourg's brothers), was a merchant "who rose to high position in the social as well as the commercial world" and became collector for the Port of New Orleans (although the sole mention of this is in the records of the Saint-Louis Cathedral).[43] He also became director of the Compagnie de Navigation d'Orléans (with Paul Lanusse and James Pitot) in February 1813, and three months later he was appointed secretary of the directors of the Compagnie d'Assurance of New Orleans.[44] The primary sources abound with examples. Boze's letters to Sainte-Gême, for instance, cite Angaud and Julien Delpit (who had a tobacco mill); Moussier, the son of a refugee; J. P. Dodart, as well as Doublet and Freyd, who owned a linen store; Mr. Ferry, a merchant on the levee; Aristide Miltenberger, an accountant and the owner of a commercial farm; Dupuy, who purchased the theater on St. Philip, where he also opened a ballroom and a gaming room; and Mr. Rochard, who opened the famous Café des Réfugiés.[45] The marriage contracts also give many examples of those refugees who went into business and shop keeping, including Henry Schmitt, François Galez, and Charles Pavet.[46] Many more examples (Jacques François Poupard, watchmaker and grocer) can also be found in the New Orleans directory.[47]

A large proportion of refugees, both whites and free people of color, seem to have gone into skilled crafts. The literature is filled with examples of refugee artisans. Among their most common crafts was that of baker. Bakers had to make a monthly declaration of the amount of flour they had used, which makes the evolution of the trade easy to trace. Between May and September 1809, at the time of the huge Cuban wave, ten new bakers started to make declarations. Among the forty-three bakers who made declarations between October 1806 and January 1813 whose birthplace was known, eight had been born in Saint-Domingue and twelve of them, although they originated from metropolitan France, had come to Louisiana via Saint-Domingue with the refugees.[48] Several names illustrate this trend: Pierre Joseph, Louis d'Aquin, who owned a bakery at the corner of Chartres and Royale, Théodat Camille Bruslé, who was Gottschalk's grandfather and d'Aquin's partner, and Pierre Baron Boisfontaine, a former tailor from Port-au-Prince turned into a baker in New Orleans, already cited for being the overseer of Daniel Clark, who became a baker at Clark's death.[49]

Many other crafts recur among the refugees' favorite occupations. Tailors were numerous (Mr. Juforgue, François Diart, and François-Xavier Olivier, a free refugee of color, among many others),[50] as were shoemakers (François Bosse and Pierre-Charles Durea, a free man of color, on Philippe and Dauphine streets).[51] Refugees are also often mentioned among goldsmiths, ironmongers, cabinetmakers, carpenters, upholsterers, and glaziers.[52] Refugee women are often found to have been seamstresses, embroiderers, and boardinghouse keepers. This perfectly fits with the already quoted assessment of the occupational pattern by James Mather, the mayor of New Orleans. The advertisements published by the local newspapers confirm that the most commonly advertised skills were plantation work and teaching, but many advertisements were also related to skilled crafts (watchmaker, joiner, painter, and glazier),

Map 3. *Pilié Map of New Orleans, 1808*. Photo courtesy of Gilles-Antoine Langlois and the Louisiana Collection, Special Collections, Tulane University, New Orleans.

overseeing, and store clerking.[53] Clerks were another category in which refugees could be found. From refugees themselves, including former planters, to their descendants, examples abound: Michel Forcisi, who was first clerk in the Mortgage Office for over twenty years, Aimable Barthélémy Charbonnet, Mr. Pilié, who was the main surveyor of New Orleans and contributed many maps to the urban history of the city, or the very famous Rodolphe Lucien Desdunes, the son of refugees, who was messenger, then clerk, at the Customs Service.[54] Other less typical occupations may be encountered frequently in the archives, from piano tuner (for instance, Louis Teinturier, mentioned by Boze in one of his letters to Sainte-Gême) to fencing master (St. Landré or Claudin de Beleurgey, the famous journalist).[55]

Quite obviously, many of the occupations mentioned here were the preferred choices of both whites and free persons of color. Except for the legal profession, which was reserved for whites, all the others were shared by both categories of population, as several of the examples cited indicate. Primary sources confirm this trend. Boze, for instance, mentions in his letters to Sainte-Gême several craftsmen who were free refugees of color or their descendants. Sainte-Gême's own racially mixed son was a joiner and cabinetmaker.[56] Other sources mention the example of the descendants of a black woman who had saved her master named Tureaud and had left Saint-Domingue with him and her two children. After being educated in Europe, both sons thrived as businessmen in New Orleans.[57] All in all, the most obvious recurring feature is the "visibility of free colored craftsmen and shopkeepers." Proportionately with the white refugees, they were much more often involved in this sector, for they were barred from other refugees' favorite sectors (like the law) by the racially biased occupational pattern that prevailed in Louisiana. A systematic study of the marriage contracts in 1804–19 shows that "fully eighty percent of the black bridegrooms whose occupations were registered in New Orleans found employment in the mercantile or manufacturing sector."[58]

A close look at the Indenture Records shows that the young refugees of color were apprenticed in almost all the fields of the craft industry. Masons and cabinetmakers were numerous. They were also apprenticed to tinsmiths, carpenters, shoemakers, saddle makers, bricklayers, blacksmiths, printers, tailors, goldsmiths, and hairdressers.[59] Several of them were found to be successfully self-employed, once their apprenticeship contract was over. Among them were François Degré, a carpenter, Honoré Besson, who became a painter, or Louis Victor Séjour Marcou (Victor Séjour's father), who "established a prosperous cleaning and dyeing business."[60] The free refugees of color were sometimes musicians, barbers, and mechanics and were found to have a monopoly on shoemaking.[61]

Free black refugee women were active as well, even more so than their white counterparts. They had their privileged fields as well. The advertisements published in the local papers show them seeking employment as wet nurses for white children or ready to invest in taverns or coffeehouses.[62] They were in great demand as nurses, both for their knowledge of tropical diseases and for their immunity to these diseases (especially during yellow fever epidemics). They were also hairdressers, washerwomen, seamstresses, milliners, and needlewomen, as was the case of Henri de Sainte-Gême's racially mixed daughters.[63] Finally, they had the monopoly on furnished room rental.[64]

This explains why James Mather, speaking on behalf of the free refugees of color, wrote to Governor Claiborne that "these very men possess property, and have useful trades to live upon," before adding that "there has not been one single complaint that [he knows] of, against any of them concerning their conduct since their coming" to New Orleans.[65] As their white counterparts, they rapidly fit into the New Orleans occupational pattern, although often in the lower layers of this pattern. There were some success stories, although less so than among the white refugees, due to the intermediate position they occupied in the New Orleans society. Desdunes mentions the example of Thomy Lafon, who taught school, then opened a store, and then became a wealthy real estate owner and moneylender. At his death, his wealth was estimated to be around half a million dollars, and he bequeathed it to charitable organizations. Desdunes also dedicates one page to Julien Déjour, who became extremely successful and gave away his fortune to those who needed it, without seeming to discriminate since, according to Desdunes, "the white, the black, the yellow—all were the same in his eyes and all received from him equal compassion and monetary assistance."[66] In short, their degree of assimilation resembled that of the white refugees, although in a slightly lower position, as was the custom in all three-tiered societies of the Americas. They were denied access to some occupations and naturally tended to concentrate on the sectors open to them. As among whites, however, there were some meteoric rises, although in lesser numbers. Women among them worked more often than white women did, as was also the norm in the other three-tiered societies.

As for the slaves, although their employment was less varied than that of the other two classes and although their status was immensely different, they also fit perfectly in the Louisiana slave group. The 1810 wave added about one-third to the slave population of New Orleans and vicinity. They remained in the service of their former masters, when the latter became planters (as was the case of Henri de Sainte-Gême) or when they were wealthy enough to keep them as servants. When it was not the case, they were either sold or hired out, and the revenue they provided to their refugee masters was often the masters' only means for survival, at least in the early days of their settlement in New Orleans. Whenever absolutely necessary, the selling or hiring out of slaves was easy, since New Orleans and the plantations of the vicinity were always in need of skilled or semiskilled manpower, which was generally the case of the refugee slaves. They were rented out or sold as sugar workers, domestics, cooks, wigmakers, or coachmen, which is consistent with the fact that they were often domestic slaves who, according to James Mather, were "trained up to the habits of strict discipline" and were mostly "faithful slaves who (had) fled with their masters" or had even assisted their masters in their flight.[67] The numerous primary sources cite the example of both whites and free people of color who lived off the rental of their slaves.[68]

Several conclusions may be drawn from this study of the refugees' occupational pattern. The first is that they found positions in New Orleans and that, after the first few months in which they sometimes needed the financial aid of the New Orleanian and except for a few widows with children who later had to resort to charity, most refugees managed to earn a living. In many cases, they found positions that were below those they had occupied in Saint-Domingue. Some former planters, for instance, became teachers, merchants, or bakers. Although their stories were not always successful, they reinforced the general occupational pattern of New Orleans. If they remained in average positions, with slightly lower incomes than their Creole counterparts, their children often rose in the socioeconomic fabric. The refugees rapidly became proprietors. Many owned at least their house in town. Those involved in business or shopkeeping owned their shops as well, some did own summer residences or plantations (as the already cited Jean-Baptiste Donatien Augustin and Henri de Sainte-Gême), and many also purchased houses for their racially mixed families. Boze's letters abound in such instances, Henri de Sainte-Gême coming first in the references, followed by many others, with the extreme case of Mr. Sauvinet, whom Boze reported was building a second house for his second companion of color.[69]

Whatever their racial status, they brought their skills to New Orleans and, with their dynamism and will to integrate, settled in the economic hierarchy of New Orleans, often giving their offspring an opportunity for upward economic mobility. That they were sometimes less wealthy than their Creole counterparts is not surprising, since they had to reconstruct their lives from nothing. Nevertheless, "they reinforced the existing urban occupational structure by adding to all sectors proportionately," and even contributed "to the city's active population without altering the sectoral distribution of occupations."[70] This is almost true, if only the sectors discussed above are taken into account, whether among whites or among free people of color. It is not entirely true, however, and requires nuancing, if their fields of specialty are considered, since the refugees gave a real impulse to certain sectors of the Louisiana economy and developed others that had not existed until their arrival.

## Fields of Excellence

Regardless of their race, their first obvious field of excellence was agriculture. In the historiography of Louisiana, the sole paternity of sugar making in the region was long attributed to them. Although some present-day historians demonstrate that refugees were not the initiators of sugar production, they were undoubtedly the promoters and technical advisors of the venture. Their agricultural expertise has always been acknowledged and has to be traced back to the dynamism they displayed in Saint-Domingue in matters of innovation and improvement of agricultural techniques. The history of Saint-Domingue abounds in testimonies of this dynamism. For the Terrien brothers, who managed the Saint-Domingan plantation of the Navailles-Bonnas family after the owners' return to metropolitan France, for instance, this innovative expertise leaves no doubt. Comparing the agricultural techniques of southwestern France (where they came from) to those of Saint-Domingue, they insist on the introduction of systematic rotation of crops, in-depth plowing, and fertilizing practices.[71] This is confirmed by a detailed study of the Galbaud du Fort sugar plantation, which attributes this tendency to experiment with new agricultural techniques to the colonists' taste for risk, to the large credits available, and to the immense freedom of action they all enjoyed.[72]

When the refugees poured into Louisiana, Louisianans had been trying to cultivate and granulate sugar for several decades. In the 1750s, Jesuits had attempted the experiment and Joseph Villars Dubreuil had succeeded in obtaining a small commercial production. It was his plantation that ended up in the Boré family in 1763. Sources confirm that the pioneer of the sugar industry was Joseph Solis, who successfully produced molasses, which he distilled to make *taffia*, a liquor common to the sugar societies of the Caribbean. His property, with the cane and the mill, was sold in 1794 to Antonio Mendez and then, in 1795, to Etienne de Boré. The reason why Boré is considered the father of Louisiana sugar is that he was the first to successfully granulate and produce sugar on a large scale.[73] Whether Boré should or should not be granted the prime role in the development of Louisiana sugar is relatively pointless. No historian denies the refugees from Saint-Domingue their essential participation in the venture. Josef Solís is sometimes even said to have had Saint-Domingan origins.[74] What is widely acknowledged is that when he purchased Solís's property from Mendez, Boré also hired his sugar maker, Antoine Morin, who was a Saint-Domingue refugee.[75] This first 1795 attempt was successful, and Boré's plantation yielded 100,000 pounds of sugar and a large profit. By 1797, 550,000 pounds of sugar were exported from New Orleans, and in 1801, 5 million pounds were produced out of seventy-five sugar mills. This implied a "gross return of $400,000 for Louisiana planters (without considering sale of molasses and *taffia*)."[76] It is thus obvious that Boré's success marked the birth of the Louisiana sugar industry and that "Antoine Morin, the experienced sugar maker from Haiti, deserves similar recognition."[77]

Beyond Morin's leading role, however, it is more useful to the present discussion to consider the numerous refugees who became involved in the process. From the Saint-Domingan slaves, who provided semiskilled labor and who were thus in high demand among the Louisiana planters, to the free refugees of color and white refugees who became managers, overseers, or technical assistants, all three groups of the refugee community played a significant part in this development. Some planters from Saint-Domingue even became involved in sugar planting, including Henri de Sainte-Gême in Gentilly, Paul Mathias Anatole Peychaud, who owned 2,240 acres and twenty slaves in the St. Tammany Parish, or Christian Miltenberger, the physician, in the Plaquemines Parish.[78] Several instances of free men of color who became overseers and technical assistants after being experienced sugar growers in Saint-Domingue may also be found in the literature.[79] Whites were also in high demand, especially former planters and those who had been trained in the science of sugar refining.[80] Many of those whites and free refugees of color had also been sugar engineers and could thus transmit their knowledge and train their Louisiana counterparts. The salary of a skilled Saint-Domingan sugar maker could be as high as $1,500.[81] They also supervised the building of the sugar mills by the slaves, who then grew sugar cane and worked the mills.[82]

The advertisements published in the New Orleans newspapers at the time attest to this involvement of the refugees in the sugar industry. In July 1809, *Le Courrier de la Louisiane* published an advertisement in which a refugee proposed his assistance "in the administration of an estate or the fabrication of sugar, if only for the season," and proved that sugar cultivation involved the whole refugee community by offering "the labor of three Negroes experienced in sugar production to the planter who hired him." In the 14 July issue, another refugee announced that he was "ready to work on a trial basis without compensation as a refiner of sugar or in a distillery." In the 30 August issue, some refugees offered to enter into partnership by providing their expertise and their slaves. There is little doubt they had much to offer and were even ready to offer it for nothing in the hope of proving their worth.

Added to the fact that sugar production had almost entirely ceased in Haiti—the world's leading exporter before the revolution left a large gap in the world's economy—the refugees' role in the birth and development of the Louisiana industry was undoubtedly immense and "imagination refuses to picture what would have been the case but for the refugees from San Domingo."[83] This had several effects on the Louisiana economic pattern. First, it created a new field of production, thus revitalizing the planter economy, which had suffered much in the previous decades. The Louisiana planters had indeed experienced an important economic recess, to such a point that, before successfully turning to sugar production, Boré was almost ruined. Because sugar production requires that industrial treatment of the cane be performed immediately after harvesting, the development of sugar production also added an industrial dimension to Louisiana's agriculture, which neither cotton, indigo, nor tobacco had done. By adding to the wealth of the plantation world, the sugar boom also created new job opportunities. The possibility to attain more self-sufficiency encouraged the planters to employ new skilled workers. The development of the sugar industry led to the hiring of more slaves as shoemakers, seamstresses, or boatmen.[84] Plantations also hired architects, carpenters, mechanics, and engineers.[85] The development of the sugar industry also tilted the ratio of female to male plantation workers, the cultivation and treatment of sugar cane requiring more males, due to the harshness of the harvesting and the skill required to operate the mills.[86] Finally, this new sugar boom induced far-reaching changes in the Louisiana landscape, participating, as all the agricultural advances attributable to the refugees (such as the coffee boom in Jamaica and Cuba), to the modernization of the countryside, to the building of roads and other infrastructures, and to the development of the rural habitat.[87] By increasing the wealth of Louisiana, it also had enduring consequences for the development of business and everything pertaining to cultivation and transformation as well as all connected activities.

Saint-Domingan refugees were also involved in privateering. Although it may seem surprising to include such an illegal activity among the economic legacies of the Saint-Domingans, the Laffite brothers and their Baratarians played an important economic role. By seizing goods and slaves on British and Spanish vessels and smuggling them into Louisiana, they launched a new parallel wealth in New Orleans. Their activity did not benefit the official economy, since it deprived the city of the import duties that should have been paid had the products been imported directly. Quite naturally, it did not benefit equally all categories of the population either. The products they sold (including dry goods and luxury products such as silk stockings or wine) and the slaves they imported, however, were in such demand in New Orleans that their activities were strongly favored by the richest categories of the New Orleans population, and the authorities closed their eyes to the traffic. Until the mid-1810s, there was no attempt to prevent those men, whose main privateering base was Barataria, from establishing a parallel economy. The refugees played an essential part in the development of Barataria, and refugees were also among the financers (and beneficiaries) of the activities, as was Henri de Sainte-Gême, for instance.

Whether Pierre and Jean Laffite were refugees is highly disputed among historians. Until recently, biographies specified that they were born at Port-au-Prince in 1779 and 1782.[88] Some sources even stress their role in transporting Saint-Domingan refugees to America. Despite the evidence advanced by others that they had been born in France, there seems to be little doubt that they had, at least, come by way of Saint-Domingue.[89] Whatever their birthplace, they had strong links with the refugee community. There is no doubt concerning their second in command, Dominique You (said by some biographers to be their brother), or the next in command, Renato Beluche (sometimes said to be their cousin), who were both refugees.[90] Even Cable, who does not expatiate on the Baratarians' origins, constantly connects them to the refugee community. Explaining their success in New Orleans, he writes that "thousands of their brethren already filled the streets of New Orleans, and commanded the sympathies of the native Creoles," and that American authorities' difficulty in ridding the city of the Baratarians could be attributed to the fact that "the prevalence of West Indian ideas in New Orleans was a secure shelter."[91]

There were refugees among the privateers beyond the four leaders. Pierre Laffite's first companion was a free refugee of color. His son, Pierre, married Marie Berret, a refugee native of Cuba.[92] Many other more obscure members were also refugees, including blacks, whatever their status. Governor Claiborne testified that "among them are some Saint Domingo Negroes of the most desperate character, and no worse than most of their white associates."[93] They were also obviously connected with the refugee community. Among their friends and defenders were Edward Livingston, who had married a refugee and defended Pierre Laffite when he was imprisoned, and General Humbert, a refugee who taught at the Collège d'Orléans and was one of the most regular patrons of the Café des Réfugiés.[94] Sainte-Gême was one of their financiers but also a friend of the Laffite brothers, and "Pierre acted as a second in an 'affair of honor' in the year 1815 along with Ste-Gême, who had no superior in New Orleans as to social position," which proves that the brothers were perfectly accepted in the New Orleans society.[95] Auguste Davezac was also among their closest friends, as well as many others, "perhaps twenty more."[96]

Among their short-term legacies was thus the creation of a parallel economy that benefited many New Orleanians, including the wealthiest Creoles of the city, and had repercussions for the economy of Louisiana. The leaders of the Baratarians were easily accepted by their fellow refugees and by the New Orleans Creole society at large. Dominique You stayed in New Orleans when the rest of the Baratarians moved to Galveston after being granted pardon by the authorities for their bravery and dedication during the Battle of New Orleans. When he died, the city council paid for his interment in St. Louis cemetery #2, and his epitaph, bearing the emblem of Freemasonry, reads that he was "one of New Orleans."[97] The Laffite brothers were also eminent citizens of New Orleans. After being pardoned, Pierre "established himself as a respected member of the Louisiana's planter class."[98] As for Jean, he had contacts with many prominent members of the New Orleans society, "he was a companion of legislators and generals," and could have played a primary part in the New Orleans political life if he had wanted to do so.[99] He had an essential role in the Battle of New Orleans, warning the authorities twice, despite his temporary estrangement and the imprisonment of his brother and of You by the American authorities, and they all fought to the point of being distinguished by Jackson and subsequently pardoned.[100] Beyond their immediate impact upon the economy, defense, and social life of New Orleans, they undoubtedly left their imprint on the "glamour and romance" of New Orleans.[101] Their "unique impact upon both history and legend"[102] is relevant to the present discussion because, whether or not Jean Laffite was born in Saint-Domingue, his supposed origins had an enormous impact upon the legendary quality of

Barataria, thus showing the influence the refugees had upon the collective unconscious.

Obviously, the refugees played an important economic part, stimulating both official and parallel economies. This is but a first deep modification initiated by the refugees or at least enriched by their presence. Refugees also gave a strong impulse to yet unexplored fields in the city's economic fabric. By the education they had received, by the habit of favoring artistic activities acquired and developed in Saint-Domingue, they fostered a strong development of the medical and educational fields and paved the way to the explosion of journalism and the arts in New Orleans.

The medical field was clearly enriched by their presence. Their expertise in curing some diseases and their immunization to tropical fevers made refugee nurses of color New Orleans favorites. Many doctors were refugees, and several acquired a long-lasting fame for their pioneering deeds. Names abound in the medical professions. Refugee doctors like Doctors Lebeau, Alliot, Rollin (who advertised in the *Moniteur de la Louisiane* his ability to cure youngsters and skin diseases), Doctors Berret, Yves and René Lemonier (on Royal Street), Yves René Lemonier (the second-generation Lemonier), Octave Huard, or Antoine-Marie Goyffon, as well as refugee apothecaries (Mr. Dufilho or Pierre Lambert) could be found in large numbers in New Orleans.[103] Their mere presence augmented a given economic category. But their dynamism and expertise also were essential to the medical field, and several of them left their imprint on Louisiana's medicine. They played an important part in military medical care, as show the examples of Germaine Ducatel, who belonged to Jackson's medical corps in 1814–15, and Maurice Bertin, who was chief surgeon of the New Orleans Militia in 1808.[104] Refugee practitioners were also among the vanguard in the treatment of yellow fever, as exemplified by Christian Miltenberger, who gave a lecture in front of the Medical Society of New Orleans to demonstrate that yellow fever was not contagious, and who was appointed by the mayor to supervise indigent health care.[105] Jean Charles Faget also left his name in medical nomenclature by discovering "Faget's sign," the distinctive mark of yellow fever (an uncommonly slow pulse), enabling the practitioners to differentiate it from malaria or other fevers. Other names remain linked with the diagnosis and treatment of yellow fever: Dr. Devèze, a surgeon who was appointed head of the hospital at Bush Hill by the U.S. government, and Dr. Billon, who made the treatment of yellow fever his specialty, both in Saint-Domingue and New Orleans.[106] Finally, Dr. François Marie Prevost, who practiced at Donaldsville, remained in the annals for practicing the first Louisianan Cesarean section, the second such operation in the United States.[107] In the medical field, the Saint-Domingan refugees both added to the existing medical staff and influenced positively the profession by initiating important advances and discoveries.

In the artistic and intellectual fields, the refugees probably did more than just stimulate or reinforce; they pioneered. By doing so, they deeply modified the economic organizational pattern of New Orleans.[108] In the late eighteenth century there was no organized artistic life, no theater, and no opera house. There were no newspapers, and education lagged far behind the rest of the North American continent. The refugees triggered and developed these activities, with almost no help from outside the community, at least in the early years.

In the New Orleans artistic fields, their predominance is obvious. Throughout the first half of the nineteenth century, all activities were pervaded by their presence. Plastic arts were enriched by the influence of Charles de Baligant, a sculptor who taught drawing, and François Bocquet, a celebrated painter and engraver.[109] Drawing and architecture were among their favorite fields. François Correjolles designed the Beauregard Keys house for Joseph Le Carpentier in 1825, and Louis Henri Pillié, the town surveyor, left hundreds of drawings of New Orleans. They also influenced the musical field, with great names such as Louis Moreau Gottschalk, a famous second-generation refugee composer, or Louis Placide Canonge, who directed the New Orleans French Opera, founded by refugees.

They also introduced the New Orleans public to ballet, as attested by the fame of the dancer and choreographer Jean-Baptiste Francis. He had practiced his art in Saint-Domingue in 1789, in Charleston in 1794, in New York in 1796, and in Boston in 1797, but it was in New Orleans that he remained after 1799.[110] The role of the refugee community, and in particular of the descendants of Saint-Domingan Creoles of color, in literature and poetry throughout the nineteenth century was significant. The field in which they had the strongest influence, however, was probably the theater, as was the case in other asylums, for instance, in Charleston, where they founded the French theater on Church Street in April 1794.[111] In New Orleans, they filled every position, founded and directed theaters, wrote plays, and acted. Alexis Daudet, the director of the Comédie du Cap Français, filled all of these positions when he came to New Orleans: he was actor, playwright, and manager of the Orleans Theater. Auguste Tessier, who had been the director of the theater of Kingston, directed the Salle de la Nouvelle Orléans on St. Philip Street.[112] Louis

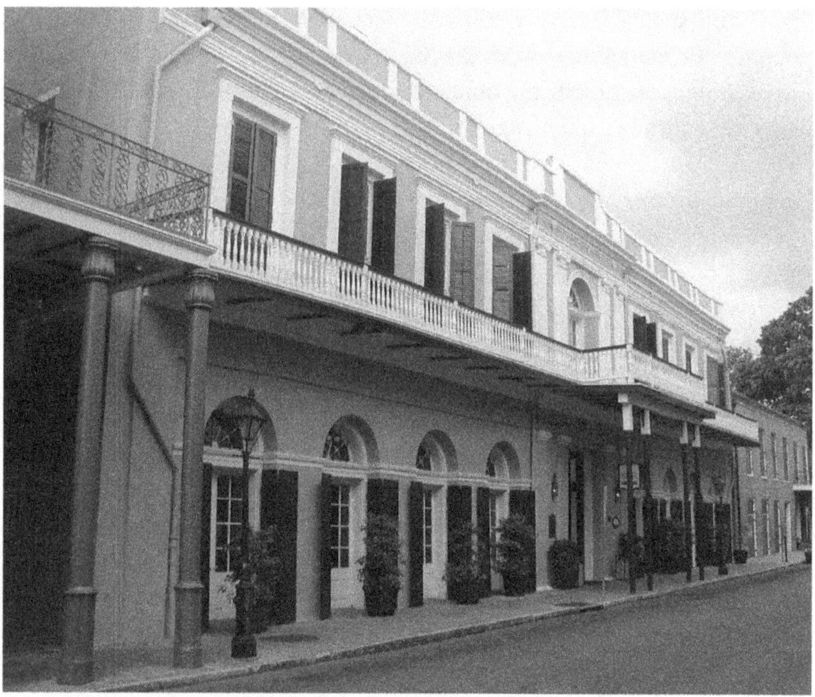

Figure 4. Théâtre d'Orléans, Orleans Street, New Orleans.

Placide Canonge is remembered as one of the playwrights of the city. Names of refugee actors abounded on the programs of the plays performed in New Orleans: Denis Richard Dechanet Desessarts, Jeanne Marie Chapiseau, Jean Baptiste Lesueur Fontaine, Louis François Clairville, Scholastique Labbé, Madame Delaure, François de Saint Just, and Rigaud.[113] Their cultural influence will be discussed later, but it may already be said that they had a definite economic impact by creating new theatrical infrastructures that did not exist in New Orleans prior to their arrival, which in turn influenced the taste of New Orleanians for this type of culture and, by reinforcing the need for these cultural activities, induced the development of a new occupation in Louisiana.

They also launched journalism in Louisiana. The 1790–1810 period was one of great dynamism, with the creation of all the main newspapers of New Orleans. In every single press venture, Saint-Domingan refugees led the way. Louis Duclot, a refugee, founded *Le Moniteur de la Louisiane* in 1794. In 1797, one year after his arrival, Jean Baptiste Lesueur Fontaine became its editor. *Le*

*Télégraphe* was founded in early December 1803 by Claudin Beleurgey and Jean Renard, who was a printer of the city and of New Orleans Parish. J. B. Thierry and J. C. de St. Romes were responsible for launching *Le Courrier de la Louisiane*, which was published from 1807 to 1860, and Jean Leclerc founded *L'Ami des Lois*. Alexis Daudet participated in the *Louisiana Gazette*, a bilingual newspaper. Among the famous journalists were Louis Placide Canonge and Baron Jérôme Bayon de Libertas, from the Breda plantation (the very plantation where Toussaint-Louverture had been a slave), who wrote both in *L'Abeille* and *Le Courrier de la Louisiane*.[114] There again, the Saint-Domingan refugees were the initiators of a new field. Saint-Domingue had long developed a journalistic tradition, and everywhere they went, the refugees launched publications that were more or less short-lived, according to the general cultural environment. In most of their other asylums, from Boston, New York, and Philadelphia to Charleston and Jamaica, they created newspapers, but nowhere did their ventures prosper as they did in New Orleans, due to the journalistic desert the city had been until their arrival and the French-speaking environment, which enabled long-lived publications.[115] By launching numerous newspapers, they created a new economic sector. As in the fields of theater, and opera, they fostered a new taste in New Orleans and ensured that it would survive their own first ventures.

Refugees also strongly stimulated education, which had been, until then, primitive in Louisiana. While the number of preexisting schools was really infinitesimal, the refugees, upon arriving in Louisiana, offered to teach in all positions and at all levels, as they did in other asylums.[116] In Louisiana, as was the case with the press, they were tremendously more successful than elsewhere, due to the local educational void and to the linguistic situation. A close examination of the newspapers at the time shows that they advertised their services in all fields. From Nicolas de Saint-Céran, who advertised his wish to teach English, Spanish, and French (*Le Télégraphe*, 28 January 1804), to Pierre Lambert, who offered his services to teach arithmetic, algebra, geometry, calculus, and navigation (*Le Courrier de la Louisiane*, 15 September 1809), or François Bocquet who offered to teach reading and writing, languages (French, Spanish, and English), history, and geography (*Le Courrier de la Louisiane*, 23 January 1809), there is great diversity. More than fifteen Cuban refugees advertised their educational services.[117] Some were private tutors, as was the case of John James Audubon or Denis-Richard Dechanet Desessarts, who tutored for the Destréhan children. Some taught in secondary schools, including Jean Boze's son (several times mentioned in the letters to Sainte-Gême), who taught in the mutual boys' school of Lafourche. Some refugees became still more influential by opening secondary schools, like the Moussier daughters who ran a boarding school, where they left their mark, according to Boze, on the knowledge and morals of their pupils (folder 268). Joseph Belzans opened an art school on Bourbon Street that he advertised in the *Moniteur de la Louisiane* issue of 20 September 1806. François Bocquet, who advertised his teaching abilities in the *Courrier,* also opened a school on Burgundy after being a private tutor, and Denis Richard Dechanet Desessarts launched a subscription to open a school (*Moniteur de la Louisiane,* 13 August 1806). The sisters of Eliza Williams opened a school in Natchez and later went to New Orleans.[118] Refugees even opened schools for free people of color, testifying to a different perception of race differences and race relations, when the teachers were white, and a stronger enterprising spirit when free people of color themselves opened the school. Although it is only one in many, the New Orleans directory of 1805 gives the example of Jean Marsenac, who taught in a school for people of color.[119]

The Collège d'Orléans, the first university in Louisiana, was founded in 1805 by refugees Auguste Davezac, Louis Moreau-Lislet, and Paul Lanusse. Davezac was its first president. Vice chancellor Jean-François Pitot, later known as James, had come to Louisiana from Saint-Domingue and had married a refugee. Moreau-Lislet and Lanusse belonged to its first board of regents, as did Hypolithe Canonge, the superintendent of public schools. Other refugees taught in it, including General Humbert, Jean Baptiste Augustin, and Pierre Lambert. The refugees' influence on Louisiana's higher education did not stop there. In 1822, the son of a refugee planter from Saint-Domingue, Paul Tulane, settled in New Orleans and financed the foundation of the Medical College of Louisiana, renamed Tulane University in 1883.[120] Obviously, the Saint-Domingan refugees contributed to the expansion of a sector that had long been neglected in Louisiana. They created positions and developed education, thus influencing the Louisiana cultural and intellectual life. Louis Guillaume Valentin Dubourg displayed an interest in the schooling activities of the Ursulines when he took charge of the Catholic Church in New Orleans. He had founded St. Mary's College in Maryland, been president of Georgetown University, and assisted in the creation of the Sisters of Charity, in which education played an important part.[121] Henriette Delille and Juliette Gaudin, the daughter of refugees, founded the school of the Order of the Holy Family.

In short, the refugees benefited some sectors by adding their mere numbers, but they either gave a strong impulse or were at the center of the creation of several other sectors. Their participation in the economic development of New Orleans and Louisiana at large was essential. They were also strongly involved in the defense sector. Primary sources abound with examples of refugees who entered the Louisiana Militia and who reached high grades in it. Pierre François Dubourg became major of the Louisiana Volunteers. Louis Buard and Louis Blanchard were appointed lieutenants of the militia in 1805, André Daniel Chastant and Claudin de Beleurgey in 1806, and Achille Bérard in 1807. Alexandre Blanche was appointed captain in 1806, and d'Esquin de Mirepoix became an officer in the Forty-fourth Regiment.[122]

The Battle of New Orleans, fought by the troops of Andrew Jackson in 1815, a few weeks after the signature of the Treaty of Ghent between England and the United States, illustrates the essential role of the refugees in the military. Whatever their color and status, they committed themselves to the defense of the besieged town. The first warnings of the incoming British attack came from Barataria through Jean Laffite, who, despite the open hostility of the American authorities toward the privateers and despite the imprisonment of his brother, did not hesitate to deny the British troops the help they had requested and offer his services to the Americans. The Baratarians, under the command of Dominique You and Renato Beluche, came to fight alongside Jackson's troops, manning two 24–pounders of the artillery.[123] Jackson's pardon for their privateering activities enabled some to settle in New Orleans and live the peaceful life of normal citizens. The rank-and-file refugee members of the militia, be they whites or free people of color, also gained fame in the fight. The second battalion of free refugees of color, which counted some 250 men, was placed under the command of Second Major Savary, the first man of African descent to reach the rank of major in the United States.[124] The battalion was later granted special commendation for bravery by Jackson, and Savary himself was rewarded for his services, benefiting in 1819 from a monthly pension "in recognition for his service in defense of the state," a measure that was renewed by the state legislature in 1823.[125] Savary was second in command behind Louis d'Aquin, a refugee who also commanded a militia battalion of white refugees and Creoles.[126] Sainte-Gême was in command of a dragoon company, and Auguste Guibert was captain of a company of chasseurs.[127] Added to the Baratarian refugees and the 256 men of Savary's battalion, refugees also made up for at least 28 percent of the white battalion of New Orleans. Not all the soldiers' birthplaces could be identified, and the proportion may still be higher.[128] Other refugees were present at various moments of the preparation and of the battle itself. For instance, Davezac walked the line of defense all day with Jackson on New Year's Day.[129] From this discussion, there is little doubt that the refugees strengthened the white troops of Louisiana and reinforced the free black military presence in New Orleans. This is but another manifestation of their essential role in southern Louisiana in the early nineteenth century.

All in all, the refugees fitted everywhere in the New Orleans occupational pattern. In many fields, they simply added their numerical presence to that of the preexisting three groups of the Louisiana population. In many other fields, they were the main engine of economic evolution. Although it is not a noble economic activity, they were at the center of the Louisiana privateering activity. The sugar industry benefited from their expertise. They were also especially innovative in the medical field. They palliated the want of cultural and educational activities by developing the public school system, creating a system of higher education in Louisiana, launching newspapers, and initiating a tradition of cultural activities. By importing from Saint-Domingue their passion for the theater, opera, and arts in general to New Orleans, they opened new occupational spaces and launched a long cultural tradition in Louisiana. Obviously, while they were thus influencing the Louisiana economy, they also influenced the organization of the New Orleans society. The refugees, as they did in the economic field, both reinforced an existing order at a transitional period in the history of Louisiana and induced several deep changes in the social organization of their new home.

# 5

# A New Social Era?

The discussion of the refugees' social influence displays close links with that of their economic impact. The mere occupational pattern of the community had consequences on the social stratification of New Orleans. The adjunction of refugees to certain sectors of the economy—artisans and shopkeepers, for instance—increased the lower and middle classes among whites and free people of color. The fact that many white refugees chose to integrate the professions also led to the reinforcement of the white upper middle class. Teachers, journalists, physicians, and lawyers added to the equivalent stratum of the New Orleans society. The development of some sectors, like entertainment or the sugar industry, also had obvious consequences on the society.

The arrival of the refugees thus partly reinforced the existing social order and partly tipped the balance. A mere numerical reinforcement of one sector is already a cause for a shift in the existing society, since it gives more weight to one category. An improvement of the wealth or dynamism of another sector is also bound to tilt the order of the existing society. The launching of new activities also created new social categories. The refugees' economic participation alone was a cause for evolution. This, however, is but an obvious and superficial vision of the social changes they triggered. In New Orleans, the arrival of the refugees meant much more than a mere socioeconomic impact.

The object of the present discussion is to show that their arrival, although it did not revolutionize the New Orleans society, did have a similar impact as that described in the economic field, both reinforcing certain existing characteristics and inaugurating new trends in society. In short, the refugees triggered evolutions, although those evolutions were not necessarily revolutionary. Because of the composition of the migrant community and the timeliness of their arrival, their influence over some areas of New Orleans society was much larger than what might be expected at first. The socioracial composition of New Orleans, in particular, testifies to this strong influence. Although historians often contend that the arrival of the migrant waves—even the last numerically important one—did not significantly alter the socioracial order in New Orleans, it did have an essential impact, linked with the political changes of the early nineteenth century.

## Impact on the Three-Tiered Society

The topic of the free refugees of color is rarely tackled by historians. It is even strangely absent from most of the studies bearing on the free people of color of the Gulf Coast.[1] The most widely shared assumption is that their arrival did not significantly alter the three-tiered society of New Orleans. A common conclusion, according to Paul Lachance, is that the refugee influx "added to all three racial castes in the city without altering significantly the proportion in the population as a whole, nor the nature of race relations." This is largely true. Indeed, the last and largest wave reinforced the white, free black, and slave classes equally. In some respects, Lachance adds, it is true that the first consequence of the refugees' arrival was an equally distributed numerical reinforcement of the three categories and a reinforcement of the "modes of interaction across barriers characteristic of three-caste societies." It seems, however, that there was much more to their coming, because of the close parallelism of the racial mix of the immigrants' group to that of the host society, while other types of migrations, those from Germany and Ireland, for instance, brought only a white increase to the New Orleans population.[2]

What seems obvious, in the still larger context of immigration to Louisiana, is that the arrival of the refugees reinforced the free class of color to a degree never attained by any other migration to Louisiana, at a time when their numerical power was strongly endangered by the takeover of the territory by the United States. Even before the Louisiana Purchase, the ratio of French to English speakers had reduced drastically, from 7:1 before 1790 to only 3:1 at the turn of the century.[3] The flow from the United States accelerated after the purchase, which means that the context was numerically unfavorable to the French speakers when the main refugee waves reached Louisiana, at the time of the purchase (from Jamaica and Haiti), and two years before statehood (for the Cuban wave).

When considering only population figures, the Cuban wave was bound to have an impact. The free class of color was a minority in Louisiana. In 1805, before the wave from Cuba, the population of the Crescent City (already influenced by the earlier waves) was composed of 3,551 whites, 1,566 free colored people, and 3,105 slaves.[4] It seems that the figures speak for themselves. Considering that the 1809–10 wave added slightly more than 3,000 persons to each class, it reduced the proportional inferiority of the free class of color. It almost doubled the white and slave categories, but it tripled the free population of color. This group, which had represented 19 percent of the city's population in 1805, suddenly represented 29 percent when refugees from Cuba poured into New Orleans in 1810.[5]

The numerical increase of the free class of color occurred at a time when this population was especially threatened by the new American takeover of the Louisiana territory. The first threat to the group was numerical. The racial composition of some migrations brought little benefit to the free group of color. During the Spanish period, all-white migrant groups reached Louisiana from the Canary Islands and Acadia. The resumption of the African trade had also added to the slave group, while the relatively more liberal manumission policies of the Spanish authorities enabled a slight increase of the free group of African descent. Before the all-white migrations of the 1840s, increasing numbers of American settlers came to Louisiana. This benefited the white class, although the settlers were likely either to come accompanied by slaves or to import slaves, even after the ban on the international slave trade in 1808 since domestic trade endured. Due to the biracial view the Anglo-Saxons had of society, despite the existence of a comparatively small free class of color in some Upper South states or in certain urban areas, the American takeover did not induce a migration of members of that class. The Saint-Domingan immigrants were thus the only free black addition to New Orleans society. Moreover, at a time when this takeover was likely to imply new political trends in favor of a biracial organization of society, the numerical reinforcement of the free class was bound to offer Louisianans an opportunity to resist the imposition of the Anglo-Saxon model. The Saint-Domingan refugees from Jamaica and Haiti thus came at the crucial moment of the purchase in 1803 and the refugees from Cuba during the early years of attempted Americanization. The refugee flow was highly influential, since it reached Louisiana at a time when, except by natural increase, the free community of color would not have evolved numerically. The thesis of a plainly equal numerical increase would have been true, but only if the migration had occurred at a different time.

The timeliness of the arrivals and the proportionately superior numerical increase to the free group of color due to the wave from Cuba was thus the first step of the deep social impact of the refugees on the New Orleans society. The arrival of the Saint-Domingan free refugees of color "dwarfed the existing free population and by the end of the decade may have composed as much as 60 percent of Louisiana's free black community. In 1810 free people of color made up nearly 30 percent of the city population; they composed a similar proportion of Mobile and Pensacola," which was obviously more than before their arrival.[6] There was, however, much more than this mere numerical and proportional factor.

The arrival of the free refugees of color also influenced some of the characteristics of the corresponding social class. Racially, the refugees were often more mixed than the Louisiana free population of color. Two explanations may account for this. First, the Spanish rules for emancipation and self-purchase (*Coartación*) had given Louisiana slaves the opportunity to attain freedom, which means that the free population in New Orleans included unmixed blacks. Although the proportion of individuals with mixed African ancestry had increased in the Louisiana free population of color (from one-fifth in the 1769 census to over two-thirds in 1791), the arrival of mostly mixed-blood free persons from Saint-Domingue tended to "whiten" the free population of color or "to reinforce this somatic marker, as the free people of color of Saint-Domingue also tended toward the light-skinned."[7]

The second explanation for this relative "whitening" of the free group of color has to do with the fact that those who left Saint-Domingue were among the lighter-skinned in the population. Due to the political turmoil that had prevailed in Saint-Domingue in the 1790s, the lighter the people were, the more likely they were to be persecuted by those in command. This was the case when Dessalines came to power in 1803, but this was even the case under Toussaint's rule. Although Toussaint's years were much quieter than the other periods of the Haitian revolution, he did not hesitate to order the execution of a large number of racially mixed persons.[8] Many light-skinned members of this group fled Saint-Domingue. This was a first significant consequence of the migrating population over the Louisiana group. A second consequence was the immediate urbanization of the free group of color. While the urbanization of the Louisiana free population of color had slowly started during the Spanish period, compared with the French colonial period, the Saint-Domingue migration strongly strengthened the phenomenon, since very few of the free refugees of color went beyond the limits of the Crescent City.

These two factors contributed to the progressive isolation of the free group from the rest of the population of African descent and were reinforced by the refugees' past experience. Since they were lighter skinned and mostly urban, they progressively diverged from the slaves, who were largely ethnically pure and rural. In Saint-Domingue the free blacks had much less in common with the slaves than did their Louisiana counterparts. Because of their more frequent access to education and wealth, because they possessed property in land and slaves, they had progressively diverged from the slave community, which was often of pure African ancestry. Moreover, the revolutionary events in Saint-Domingue had estranged the free people of color from the slaves. There, they had been politically threatened by the former slaves, who resented their alliances with the whites. Some had witnessed the murder of their peers by the infuriated slaves. The free immigrants of color were strongly conscious of the differences that existed between them and the bondsmen. The arrival of the refugees tended to separate more radically the free blacks from the slave community. That the newcomers had little to do with the Louisiana slaves is obvious. As Ira Berlin writes, "The shared history reaching back to the Natchez revolt had but slight meaning to the newcomers. Men and women chased from their homes and disposed of their property—often including slaves—by Toussaint's armies could hardly identify with saltwater Africans and the plight of the plantation slave." He adds that "colored refugees from Saint-Domingue may well have tutored their mainland counterparts—the free Creole slaves—on the dangers that an alliance with plantation slaves posed to the free people of African descent."[9] Although there is no evidence of this tutoring, the probability of its reality is indeed high.

While becoming progressively estranged from the slave population, the free population of color had also diverged from the white class in Saint-Domingue. The early political movements on the island had been triggered by the denial of the rights of the free group of color by the whites and by their refusal to implement the principles of equality celebrated by the French Revolution. It is easily imaginable that they resented the uncompromising position of the whites that had prevented any further joint action between the two groups and had eventually favored the accession to power of the slave group—although not voluntarily. Moreover, because of their relocation in Louisiana after its takeover by the United States, they could not openly intermarry with whites any more than they could with black slaves. It tended to create a stronger homogamy among them. There was a close similarity of the Creoles of color of both Saint-Domingue and Louisiana, with a remarkable tendency to marry "within their class," so that they sometimes "formed entire clans tracing descent from a single European ancestor."[10] The free Creole group, thanks to this new addition, had become self-sufficient, so to speak. It had more than doubled in number and wealth and could now easily increase through intermarriage.[11] The Saint-Domingan refugees had undoubtedly brought new blood to the group, and their disinvolvement with the other two groups favored the birth and development of a stronger group consciousness among the free people of color in Louisiana.[12]

The stronger sense of identity was reinforced by one of the rare negative consequences of the arrival of the free refugees of color. The sudden increase of the group, especially when the Cuban wave reached Louisiana, reinforced the fears of the Americans—who had gained command of the territory six years earlier—against this population they were not necessarily used to, especially since the privileges of the free people of color, both in Saint-Domingue and Louisiana, had been far more important than in the American South.[13] This concomitant increase in the numerical presence of the free group, a stronger class consciousness, and widespread fears among white Americans prompted a stronger feeling of defiance and new restrictive legislation against them. They were, of course, denied franchise as well as the benefits of the free school law. They had to carry proof of their freedom at all times, be noted as free men or women of color in the records, request permission to leave the city, and, for a while after the arrival of the refugees, respect a 9 p.m. curfew.[14] They could not wear masks during carnival, and there were separate balls for whites and people of African descent.[15] After 1850, they were denied the right to open schools, and the schools already in existence were progressively closed down, while the societies they had founded, be they "religious, charitable, scientific, or literary" were dissolved. A number of activities were also forbidden to them, such as operating "billiard halls, coffee halls, and liquor stores," and they could not work as riverboat captains.[16] These restrictions against the group led them to unify further and had the advantage of pushing them to define much more clearly their position within New Orleans's social fabric. At first, before the legislation became too restrictive, they manifested this consolidation of their group consciousness by forming their own religious orders, associations (religious or charitable), schools, and literary societies.[17] When legislation became too restrictive, they strengthened their political resistance. As early as 1804, that is, before the largest addition of the Cuban wave, the propertied free people of color had petitioned the federal government for the right to vote on tax issues. Throughout the nineteenth century, "they were intensely political,"[18] a reaction that marked a clear dissent from the rest of the American South, where the biracial order had silenced any political claim by people of African descent.

The more threatened the refugees' identity was, the stronger their sense of identity. Unity making for strength, the group prospered. The arrival of the Saint-Domingan refugees triggered monopolistic involvement of the free group of color in some economic sectors. It also led to the emergence of a stronger elite among them and increased their visibility. They were active in the world of trade; they were also much sought after as artisans and shopkeepers. They totally dominated the leather working industry. They were devout Catholic, rarely involved in crimes, and thus lived relatively quietly. The strengthening of the group led to the creation of a true free elite of color, similar to, although less prosperous than, the Saint-Domingan one. When examining the marriage contracts or wills involving free refugees of color, it is clear that they possessed some wealth.[19] They often owned their houses, movables, and even jewels, and they often possessed their shops and owned slaves.[20] They widely owned property in the Faubourgs Marigny and Trémé.[21] They owned schools, attended mass at the St. Louis Cathedral, organized balls, acted in the theater plays, and attended theatrical performances.

This increase and stimulation by a class that was both educated and accustomed to being socially recognized as well as economically independent and powerful undoubtedly influenced the Creoles of color of New Orleans. They reinforced a group that eventually emerged as "one of the most advanced black communities in North America."[22] The arrival of the refugees coincided with the development of black education in New Orleans. Most of the schools for free people of color were run by Saint-Domingan refugees, as was the Couvent School, which included Armand Lanusse among its faculty.[23]

The militia offered Creoles of color a good chance for promotion, both in Saint-Domingue and in Louisiana, and the free refugees of color never refused to participate, as exemplified by the battalions that assisted the American troops during the Battle of New Orleans. The example of Savary attests to the obvious success of the free refugees in those ranks. The militia had the advantage of reinforcing the group cohesion and sense of identity, making them more visible, and linking them to the municipal activities in New Orleans. The militia could even be described as the framework from which all political actions originated, for instance, the petitions of free people of color for the permission to hold dances, the Dorville petition, and the petition to the territorial government to maintain the militia.[24]

The higher visibility of the free group of color was thus favored by the influence of the Saint-Domingan refugees. They tried to turn the group they integrated into what they had known in Saint-Domingue, while fighting with still more vigor against the further restrictions the Americans were trying to impose on them. There is hardly any doubt that, without the new energy brought by the numerical increase of the Saint-Domingan refugees, by their higher level of education and political awareness, and by their habit of much greater privileges granted in Saint-Domingue, the American attempts at imposing their biracial vision of society would have prevailed easily and rapidly in New Orleans. The Creoles of color no doubt would have been in such a minority that they could not have made their claims heard. They probably would have had to submit almost immediately to the American will and to their vision of races and interracial relationships. The refugees' influence was especially strong because their conception of racial differences and race relationships was certainly still further away from the Americans' than the Louisianans.' The refugees clearly dissented from the American perception of the social order, and they reinforced the Louisianans' resistance to the rigid racial order that the new American owners were trying to impose.

## An Altered Conception of Races Relations?

The refugees probably exerted a strong influence on racial differences and race relationships. In colonial Louisiana, be it French or Spanish, a great amount of race fluidity had been the norm, compared with the Anglo-Saxon South, especially in rural communities.[25] Still more fluidity had apparently existed in Saint-Domingue, however. This explains why it might be thought that the arrival of refugees so numerous as to double the population of New Orleans probably influenced race relations in New Orleans. The coming of the refugees apparently gave slightly more independence to urban slaves. The practice of leasing slaves out was common in both Saint-Domingue and Louisiana. In Louisiana, however, slaves were leased out by their masters, and the masters chose the person to whom they leased their slaves. In Saint-Domingue, the slaves were relatively often free to seek work, providing that they returned a certain amount of money to their masters. The Saint-Domingan refugees imported the practice into Louisiana, which contrasted with local customs.[26] This granted slightly more opportunity to the New Orleans slaves and gave them more independence.

Moreover, the ties between the whites and free people of color were stronger in Saint-Domingue than in Louisiana. In Saint-Domingue, there was no residential segregation, and when the refugees reached New Orleans, they all flocked into the same areas of New Orleans, without any racial distinction, principally to what is now known as the French Quarter and to the Faubourgs Trémé and Marigny. The white refugees also introduced the practice of endowing their racially mixed children as they did their white offspring. The

Books of Wills of New Orleans show the pains they took to ensure that their children, legitimate and illegitimate, would inherit their property.[27] There are also many signs that they endorsed the education of free people of color. It was common practice in Saint-Domingue for white fathers to provide generously for the education of their racially mixed sons, even to send them to metropolitan France to get an education. Being more educated than the Louisiana Creoles of color, the free refugees of color transmitted their knowledge to their comparatively undereducated counterparts. The number of schools for people of color that were opened by white refugees is proof that they did not abandon either the belief that they deserved an education or the practice of educating them when they came to Louisiana. It is, of course, difficult to appraise to what extent their practices and principles spread to Louisiana society. Determining whether or not they influenced the Louisiana Creoles is impossible to sustain scientifically. What is clear, however, is that seeing their example must have led the Louisianans—whose attitude in matters of race relations was already relatively relaxed—to become accustomed to this slightly unusual view of race relations, at a time when they could have been influenced by the Anglo-Saxon biracial model. Whether the refugees influenced the perception of the white Creoles of Louisiana is disputable. That they made a clear mark on the perception that the free Louisiana Creoles of color had of their group and their status is easier to confirm. By intermingling, the refugees caused them to become more openly conscious of their peculiar status and their capacity for economic viability, social visibility, and much more. In the political and cultural fields, indeed, they vitalized the free people of color, giving them faith in their abilities and much more weight in New Orleans, strengthening them to counter the American model.[28]

The perception the white Saint-Domingans had of their racially mixed offspring and their descendants also tended to further desegregate the free people of color, even as the latter were considering themselves different and belonging to a group with singularities that prevented any kind of assimilation. When *L'Abeille* was founded in 1827 by white refugees, the editors displayed a clear tendency toward progressive beliefs in matters of race and race relations. Several free blacks, using pen names, contributed to its columns. This tendency was not limited to the press. Refugee Grandjean, for instance, supposedly attempted to organize a revolt against Americans in 1805 by agitating slaves and free people of color.[29] Whether the coalition between refugees—whites and free people of color—is real or slightly mythologized, it clearly shows that the Louisianans perceived the refugees as much more progressive in matters of racial differences and race relations. Although the Louisianans' view of race relations was not tremendously different from the Saint-Domingan refugees' principles, the "French West Indian tincture" reinforced resistance to contamination by the Anglo-Saxon perception of races.[30]

The refugee influx revitalized the free Creole population of color, conferred on them much more weight and visibility in New Orleans, and gave them more power of resistance against the Americans. According to Joan M. Martin, "During the decade between 1830 and 1840, the free colored class had reached such a level of culture, wealth, and influence, that they attracted notice of all persons traveling to New Orleans." The free community of color, because it had been reinforced, because it had to resist the Americans' will to dispossess them of their privileges, because it had developed a culture of its own, different from those of the whites and the slaves, became more group conscious or "a separatist, self-focusing community."[31]

The arrival of the refugees at least produced this great evolution in the New Orleans society. Whether it had a wider impact on society at large is difficult to assess. It is obvious, however, that by merely affecting the self-perception of the free group of color and by showing the example of a very relaxed perception of race relations, it undoubtedly reinforced the lack of segregation against the free group of color by the Louisiana whites. If it did not altogether change the Americans' perception, it showed them that there could be other models.[32]

## Consequences on the Religious Community

Beyond this impact on race relations, the arrival of the refugees also influenced other areas of the New Orleans society. One of the obvious consequences of the massive arrival of refugees in the first decade of the nineteenth century was a numerical reinforcement of the Catholic community.[33] Since the refugees more or less doubled the population of New Orleans, they more than doubled the Catholic community. It would not have been of much importance per se, had it not been at the crucial turning point of the Louisiana Purchase or soon thereafter. Until Anglo-Saxon American immigration started in the late colonial period, all migrations to Louisiana had been largely Catholic. From the original French settlers to the Spanish representatives, the *Isleños*—those immigrants from the Canary Islands—and the Acadians, there had been a remarkable religious homogeneity until the beginning of the migration from the United States. Very slow at first, the Anglo-Saxon Protestant flow accelerated after the Purchase. In the resistance of the Creoles against Americanization—and thus against Protestanticization—an addition of over 15,000 Catholics was bound to play an essential part. The refugees, whatever their racial and social status, flocked into St. Louis Cathedral and filled the sacramental records of the Archdiocese of New Orleans, thus reinforcing Louisiana's Catholic identity in an overwhelmingly Protestant South.

The influence of the refugees was probably still more important than this mere numerical reinforcement. Several Saint-Domingans occupied important positions in the Catholic Church of Louisiana. Mary Joseph Chanche was appointed bishop of Natchez.[34] Other instances may be found in history, including Father Flavian.[35] Louis Sibourd, the vicar general who supervised lower Louisiana, was "originally from Saint-Domingue, the ill-fated French colony in the Caribbean."[36] Father Antonio de Sedella's two assistants, Fathers Claude Thoma and Jean Koüne, were also refugees. They held the sacramental records for years, which may explain the care with which the refugees' connection to Saint-Domingue was noted, sometimes even by a mere marginal mention.[37] Another important contribution of the refugees to the Catholic Church was Juliette Gaudin, co-founder with Henriette Delille of the Sisters of the Holy Family, in 1842. Although she is sometimes simply said to be "of Cuba," she was clearly part of the large refugee wave of 1809–10. Her father was one of those refugee professors "at one of the principal young men's high schools in the French part of New Orleans."[38] The assistance she gave Delille in founding the order and her long-lasting proximity to the founder until Delille's death in 1862 leave no doubt about her influence. After she became Mother Superior at Delille's death, her influence receded. Indeed, after a scission in the order, she remained Mother Superior of only the Bayou Road branch, which housed but a few elements of the congregation. She still ran the school, however, and the congregation was reunified in the early 1880s at the old Quadroon Ballroom of the Rue d'Orléans. There is no doubt that her influence on the religious and scholastic education of the female students of the order was great. To her enterprise is often associated St. Mary's Academy, as well as all the educational facilities for girls of African descent in Louisiana and throughout the United States.[39] Saint-Domingan connections are sometimes attributed to Henriette Delille.[40] It seems, however, that there was none other than her lifelong friendship with Juliette Gaudin.[41]

Finally, among the most distinguished members of the Catholic Church with connections to Saint-Domingue was Archbishop Guillaume Dubourg.[42] He is often not counted among the refugees, for various reasons. He did not live in Saint-Domingue. After his mother's death, when he was two, he was raised and educated in France. Moreover, he did not come with the refugee wave. There are many reasons, however, why he may be counted among those influential persons who had close connections with the lost colony. He was born there, and his family resided in the French colony until they had to flee at the time of the slave rebellion. His maternal uncle, Father Jean Vogluzan, was the pastor of the church of Trou Dondon, in Saint-Domingue.[43] When Guillaume went to France, his father and older brothers stayed in the French colony. All his stepsisters and brothers were married there. His father owned coffee plantations on the island, did business at Le Cap Français, and owned property in Marmelade, Port Magot, Petite Rivière, Mirebalais, Port-au-Prince, and Rivière Marion. His whole life on the American continent was punctuated by encounters with Saint-Domingan refugees, and he sometimes gave the impression of being a refugee by proxy, or of having been pervaded by the ideals of the refugees, as if those ideals were, so to speak, contagious. Indeed, "during the bishop's some twenty years in the United States, there had never been a time when his life was untouched by the goings and comings of Dominican refugees." First, he was "contaminated" by his family, of course, whose members repatriated to Louisiana and appears to have been "indelibly marked by the characteristics of Haitian colonial life."[44] What is obvious is that, throughout his years in America, he was surrounded by refugees. He baptized, married, and interred them. He became "the chaplain of the French colons from the island."[45] In most of his American appointments, he was surrounded by refugees: he was first in Baltimore (in 1794), then he went to Havana (in 1799), where he founded a college. In 1802, he went to New Orleans, where he unsuccessfully attempted to establish a school, before going back to Baltimore, where he founded St. Mary's in 1804. His appointment to Louisiana, first as apostolic administrator, then as bishop of New Orleans in 1815, took him, once again, to one of the refugees' favorite asylums. Be it Baltimore, Havana, or New Orleans, his track followed the refugees. This close proximity with the refugees, be they his kin or not, most certainly influenced his mind and life. There are several indications that they may have influenced his perception of races. His life attests to a constant commitment to slaves and free people of color, both in Baltimore, where he began to work with them, and in Louisiana, where he always protected attempts at educating them.[46]

By their involvement in religion, refugees probably caused Louisiana society to introduce the people of African descent to the Catholic religious principles as well as to the basics of education. They are also often said to have had a negative influence on morals. Discussing the customs of the refugees, in particular concerning religious principles, Bishop Carroll wrote in 1812 that New Orleans was contaminated by foreigners, adding that "what has put the peak to scandal is the arrival of a very great number of girls of color from Santo Domingo who spread corruption everywhere."[47] He added, as many witnesses have, that this corruption of morals and religious principles was all the worse as members of the Church were also concerned: "If the conduct of Père Antoine and his two assistants Thoma and Kuan (Koüne) were above reproach I would have less to lament." Both Thoma and Koüne are said to have come from Saint-Domingue via Cuba with their racially mixed housekeepers, and Koüne's critics "claimed that the children ate at table with him and called him 'Papa.'"[48]

Whether their "nefarious" influence was real or fantasized, they had an impact, if only psychological, on Louisiana society. If what was said about them is true, they may have altered the moral principles of their new homeland. If not, the amount of criticism against them shows that they were influential enough to trigger opposition and criticism and that some residents of New Orleans were intent on sullying their reputation, thus lessening the influence they might have on the population. What has remained is the notion that they "lowered morals and disturbed order," as Cable writes, and that their "ideas of public order and morals" ran counter to the Americans,' even though all testimonies of the local authorities (from Governor Claiborne to the mayor of New Orleans) took pains at writing on their behalf, testifying that they were perfectly law-abiding.[49]

## Altering Social Practices

Beyond influencing the social hierarchy, the vision of races and race relations, and religion, the refugees also had an impact on Louisiana society by introducing new practices or reinforcing others already in existence. A certain number of features introduced by the refugees may have contributed both to making Louisianans certain that they were lowering the morals of the Crescent City and to granting them a certain visibility, to the point that Cable mentions "a French West Indian tincture," and speaks of the "prevalence of West Indian ideas in New Orleans."[50] Among their many creations, as in many other asylums, in particular in Jamaica and Cuba, they opened billiard houses, gaming houses, and lottery offices. To quote Cable and his usual flowery style, "the West Indian was a leader in licentiousness, gambling and dueling."[51] It is true that the opening of Davis's ballroom, which also contained a gaming room, confirmed this sentiment. Refugees opened coffee and drinking houses, as exemplified by the renowned Café des Réfugiés.[52] Their contribution to the development of more cultural forms of entertainment, such as the opera and theater, also reinforced the impression that, whether their contributions were cultural or not, the refugees were intent upon introducing new pleasures to the Louisianans. Protagonists of the period (such as Paul Alliot and Governor Claiborne) confirmed that they were considered leaders in the importation of "European culture, with all its pleasures and vices to the erstwhile provincial town."[53] They were also accused of importing the habit of dueling to Louisiana. The practice had long existed in most of the South, but it is true that there were fencing masters among refugees, in Louisiana as in other asylums (in Charleston, for instance), and that the practice of dueling rose after the refugees' arrival. Saint-Domingans were also among the best aficionados of the Congo Square slave dances, considered by the Americans as vile practices that gave too much freedom and cultural weight to the slaves, who could be seen performing "indecent" dances to "far too" African rhythms.

The refugees are also said to have reinforced such practices as *plaçage*, the tradition of unions (not legally sanctioned but perfectly official) between free women of color and white men. This practice already existed in Louisiana, but it was still more widespread in Saint-Domingue. The women of exotic beauty produced by successive race mixings in Saint-Domingue were known as "Les Sirènes."[54] The Saint-Domingan refugees influenced *plaçage* and quadroon balls, especially the Bal des Cordons Bleus. Most sources date the development of the practice of quadroon balls after 1805. Those festivities were reserved for women of color and white men, which often led to further relationships between the two groups and to the establishment of racially mixed families, either as primary ties or in parallel with official unions. The Quadroon Ballroom, located at 717 Orleans, was especially important in this respect.[55] This "licentious" influence probably also partly accounts for the criticisms bearing on the refugees' impact on the morals and Catholic principles in Louisiana. Although these practices were known among Louisianans before the refugees' arrival, they were conducted much more discreetly. The refugees apparently reinforced the practice, which was one of theirs as well, but also gave it more visibility by being much more open and less hypocritical about it. To the Protestant Anglo-Americans, these traditions, practiced so openly by the refugees, were most obviously licentious. They were also a plain assertion of the refugees' and Louisianans' difference and refusal to conform.

Added to these alterations or reinforcements of already existing social practices, the refugees may well have contributed to the refining of social mores and to the modernization of New Orleans. Louisiana had long remained a frontier territory, although the Spanish period had brought more refinement, especially in New Orleans. Whatever the degree of polish the city may have acquired in the late colonial period, it was still less a real capital than the "Pearl of the Antilles" had been. This name alone reveals the advancement of the French Antillean colony. The refugees found New Orleans backward in many respects. Some of them even participated in its improvement. Alexis Daudet, who wrote a column known as "Feuilleton," was probably "the first newspaper columnist on the New Orleans scene."[56] His main mission was, so he said, to echo the complaints he heard in New Orleans, to try to help improve the city. Among his most often repeated complaints was the scarcity of street lighting, the dilapidated sidewalks, and the necessity for more safety on the streets. Some of his readers or co-workers acknowledged the effectiveness of his criticisms. In the 4 May 1820 issue of the *Louisiana Gazette*, for instance, one may read: "Last year, our pavements were in many parts too bad to walk in wet weather. Le feuilleton attacked the nuisance in a sarcastic jocular way, and the bricklayers were soon seen in activity to mend the pathways." Whether this was the direct consequence of Daudet's action cannot be ascertained. That these improvements were said to have originated in his criticisms is of deep interest to the present study, however, since it apparently acknowledges the dynamism and influence the refugees had or appeared to have in New Orleans. What might confirm the veracity of this will, energy, and ability to modernize the existing structures is that the refugees had a similar influence in the various American refuges. The improvement of infrastructures, the building of water drainage systems, and the creation of gardens were the legacy of the Saint-Domingans to Jamaica and Cuba, for instance.[57]

In all the refuges, the spread of luxury and the development of more refined fashions were also attributed to them. This was the case in the cities of the northeastern United States as well as in the various Caribbean islands that welcomed them. They are said to have refined the mores of worlds that had remained rustic by launching newspapers, schools, and theaters but also by opening Masonic lodges, clubs, and societies. They also introduced clothing and architectural fashions, and these essential influences are especially perceptible in Louisiana, where they left traces that are still very strong today.[58] This already interferes partly with the study of their cultural legacy, but the question of fashions is in close connection with social practices and is also the direct consequence of the refugees' occupational pattern in Louisiana. As the refugees formed a large majority among artisans, especially in such fields as clothing and furniture building, they could easily interfere with local traditions. The refugee tailors, embroiderers, and seamstresses undoubtedly modeled the fashion of New Orleans. By the models they chose to create and by the adornments they added, especially laces, they left their imprint on New Orleans. They are also said to have introduced new types of fabric, of "embroidered muslins, embroidery, gold spangle, lace," and of new jewelry.[59] As for the joiners and cabinet makers, it seems hardly believable that they could have discarded their Caribbean customs and that they may have totally bent their tastes to those of their new homeland.[60] What all testimonies state is that "it was the refugees from the West Indies that brought the love of luxury into the colony."[61] Several explanations may be given to this influence. The Louisianans had remained relatively simple in their tastes, probably due to the developmental difficulties the colony had experienced in the early eighteenth century. They were said to be "simple in their tastes and plain in their living."[62] The timely arrival, at the crucial turning point of the passage from a frontier colony to a United States territory, of immigrants whose original society had been far more advanced than the Louisiana colonial society, was of prime importance, all the more so since they numerically counterbalanced the influx from America, which, comparatively, still lacked polish and refined social practices.[63] Again, the refugees largely contributed to reinforcing Louisiana's difference within the United States. That they reproduced what they had known in their former life is only natural. It might even be contended that they had interest in initiating new needs among the New Orleans population, since "all these demands the refugees could cater to and capitalize on."[64] This might be true as well, although this kind of calculation was probably not the first motive of the refugees' actions and is impossible to prove, for lack of documentary evidence.

The refugees' reputation for luxury and refinement may also explain the fostering of some legends about the West Indian newcomers. When examining family legends, the most often encountered common characteristic is that "the tropical ease and languor of the West Indian women were as much a novelty then in the feminine world as the always emphasized distinction, the literary tastes and accomplishments of the West Indian men were in the masculine world."[65] This general mythologizing may enlighten the mystery of Jean Laffite's origins and account for his aura in Louisiana and for the persistence in literature of his representation as a mysterious seducer who was able to charm Governor Claiborne's wife at a time when he was at odds with the new Louisiana authorities.[66] The seductiveness that has always been attributed to the West Indians made them legendary in Louisiana. This partly explains the pride many of their descendants display for their Saint-Domingan origins. Be it myth or reality, or both, this tendency to single them out attests to the social importance they had in the early nineteenth century.

Last but certainly not least, it is essential to mention among the refugees' influences the reinforcement they brought to the Gallic community, although not in terms of cultural influence here. The mere numerical addition of over 15,000 French speakers was sufficient to strengthen the Gallic presence at a time when the Creoles were being submerged by the Anglo-Saxon immigrants. This was probably their first contribution to New Orleans society at the time, since they did "alter the existing *rapport de force* between two social groups."[67] Cable had also noted that this influx strengthened the Creoles' power "with which they had begun to wage their long battle against American absorption."[68] This reinforcement had a clear influence on the New Orleans social balance. Moreover, by creating places where the specific Creole cultures could be transmitted, such as schools, theaters, or newspapers, they contributed both to the maintenance of the French language in American Louisiana and to the persistence of a definitely Creole legacy. They imprinted a different sociocultural refinement on their host society and accented the Creole character of New Orleans. To pursue the path of legend and exoticism, they "permitted New Orleans to preserve for a few more years its colonial character, its exotic charm, and a lifestyle similar to that of an island just offshore from the continent."[69]

To conclude, the refugees undoubtedly left their imprint on the early-nineteenth-century society of New Orleans. Inducing a shift in the social balance through their occupational patterns, altering the perception of races and race relations (at least in the new Anglo-American environment), strengthening the Gallic community at a time when the Creoles needed new battalions to resist the unavoidable Americanization that followed their new territorial and national status, they visibly influenced the New Orleans social pattern in the short term. Bringing with them new social refinements, they left a longer-lasting imprint on the Louisiana fabric. They had a similar kind of influence on all the societies they encountered in their flight. In New Orleans, however, the influence was both different and stronger. Because of the religious, linguistic, economic, and social proximity of Creole New Orleans to their original homeland, the influence they had in some areas may have been more discreet there than in other asylums that had different religious, linguistic, and social patterns. Nevertheless, it is also because the society was similar and because they could thus strengthen already existing patterns that their influence lasted longer. Because of the fluidity and diversity of the New Orleans society, because Louisiana was accustomed to new population influxes and to relatively relaxed race relations, this influence was easier. The already Creolized Louisiana society was less rigid and much more open to further influences.[70] The only part of the United States with such a different colonial past, Louisiana could not help but benefit from their presence, which "added a gaiety and liveliness to the atmosphere of New Orleans which contrasted with the staid customs of the Americans."[71] That their influence took on a more legendary or even mythic resonance is beyond question. This, however, does not reduce this influence in any measure, and it rather tends to confirm its existence and strength.

Because they had lived a different life in Saint-Domingue and because they had gone through a traumatic period during the slave rebellion, migration, and resettlement, they displayed a specific dynamism, as if "the misfortunes they had suffered and their degree of need was the impetus for ingenuity and creativity. They infused New Orleans with their endeavors."[72] Finally, because they came to Louisiana when the territory was struggling through the turmoil of a new national destiny, they were both accepted by part of the population and strongly rejected by another portion of it. Both this acceptance and this rejection gave them still more influence and more dynamism to exert their influence. Moreover, the new political deal, due to the Louisiana Purchase, created specific conditions that benefited the refugees. Beyond the economic and social impact they had on Louisiana, they also displayed dynamic political activism and are to be credited with several political achievements that have long remained in oblivion.

6

# The Refugees' Politics

## From Visibility to Influence

The political aspect of the refugees' impact on Louisiana, long neglected in the historiography of the past 200 years, is yet another topic that reveals much about the Saint-Domingan migration to the lower Mississippi valley. The main difficulty here lies in determining whether their influence went beyond the normal visibility due to their number and proportion to the New Orleans population. It seems, however, that the timeliness of their arrival made their role still more palpable and their influences—direct and indirect—stronger. It is clear that white refugees filled influential positions and that the free refugees of color spurred the development of a clear group consciousness and intervened in the life of their new homeland by launching petitions or trying to weigh in on the state's and country's policies, especially when their group's prerogatives were concerned. This is only a first-degree interpretation, and the refugees' political involvement went far beyond this influence.

On the one hand, arrival in New Orleans occurred at a time that was doubly important historically. First, they reached Louisiana at a turning point in the destiny of the territory, which made them an essential tool in the hands of the different groups confronting one another locally. They also made Louisiana their home in the early days of the debate over the institution of slavery, and their influence—whether direct or not—was great. On the other hand, their Saint-Domingan experience made them much more keenly aware of political activism than their Louisiana counterparts, whatever their racial status. Moreover, the revolutionary years and their forced flight tended to render them still more politically active than they would probably have been without this unusual experience.

Some features of the refugees' influence on the Louisiana political sphere in a broad sense, mainly the consequence of their arrival on the life of the territory as well as their civic commitment and political involvement, were relatively usual in their various American refuges. Their political influence in Louisiana, however, went far beyond, and it might be said that they ended up shaping not only political activism but also the politics of their new homeland. The following discussion will thus bear first on their unintentional influences on the local and national politics (mostly the implementation of a repressive legislation), then on their role in modeling the Louisianans' psyche, on the way they shaped nineteenth-century political activism, and eventually on their direct role in inflecting the political scene of the state and of the nation as a whole.

## Distrust and Repression

In all the Caribbean and continental host societies, the arrival of the refugees went together with an increased repression of the blacks, whatever their status. The free people of color, who had been politically active and who had sometimes participated in the early revolutionary movements, were suspect. Most of the time, the result of their arrival was the implementation of increasingly more restrictive policies against the group.[1] Everywhere in the United States, the events in Saint-Domingue and the outpouring of refugees into American harbors promoted legislation banning the entry of blacks. South Carolina legislated against the entry of slaves in 1792 and against the entry of blacks, whether free or slave, in 1803, and decreed in 1805 that "any person in any way to aid an insurrection" could be executed. Georgia banned entry of blacks from the West Indies, as did Virginia in 1792, North Carolina in 1795, and Maryland in 1797. In a law of 1793, Virginia threatened death to any free black "exciting slaves to insurrection or murder."[2]

Louisiana authorities feared that the refugees might ally with slaves and incite a revolution. So they restricted the rights and prerogatives of free people of color. When the first immigrants reached Louisiana in the 1790s, the terror of ideological contamination and increased risk of slave rebellions apparently had three immediate consequences: reinforcement of the Creoles' loyalty to Spain, since the Spanish seemed more fit to ensure their protection than the French; restriction of the slave trade in 1795; and finally a total ban on it in 1796.[3] The stories the refugees told their Louisiana counterparts apparently affected political thought and beliefs, forcing "all parties to consider again the ramifications of revolutionary politics."[4] The fear of revolutionary contagion had direct effects on the policies of the Spanish authorities, for instance, the reinforcement of patrols, transfer of troops from Vera Cruz and Havana, ban on slave imports, deportation of people with Saint-Domingan origins, and the closing down of cafés and cabarets. In the American era, when more refugees came flocking in, the possibilities of emancipation were reduced by the territorial legislation of 1806, as were the privileges of the free persons of color:

they could no longer carry guns; free black criminals were punished more severely than white criminals; and slaves, who otherwise were not allowed to testify against free persons, could testify against refugees. Legislation expressly forbade free people of color to insult or strike white people, and their attitude had to show due respect to their white interlocutors. They also had to carry their freedom papers with them at all times, and they were compelled by the 1808 Civil Code to indicate in all official documents that they were free persons of color. The 1828 Louisiana Code prevented illegitimate children from being recognized and from inheriting (unless their parents were legally married). New Orleans segregated public transportation in 1820 and theaters in 1826.[5] This type of restrictive legislation was common to most of the asylums reached by the refugees.[6] It did not prevent the free people of color from attempting to obtain equality, and although they did not manage to do so in the early nineteenth century, they were granted a certain leniency, Claiborne having understood from the Saint-Domingan lesson that they should not be pushed to react against the white community.[7]

This fear of free black agitation led to two policies: a repressive one that led the authorities to ban the entry of free black males over fourteen from the French West Indies in 1806 and attempt to control the free black militia, and a more conciliatory one that led Claiborne to maintain dialogue with them and reinforce the prerogatives and official existence of the militia. At any rate, the Saint-Domingan events and massive arrival of free refugees of color undoubtedly deepened the division between the racial groups.

Even the white refugees were considered potentially dangerous politically. In Cuba, Jamaica, Trinidad, and the United States, they were suspected of potentially revolutionary influences.[8] Before Louisiana even became a U.S. territory, the presence of the refugees on the eastern coast probably contributed to the passage of the Alien and Sedition Acts. The intense political activity they displayed in newspapers, clubs, lodges, and associations in New York, Philadelphia, and Baltimore probably frightened the U.S. government into devising means to get rid of dangerous aliens. Whether royalist (like Gatereau, who edited *Le Courrier Politique de la France et de ses Colonies*, printed in Philadelphia by Moreau de Saint-Méry) or staunchly republican (like the editor of the Philadelphia *Courrier Français* or Claudius Beleurgey and J. J. Négrin in Charleston and New Orleans), the refugees were seen as extremists.[9] This relative anti-French sentiment, exacerbated by the excesses of the French Revolution, the XYZ affair, and French seizures of American ships, generally spared the mass of the refugees, however, since they were mostly considered the first victims of one of the most terrible consequences of the French Revolution. This was especially true in Louisiana, where the Creoles tended to identify with the refugees and welcome them.

Throughout the United States, events in Saint-Domingue and the narratives the refugees made of them may also have favored colonization plans in the early nineteenth century. Conscious as they were of the involuntary role of the free Creoles of color of Saint-Domingue in triggering the slave revolution, the partisans of colonization became sure of the danger caused by the presence of free blacks alongside the slaves in the American South. Before the Liberian solution occurred to the partisans of colonization, Jefferson had seriously thought of colonizing the free blacks of the United States in Haiti. Following Denmark Vesey's attempted rebellion, Governor Monroe wrote to Jefferson in 1801 to promote the idea of colonization. Although Haiti was by no means the only solution (purchasing land west of the Mississippi River, in Sierra Leone, or in Portuguese Latin America was also considered), it bore heavily on American leaders' minds.[10]

Finally, the events in Saint-Domingue and vivid narrations of the refugees probably also reinforced the hesitations of Americans to acknowledge the independences of the Latin American republics in the 1820s. An official recognition would have meant considering the case of Haiti, which the Americans thought dangerous and adverse to the positions they still mostly defended on the blacks' inferiority and need for tutelage. Interestingly, Latin American independences seemed important to the free refugees of color of Louisiana, because Savary and several other Saint-Domingan veterans of the Battle of New Orleans joined the republican insurgents in Mexico and supported the Latin American revolutionary movements.[11] Everywhere in their American asylums, including the United States, and more specifically Louisiana, both in the late colonial era and after the Louisiana Purchase, the refugees involuntarily triggered attitudes of distrust and a general increase in the repression against people of African descent, both free and slave, especially since the Saint-Domingan slaves were widely associated with conspiracies and attempts at overthrowing the established order.[12]

## Slave Agitation and the Louisiana Psyche

The role of the Saint-Domingan slaves on the Louisiana political scene was necessarily reduced, but they had a significant role in modeling the Louisiana psyche. They were always incriminated when slave rebellion occurred. The quasi-paranoid fear of slave rebellions, spurred by the revolution in Saint-

Domingue, tended to attribute most rebellious events to those slaves, sometimes rightly but sometimes also abusively. The Saint-Domingan example did promote rebellions, and some slaves imported by the refugees did initiate revolts. But not all slave rebellions were led by Saint-Domingan slaves.

Following their arrival, there was renewed rebellion in most of the territories in which the refugees settled with their slaves. It is often difficult, however, to ascertain that they were the initiators. In Cuba, for instance, the multiplication of slave rebellions between 1795 and 1800 (including the Puerto Príncipe rebellion) followed the arrival of the refugees' slaves and is always linked with their spreading the message of liberty and equality.[13] José Antonio Aponte, the leader of the 1810 rebellion, is said to have been in contact with narratives of the Saint-Domingan revolution and with Haitian leaders.[14] An 1801 French report indicates that similar troubles were to be encountered all over the Caribbean and, quite clearly, if one follows the route of the refugees, in all the islands where they found shelter: Danish St. Thomas, Dutch Curaçao, Spanish Puerto Rico (Aguadilla 1795), French Martinique (Jean Kina's rebellion of 1800), and Spanish Venezuela (Coro 1795, Maracaibo, 1799).[15] In Jamaica, the local planters were terrified by the Saint-Domingan slaves, "who had been heard to sing Jacobin songs, and were not respectful to white people."[16] Even in the cases when there were no Saint-Domingan slaves involved in the rebellions, the knowledge of the revolutionary events of the French island and of their outcome had obviously spread to the local slave populations. Wherever they were employed, the Saint-Domingan slaves told their story and that of their island. They obviously knew about the revolution and were informed of the ongoing events. The world of the slaves was indeed not hermetically shut off from the rest, and the slave societies were porous, especially in New Orleans. The Crescent City was a very active port with ceaseless movements of boats and sailors. It was a land of passage and immigration, and the slave community was certainly not isolated.[17] Both refugee slaves' narratives and sailors' songs were good modes of propagation of knowledge of the revolutionary events. In a letter written by planters to Claiborne in November 1804, the Louisianans warned their governor: "The news of the revolution of Saint-Domingue and other places has become common among our blacks."[18]

Although it seems difficult to distinguish reality from collective psychosis, the slave rebellions of the American South and in particular of Louisiana have followed the same tradition of being attributed to the Saint-Domingan slaves, either for incitation or for leadership. From Gabriel Prosser's rebellion in Virginia in 1800 to the main rebellions or attempted rebellions of Louisiana

(Pointe Coupée, 1791 and 1795, as well as German Coast, 1811), to Denmark Vesey's 1822 Charleston rebellion and Nat Turner's rebellion of 1830, all of them clearly bear the stamp of the Saint-Domingan influence.[19] For decades, rumors spread throughout the South from all the main refugee centers. In Norfolk, in Richmond, but also in South Carolina, there were repeated mentions of plots organized by Saint-Domingan slaves.[20] There even were persistent legends connecting Gabriel Prosser to Saint-Domingue, referring in particular to his supposed attempt to flee to the island. There is no evidence that he intended to go to Saint-Domingue, and the rumors probably purport to the collective fears mentioned earlier. Several sources, however, mention the fact that French people were thought to be behind the rebellion. Two Frenchmen were apparently involved in the trial, and the rebels supposedly declared that they wanted to kill all the whites except the French.[21] In the case of Vesey's rebellion in Charleston, the link is far easier to establish. Vesey had been a slave in Saint-Domingue. He had been purchased from Saint-Domingue by Captain Vesey in April 1782. He had bought his freedom in December 1799.[22] From then on, he had always been involved in the fight against slavery, especially by instructing the people of African descent about the Bible.[23] Although he had left Saint-Domingue long before the slave rebellion, he knew that the former slaves had taken power there and that the former French colony was now independent. Indeed, he had written to President Boyer in Haiti to request his assistance and was apparently positive he would obtain it. He expressly declared that he wanted to sail there, and most of the rebels were found to have connections with the island. The name of Saint-Domingue was repeatedly mentioned once the plot had been uncovered.[24] There is recurrent evidence that the slaves knew what had happened and was still happening in the Caribbean island. Only in the last rebellion of the antebellum American South, Nat Turner's, is there much less evidence of Saint-Domingan connections, and conflicting theories have developed on the influence Saint-Domingue may have had on Turner's actions. There were refugee families in Southampton County, and it is most probable that Nat Turner had been in contact with information on Haiti. Contemporaries clearly connected the rebellion with the Haitian revolution. There were, however, no known direct links (whether real or virtual) between Nat Turner and Haitian rebels, as had been the case with Prosser and Vesey. All white contemporaries, however, established the connection, since there was no way Turner could have been ignorant of the Saint-Domingan revolution and subsequent independence of Haiti. He probably found some—even if remote—inspiration in it, but "whether or not Nat

Turner consciously imitated the example of Saint-Domingue, many whites were reminded of that example and some were convinced that his inspiration came from his black brethren in the Caribbean."[25] Either from real signs or from slightly paranoid fears, southern whites always firmly believed that their rebellious slaves had been influenced by the Haitian example.

The Louisiana abortive or effective slave revolts (or attempted revolts) obviously display similar connections to this culture of rebellion. From the Pointe Coupée plot of 1791 to the German Coast rebellion of 1811, Louisiana's rebellious episodes all bear the mark of the Saint-Domingan revolution. They reveal both the leadership of Saint-Domingan slaves and the slightly paranoid trend of exaggerating both their visibility as rebellious leaders and the role they played in those revolts. Two rebellions have been more documented than the others. There are, however, several other occurrences mentioned in the literature. A plot at Pointe Coupée in 1791, evoked in a letter of Governor Miro, "had supposedly unmasked free mulattoes from Saint-Domingue as instigators." During the trial of the suspects, a free racially mixed man named Pierre Bahi said that he and his companions were expecting orders from Cap Français "to start a coup that would have resembled the one in Cap Français."[26] In 1805, the uncovering of the plot incriminating the Saint-Domingan white refugee Grandjean tended to confirm the common belief that there was a close tie between the refugees and the rebellious episodes of Louisiana.[27] The main two attempts at large-scale rebellion are still clearer in this respect, although there is an ongoing historiographical debate as to whether the involvement of Saint-Domingan slaves was real or fantasized.

The first case is the attempted Pointe Coupée rebellion of 1795. At the time of the rebellion, some sources incriminated a free refugee of color, Louis Benoit, for initiating the plot. Both a letter from Governor Carrondelet to Las Casas in June 1795 and an account by Paul Alliot clearly lay the blame on him. Alliot mentions "an inhabitant of New Orleans, famous at Jérémie, on the island of Saint-Domingue, for his murders, thefts, and devastations" who convinced the slaves to rebel by revealing to them the success of the revolution in the island and the advantages the former slaves now enjoyed.[28] Louis Benoit was declared "ungovernable and audacious" and was later banished from the colony by the Spanish authorities.[29] Sources diverge on the Saint-Domingan origins of the plotters.[30] Indeed, Alliot's word might be considered unreliable because in March 1803 he himself was accused of inciting slaves to revolt, deported, and imprisoned in France, although he was later granted permission to reenter the United States.[31] When examining the Pointe Coupée conspiracy, several conclusions may be drawn. Whether these Saint-Domingan blacks, free or slave, were involved or not, they were always accused of being at the center of this revolt.[32] There may have been other obvious connections with the French island, since Julien Poydras himself, the owner of the plantation where the rebellion was planned to occur, had lived in Saint-Domingue.[33]

If there was no direct involvement of the Saint-Domingan slaves, their being held responsible for the organization of the abortive rebellion shows the measure of the fears their presence provoked among the Louisiana planters and authorities. It also reveals their reputation and visibility in Louisiana, as well as the indirect role that the revolution on the French island played in Louisiana slave rebellions. Indeed, if there can be doubt about the direct involvement of slaves from Saint-Domingue, no one has ever questioned the ideological link between the conspiracy and the revolutionary events that had occurred in the Caribbean island. Berquin Duvallon, for instance, asserted that the Louisiana slaves were aware of the revolutionary events and "were much more ready for a general insurrection than they were in San Domingo at the time of the revolutionary crisis."[34] All sources confirm that the slave insurrection planned at Pointe Coupée was ideologically inspired by the Saint-Domingan revolution, by the news the slaves had of their brothers' successes in the Caribbean island, and by the narrations they had heard from the Saint-Domingan slaves.[35] Even when attempting to destroy the "historical myths . . . deeply implanted into the consciousness of white Louisianans," according to which the leaders at Pointe Coupée were from Saint-Domingue, Gwendolyn Hall, studying the trial summary, concludes that there is no doubt that the slaves of Pointe Coupée were perfectly aware of the revolutionary events, which inspired the conspiracy.[36] There are clear indications of the similarity between Louisiana and Saint-Domingue, since, in both places, slave rebellions presented the originality of being secular. Contrary to the religiously inspired rebellions (such as Nat Turner's) where destroying the leader was sufficient to suppress the rebellion, the pattern in Louisiana closely resembled that described by Toussaint, who said that revolution would survive him, for "he was the trunk of the revolution: it would spring up again by its roots, because they were many and deep."[37]

The other main rebellious occurrence in Louisiana which had clear links with Saint-Domingue was the 1811 German Coast rebellion, which is sometimes labeled "the largest slave rebellion in United States history."[38] In January 1811, several hundred slaves (figures vary from 180 to 400 to 800, according to the sources) of the Parish of St. John the Baptist on the German Coast (35 miles north of New Orleans), wounded their master and killed his son, and then went from plantation to plantation trying to recruit more rebels. They were stopped by a large coalition of local planters, militiamen, and federal troops, in a fight which ended with the death of sixty-six slaves, seventeen missing slaves (some of them probably killed as well), and the arrest of thirty, twenty-two of whom were executed. The leadership was attributed to Charles Deslondes, a racially mixed slave driver from Saint-Domingue. Many sources also indicate that the outcome of the trial proved the involvement of Saint-Domingan slaves, some of them supposedly coming through Barataria.[39] Links are even established between the outset of the rebellion and the announcement in Louisiana of the success of Henri Christophe's troops over those of *quarteron* Petion in Saint-Domingue, a victory that supposedly encouraged the rebellious leaders of the German Coast.[40] However seductive this thesis might be, it is doubtful that, even if the news broke in New Orleans that day, the slaves of German Coast could have been immediately informed of the victory of the black troops. What is obvious is that the planters and authorities were terrified. Some planter families, warned of the beginning of the rebellion, fled to New Orleans and martial law was declared. Observers considered that this was a "miniature representation of the horrors of Santo Domingo,"[41] which had a tremendous influence on the Louisiana white psyche at the time. Both slaves and whites were undoubtedly influenced by the narratives they had heard: slaves were influenced into rebelling, since the message delivered from Saint-Domingue was that they could obtain freedom from subjugation by violent rebellion; whites reacted in fear, "all the more so in Louisiana because the white refugees from that holocaust were available in numbers to remind the nervous Louisianans of their potential powder keg."[42]

This discussion on the influence of the Saint-Domingan slaves shows the leadership and involvement of some Caribbean slaves in the rebellious events of Louisiana. It also shows the clear ideological role played by the Saint-Domingan revolution in Louisiana. That the slaves imported by the refugees were the main vehicles of the history of the French island leaves little doubt. Their role in spreading the revolutionary ideology might be sufficient in the discussion of their role in shaping their Louisiana counterparts' activism. It also teaches much about the white Louisiana psyche and about the role of the refugees in maintaining and reinforcing the specter of rebellions. The fact that most rebellions or conspiracies were immediately attributed to Saint-Domingan slaves—whether true or fantasized—is also of deep interest. The total absence of nonwhite contemporary sources is a factor contributing to this distortion. The fact that the leaders were sometimes killed before they could even be tried—as was the case for Deslondes—also helps maintain a high degree of doubt about their identity and origins. For this reason, the part played by rumors is essential, as exemplified by the supposed responsibility of the Baratarians in the German Coast rebellion. Whatever the reality of the involvement of Saint-Domingan refugees and slaves in all these episodes of Louisiana history, the fact that they were systematically incriminated proves that their presence was topical in early-nineteenth-century Louisiana politics. The refugee group was thus highly visible and clearly present in the lives of Louisianans and in the Louisiana psyche. They were all the more so because many of them occupied prominent positions on the Louisiana political scene, to the point that they shaped much of the political activism of the nineteenth century.

## Shaping Political Activism

The refugees' highly developed political conscience seems to be a widely accepted fact.[43] This was probably the result of the long practice they had had in Saint-Domingue of the political life. Even before the last autonomist drive of 1789, the Saint-Domingan whites had a long history of contestation and political demands, especially since they had also been granted certain prerogatives that had made them accustomed to exerting some kind of control if not power. The superior councils of Saint-Domingue, for instance, had judicial functions and the power to defer the implementation of a law that ran counter to the interests of the colony. When the General Estates convened in the late 1780s, the colonists did not hesitate to request representation. Despite the refusal of the French authorities, they sent representatives to Paris and, in March 1790, they created their own political body: the Saint-Marc Assembly. The first decisions made by the assembly were very revealing of the colonists' political activism. Calling themselves "Assemblée Générale de la Partie Française de Saint-Domingue" (General Assembly of the French Part of Saint-Domingue), they adopted a constitution that read as a declaration of independence. They granted themselves all legislative powers and proclaimed their right to invalidate any decision made by the metropolitan government. They later decided to open all the colony's harbors to foreign trade and to replace the French troops by a national guard. The slave rebellion in Saint-Domingue began with their determination to participate in the French revolutionary activities, in the rebuff they had first faced when they had attempted to have their say at the General Estates and to their local political initiatives and decisions after the French Revolution began. The spontaneous emergence of provincial assemblies, together with the repeated attempts to have their delegates accepted in Paris, the organization of the Saint-Marc assembly in 1790, the framing of a constitution, and the proclamation of a veto power over any decision made by the metropolitan government that might run counter to their specific interests—all this testifies to their political vitality and experience. There is no doubt that, even before their flight and relocation in their various asylums, they had a long practice of contestation and were both politically conscious and trained, a trait also found among the free people of color who had not hesitated, under Vincent Ogé, to try to obtain—first peacefully, then by force—the equality of rights to which they deemed themselves entitled.

The refugees carried this unusual political conscience in their flight. In Spanish Santo Domingo, for instance, descendants of the refugees played an important part during the first independence and during Spanish restoration.[44] In the northeastern United States, they even displayed a strong tendency toward inner political oppositions (between conservatives and prorevolutionaries), although this tendency was unnoticed in their other asylums. Nowhere like in Louisiana, however, did they have such a tremendous role in shaping the political activism of all three groups they integrated, most probably because of the favorable conditions they encountered upon arrival. Throughout the two decades of the migration to Louisiana, the political life of their new homeland was marked by events that conditioned their participation. From the brief French period of the late eighteenth century, to the 1803 American takeover and 1812 statehood, the territory was marked by a series of political alterations. This ferment offered the refugees space for influence.

The refugees' civic, institutional, and political presence was felt by all protagonists of the period. Be they whites or free people of color, the refugees may be described as politically aware, civically active, and ideologically influential. The three groups had been uncommonly active in prerevolutionary and revolutionary Saint-Domingue. The whites had shared a long tradition of activism and had played a privileged part in the political life of the colony, undoubtedly more so than their Louisiana counterparts, who are said to have "lagged almost hopelessly behind in education and political experience." From a long tradition of autonomist trends to their participation in the life of the colony, the Creoles of Saint-Domingue had been politically active. This made them ready for "political tutelage and leadership."[45] They were accustomed to exercising self-government, to a large measure, and they put forward their claims with a boldness unheard of in Louisiana, where the

Spanish mode of government had been much more centralized. They were also clearly ahead in civic awareness—as proved by the dynamic colonial press of Saint-Domingue—compared with Louisiana.

In Saint-Domingue, the free people of color had very rapidly followed in the whites' footsteps, intent as they were to see the revolutionary principles of equal civil rights applied to their class. As for the slaves, they had triumphantly attempted to have their share in the benefits of the French Revolution, their action resulting in the implementation of general emancipation in Saint-Domingue and the rest of the French colonial possessions. All the refugees were undoubtedly accustomed to active participation in the political life of their colony, whatever group they belonged to. All the refugees had also experienced the ultimate stress of forced removal. This was true for the whites who had been submerged by the slave rebellion, for the free Creoles of color who had been accused of collusion with the planter class, and for the slaves who had followed, willingly or not, their masters in flight. All of them had undergone the stressful experience of relocation in a strange land; some of them had even suffered it several times. Whether from their initial political awareness and experience or from their reaction to migration, they were all ready to engage in uncommon activity.

White refugees undoubtedly participated in local politics as soon as they reached Louisiana, regardless of the migratory wave. The first decades of Louisiana's American history testify to their visibility. From the founding and running of the Louisiana press to their role in the political confrontation between Louisiana Creoles and Americans, they were unquestionably present. They helped defend the territory; they also helped forge some of the institutions of the state of Louisiana. Some of them reached prominent political positions in such brief intervals that it might puzzle present-day readers.

Refugees held important offices in New Orleans. Paul Lanusse, who reached New Orleans in 1801 (from Philadelphia) almost immediately became a member of the *Cabildo* before being appointed attorney general; Diego Morphy became Spanish consul in New Orleans.[46] As the occupational pattern of the refugees clearly indicates, many judges were chosen from among the refugees: Gallien de Préval (city judge of New Orleans), Jean-François Canonge (judge of the Criminal Court, member of the Louisiana Upper Court of Appeal), Jean-Baptiste Donatien Augustin (district judge), Pierre Bailly (judge of Iberville Parish), Augustin Dominique Tureaud (judge of St. James Parish), Pierre Dormenon (parish judge at Pointe Coupée), and many more.[47] The refugees also filled many state and city political positions. Among the lower positions,

Jules Davezac was secretary to the mayor of New Orleans in 1812; Jean-François Canonge was clerk in the Louisiana legislature; Jean-Baptiste Donatien Augustin was secretary to the municipal council and sheriff; Charles Bougeois was clerk to the municipality and secretary to the municipal council as well.[48]

Other refugees filled higher positions, sometimes several positions either concomitantly or successively. The refugee group gave mayors to the city of New Orleans. Jean-François Pitot—who was not a native of Saint-Domingue but had lived there, married a Creole and had come to Louisiana with the other refugees in 1796—became the first appointed mayor of American New Orleans. He was appointed to the city council in March 1804 by Claiborne, then became mayor three months later, after Etienne de Boré's resignation.[49] After being city recorder, Denis Prieur became mayor of New Orleans, a position he held from 1828 to 1838.[50] Several refugees also held offices in the state legislature. Pierre Dormenon, for instance, was representative of Pointe Coupée. Jean-François Canonge was also elected to the legislature. When he resigned, he was replaced by another refugee, Damien Augustin. Thomas Théard held several local and state offices. Pierre Auguste Charles Derbigny held many offices. He was, for instance, Claiborne's official interpreter and a member of the state legislature and the state supreme court. In 1828, he even became the fifth governor of Louisiana.[51]

Their descendants followed in the refugees' footsteps. Hypolite Canonge was superintendent of public schools, Diego Morphy's son was a member of the state supreme court, and Paul-Emile Théard held local and state offices, as his father had before him.[52] All their political activities tended to remain within the municipal and state spheres. One of the rare exceptions to this rule was undoubtedly Auguste Davezac. He was sent by President Jackson to The Hague and to Sicily as chargé d'affaires, and his appointment to The Hague was renewed by James Polk.[53] At any rate, their local involvement shows their determination to influence the political life of their new homeland. One single example may illustrate the visibility some refugees acquired in Louisiana: that of Louis Casimir Moreau Lislet.

Moreau Lislet was indeed an important local figure, exceptional for all the offices he held, for the swiftness of his rise, and for the imprint he left on the state. Before he came to Louisiana, his records were already impressive, a proof of the dynamism some refugees had displayed before the demise of the French colony. He had been attorney in the Parliament in Paris, then deputy attorney general of the Superior Council at Cap Français. When he came to Louisiana in 1804, he immediately started a new career as official interpreter of the territory. He then became justice of the Orleans Parish (in 1805) and member of the Parish Assembly; he represented the city of New Orleans in all judicial proceedings. After such promising beginnings, he was successively member of the State House of Representatives, a state senator, and attorney general for the New Orleans City Council. He is said to have written a huge proportion of the legal proceedings of nineteenth-century Louisiana. He is still more famous for his primary legacy to the state of Louisiana: the Civil Code, which he wrote and revised in collaboration with other prominent figures of the Louisiana legal world.[54] The white refugees were in the limelight for a good half of the nineteenth century in Louisiana. Although the racial situation in Louisiana prevented free refugees of color from holding important offices and directly influencing the political decisions of the state, they played an essential role in Louisiana politics for over a century.

The free refugees of color definitely shaped political activism in nineteenth-century Louisiana.[55] Those who reached Louisiana with their white companions of misfortune had been born and raised in a society where this category of population had a definite weight in the life of the colony. They had sometimes fought during the revolutionary years to try to improve their civil and political condition in Saint-Domingue. When it was not the case, they were aware of the role their peers had played in this fight. Louisiana was a relatively favorable environment for local activism, even though their Louisiana counterparts had been less active. As in the case of the white refugees, the conditions of their migration and resettlement tended to render them still more active. All conditions were thus met to make them the leaders of their class, beginning with the fact that they outnumbered the free Creole population. They were clearly public-spirited, as their involvement in the militia and in the 1815 Battle of New Orleans proved. They were the engine of a new class consciousness among New Orleans free people of color. They were also politically aware and active.

In the free group of color, both the refugees and their descendants gave the Louisiana Creoles of color political leaders, and they were involved in all the political actions concerning free blacks' rights. In the late Spanish period, a study of the legal actions initiated by free people of color shows that a large proportion of these cases involved men with West Indian origins.[56] After Louisiana's inclusion in the United States, free black activities often involved refugees, most likely in leadership positions. Because of their prominent role, they may be described as "intensely political."[57] When Louisiana free blacks attempted to petition Congress to obtain the right to vote on property issues, Saint-Domingan refugees were actively involved. Some of them wrote in newspapers, in *L'Abeille*, for instance, under pen names, to try to influence Louisianans on questions of franchise. The Grandjean conspiracy of 1805, aimed at opposing the Americans, is another sign of this involvement.[58] Another petition, mainly organized by refugees, was also addressed to the State House of Representatives in 1838 to try to obtain the right for property-owning free blacks to vote in state elections.[59]

The free group of color in Louisiana never attempted to fight for the liberation of the enslaved population. While abolitionism was the main battle fought by northern free blacks, the Louisiana free blacks never opposed the system of slavery. Their presence in the militia was the sign that they accepted to serve as a policing force to protect the institution. Historians agree that slaveholding was the best proof of their special rights, which made them tacitly support the maintenance of the system.[60] Their fight was focused on their own rights, in particular that of political equality through franchise. This essential difference—although it is difficult to scientifically document the refugees' influence in this matter—was probably the result of the Saint-Domingan free blacks' presence among them. The refugees were perfectly aware of the effects that abolition had had on the prerogatives of the free Creoles of color in Saint-Domingue, since their flight had been one consequence of abolition. They had also been involved in the fights for the civil equality of their class in Saint-Domingue. There is little doubt that their narrations directed Louisiana politics toward militancy for free black equality instead of general emancipation.

Besides direct political activism, the refugees can be credited with importing republicanism into their new homeland. The ideology of the French Revolution "entered as if clandestinely through the harbors, conveyed by immigrants, sailors, corsairs, and freemasonic lodges."[61] Free black republicanism was undoubtedly part of that—sometimes not so clandestine—movement. The refugees were as intent as their Saint-Domingan counterparts had been about obtaining the franchise and thus gaining political weight, and "among the West Indian newcomers were even more skilled, better educated, and probably more assertive leaders—both free and slave—than those who had already disturbed the Americans in 1803."[62] This was probably favored by the status of "quasi-citizenship," of the free group of color in Louisiana.[63] They had the right of petition, which may be considered "a kind of left-handed representation" and were fully counted in the apportionment of representation in

1852, both facts which gave them a definite, although indirect, weight on the political decisions. Some of the free refugees of color even managed to vote at times.[64] In 1844, for instance, a group of free refugees of color sufficiently light-skinned to "pass" formed the Clay Club, a pressure group supporting Henry Clay's candidacy in the presidential election. Some of them apparently managed to vote, despite the regulations depriving free people of color of the franchise.[65] There were also times when, if votes were close, they were asked to vote in local elections. This happened several times in the Rapides Parish between 1830 and 1860, especially in the Ten Miles community.[66]

Throughout the antebellum years, even as the civil rights of the free group were being reduced, the free refugees of color took part in (and often led) public actions aimed at ensuring the maintenance of the few rights they had and at advancing their situation. In 1853, for instance, free black veterans of the Battle of New Orleans, in majority refugees, founded the Association of Colored Veterans to ensure their visibility in all the celebrations of the Louisianan victory.[67] Beyond their visible political actions and organizations, they mostly inflected the political thought of their Louisiana brethren by importing a relatively radical republicanism into their new homeland. Joining forces, for instance, Baratarians, including Louis Aubry and Renato Beluche, and Veterans of the Battle of New Orleans, led by the most famous hero of the free troops of color, Colonel Savary, openly supported the revolutionary government of Manuel Rodriguez in Colombia in 1811.[68] The same Savary, together with General Humbert (himself a white refugee) rallied men to the service of the Mexican republican revolutionaries, which could lead to the conclusion that "Colonel Savary and his soldiers nourished a republican revolutionary tradition within the black Creole community."[69]

Without any doubt, the refugees' strong commitment to republicanism, a political trend that had ensured the Saint-Domingan population of color access to civic equality and freedom, their active leadership in New Orleans, and their strong proportion within the New Orleans free population of color had several consequences. It reinforced their sense of community and their wish to improve the general situation of their class, and it most certainly fashioned their cultural identity. Their presence was found in all the important ventures undertaken by free people of color at the time. When the Société des Artisans was founded by free artisans and war veterans of color, the initiator was a refugee, Louis Victor Séjour, who had fled Saint-Marc in 1794, had settled in Louisiana, and had been part of the free battalion of color under Savary and Daquin. The society also included active refugees' children, including Séjour's son, Victor Séjour, but also Michel Séligny and Camille Thierry. When the Société Catholique pour l'Instruction des Orphelins dans l'Indigence was founded in 1848 to administer the Couvent estate, many refugees of color or descendants of refugees were among the members of the board of directors, including Armand Lanusse, the school's principal, Paul Trévigne, Aristide Mary, and Rodolphe Lucien Desdunes.[70]

It is clear that the free refugees of color had an undeniable political and civic dynamism. Their long-term influences on the Louisiana political world are more difficult to document. What is clear, however, is that political dynamism did not die away when the first-generation refugees disappeared because, as the previous discussion suggests, their offspring are to be found among the most indefatigable leaders of Louisiana's free Creole politics. The first manifestation of this leadership is the romantic literary movement of the mid-nineteenth century. The descendants of free refugees of color were famous in the literary world, and their contribution to Louisiana literature and poetry was made obvious by the place they held in the collection of poems written by seventeen Louisiana Creoles of color, entitled *Les Cénelles*, and published in 1845.[71] The poems are generally related to the situation of the free people of color in Louisiana, their bitterness at racial injustice and prejudice, and their wish to see the wrongs they endured throughout their life redressed. The topics of these poems clearly point to political militancy, and if their poems are read in parallel with the articles and editorials they wrote, it may be concluded that these poems had a definite political weight and bore the clear mark of French revolutionary republicanism as expressed in the French cultural tradition.[72] Their republican heritage was most certainly canalized in the romantic literary movement of the 1840s, which the "Haitian émigrés, their offspring, and Haitian-educated native Louisianans spearheaded."[73] Their poems published in *Les Cénelles* and in the literary journal they had founded in 1843, *L'Album Littéraire: Journal des jeunes-gens, amateurs de littérature,* and the editorials they wrote for the journal were a clear denunciation of Louisiana society.

During the Civil War, Louis Charles and Jean-Baptiste Roudanez, both of refugee descent, founded *L'Union*, a newspaper which took part in all the fights fought by the Creoles of color, from the condemnation of slavery to the attempt to obtain the franchise for free blacks. In 1863, J. B. Roudanez and E. A. Bertonneau went to see President Lincoln in the hope of securing the franchise for free Creoles of color. *L'Union* editorials claimed as the undisputed models of the Creoles of color Chavanne and Ogé, leaders of revolutionary Saint-Domingue, as well as Savary, the hero of the Battle of New Orleans.[74]

In 1864, *L'Union* became *La Tribune de la Nouvelle Orléans*. Louis Charles Roudanez was still among its active members, and Paul Trévigne, another descendant of refugees, was its chief editor. They constantly fought for free black suffrage, insisting on Louisiana's exceptionalism. They wrote editorials, political articles, fiction, and even poetry to promote racial equality and universal male suffrage.[75] In 1862, they launched a campaign for the desegregation of public schools and streetcars. They later created the Louisiana Chapter of National Equal Rights League and founded the Friends of the Universal Suffrage in 1865. Their ceaseless fight against segregation resumed in 1867, when they tried to obtain civic equality, voting rights, and desegregation of public facilities. They even launched an assault against the New Orleans streetcars. Their movement had far-reaching requests, all linked with total equality for free people of color. Trévigne also militated vigorously in favor of the desegregation of Masonic lodges. They even published an English version of the newspaper and sent it to members of Congress in Washington.[76]

The Reconstruction and post-Reconstruction years were also periods of intense activity, particularly under the influence of Rodolphe Lucien Desdunes, the son of a Saint-Domingan father and a Cuban refugee. He was rightly considered "the primary strategist of Creole resistance." He militated in all the causes of the Creoles of color and participated in all their actions: a militant for the Association of Equal Rights in 1881, he helped found the *Union Louisianaise* in 1887. He contributed to the *New Orleans Crusader*, a bilingual newspaper which has remained famous for being "an aggressive vehicle for racial protest in New Orleans."[77] He even became, in 1895, associate editor of the *Crusader*. The newspaper called itself a "Labor and Republican" paper and supported both labor unions and the Populist Party. It is one of the best proofs of Louisiana's free Creole group's vitality, since it was, in the 1880s, the only African American daily in the United States, a leader in matters of militancy for the civil rights of people of color. It was involved in all the fights opposing segregative and discriminatory measures (segregation in railroads, denial of the right for people of color to sit on criminal juries, literacy and property requirements for the franchise).[78] Desdunes and his friends (including Arthur Estèves, who became president of the committee and who, according to Desdunes, "was of a Louisiana family, but was Haitian by birth")[79] also launched, in 1891, the Citizens' Committee in an attempt to end segregation on railroads. Beyond proving Desdunes' political commitment, the activities of the Citizens' Committee are a sign that the family's involvement did not end with the second generation, since Rodolphe's son, Daniel, was the engine of a successful action against segregation on interstate railroads, before Homer Plessy was sent by Rodolphe Desdunes and his supporters to solve legally the case of segregation in the intrastate railroads. In the case of the interstate railroads, the segregation law was deemed incompatible with the Constitution. In *Plessy v. Ferguson*, their plan only resulted in the legalization of segregation—or, as Desdunes writes, the outcome of the case "sanctioned the odious principle of the *segregation of races*"—but it illustrates the vitality of the New Orleans Creoles of color and, more particularly, of the refugees' descendants.[80]

Desdunes also initiated an organized plan for the immigration of Creoles of color to Haiti, which met with some success before being abandoned after the return of most of the Louisianans who had migrated to the Caribbean island. Desdunes never ceased to be involved in all the questions of race and racial equality, as evidenced by his official opposition to W.E.B. Du Bois—who is himself said to have claimed Haitian ancestry—in a 1907 pamphlet entitled *A Few Words to Dr. Du Bois "With Malice toward None,"* in which he lists the educated Creoles of color of Louisiana to disprove his opponent's argument, once again stressing the exceptional character of the Creole community and using it as an example (together with that of Toussaint Louverture) of what his people could achieve.[81] Finally, the 1911 publication of *Nos Hommes et Notre Histoire* may also be considered another of Desdunes's political legacies through its exclusive focus on Creoles of color in all fields of Louisiana life. The book, when read with the knowledge of the Saint-Domingan origins of many of the characters involved, is an excellent proof of their vitality. The translator of the English version of Desdunes' book, Dorothy McCants, makes it clear in her preface that the refugees had a leading role. She even defines, slightly abusively, the Creoles of color as "free, mixed-blood, French-speaking descendants of Immigrants from Haiti," adding that the group known as the *gens de couleur libres* was composed of "these Creoles of color with Latin blood, and certain other free blacks."[82]

The community of the Creoles of color was doubtlessly active in nineteenth-century America. The refugees—who were so numerous among them—were especially active. They were more literate, politically trained, and more conscious of their potential weight. They led and tutored the free black community of Louisiana. They used their previous experience or that of their fathers to attempt indefatigably to prove that they were worth much more than what the United States granted them. They constantly challenged the dual racial order that the Anglo-Saxon tradition was trying to impose in Louisiana as well as the later white supremacist trends. As their white counterparts, free refugees of color and their descendants occupied the forefront of the Louisiana political scene and imprinted on their class a tradition of political activism unique in the nineteenth-century American South (and even in nineteenth-century America). The refugee community thus displayed uncommon dynamism and clearly shaped political activism in Louisiana. What remains to be assessed is the degree of influence they had in shaping the politics of the state and of the nation.

## Louisiana Politics, American Politics.

The refugees shaped political activism. Because they occupied key positions in Louisiana politics, they acted on the institutions and legislation. Because leading law specialists were among the refugees, but also because the refugees exerted pressure on their new homeland, they most certainly helped to retain Roman Law as the main source of legal influence, to the detriment of the Common Law. Moreau Lislet was a member of all the commissions that elaborated and revised the Civil Law of Louisiana, both during the territorial phase and after the admission of Louisiana into the Union as a state. With Pierre Derbigny (himself a refugee), Edward Livingston (married to a refugee), and Etienne Mazureau, in 1805 he ensured the persistence of Roman Law in Louisiana's legal institutions. In 1808, with James Brown, he wrote the Digest of the Civil Law in Force in the Territory of Orleans, which was adopted by the Orleans legislature in 1808 and is said to be "the first Civil Code in the Western Hemisphere." Upon request from the legislature, he translated with Henry Carleton the portion of the *Siete Partidas* that had been in force in Louisiana during the Spanish era. In 1822, Moreau Lislet was again selected, by a joint vote of the House and Senate, to revise the Civil Code with Livingston and Derbigny. The outstanding reputation of this refugee is to be seen in the results of the vote: he obtained 43 votes, while the two other persons selected, Livingston and Derbigny, themselves closely connected to the refugee community, were granted 25 (which was, of course, more than all the other rejected candidates to the appointment). Moreau was appointed chairman of the commission designed to revise the Civil Code and prepare the Commercial Code. The commission thoroughly mixed the French and Spanish practice with whatever they deemed good in the Common Law and produced a Compact of Civil Code Procedure composed of 1,161 articles. Many of the provisions of the Code remained when it was revised in 1870, which means that part of the work of the commission is still operative in Louisiana.[83]

In devising the civil and commercial laws of Louisiana, the refugees ensured the prevalence of Roman Law. As shown by a pamphlet published in New Orleans in 1806 by Jeremiah Brown, they even came to embody the success of this law so untypical of the rest of the country. They became the focus of all opposition to it because, in the eyes of the rest of the Louisiana population, "not content to practice law *in* the territory, these newcomers desired to dictate laws *for* the territory."[84] It is sometimes even contended that they did so to keep the monopoly over the legal profession, where they could in no way be challenged by American lawyers who were unfamiliar with the proper proceedings. Without going that far, it seems logical to think that they used their knowledge and experience, and that it was to be expected that the legal system they had practiced all their lives was the one they favored when devising the Louisiana Codes. What made the role of the refugees in the legal world still more obvious is that, although the code was published both in French and in English, it was the French version that was authoritative in all legal proceedings because the native language of the codifiers was French. This was undoubtedly, after the adoption of Roman law as the main principle, the second Louisianan exception introduced by the leading refugee lawyers. Moreover, the public printer of the laws of Louisiana at the time was Jean-Bastien Thierry, himself a refugee.[85] When Moreau Lislet died, his eulogy mentioned his "insight" and "wide experience" and declared that his "task, fruit of his long vigils and of his deep meditation, is a monument" for the benefit of "future generations."[86] This is clear proof that his participation, together with that of other refugees, was properly acknowledged by the Louisianans.

The role of the refugees, however, was not limited to the legal field. Because they held offices, they could influence local life. This also conferred visibility on them. For instance, a refugee, J. B. Vernet, signed the welcome address from the inhabitants of Louisiana to Prefect Laussat in 1803.[87] As Claiborne's official interpreter, Derbigny delivered the main oration in French at the first celebration of the Fourth of July in Louisiana in 1804.[88] As the first mayor appointed in American Louisiana, Pitot headed the municipality when the principles of municipal government were organized. He saw the first census of American Louisiana in 1805 and was also in command when the first elections took place. The "various improvements in municipal services, such as voluntary police protection and better sidewalks and street paving"[89] occurred during his term. This is in perfect agreement with the attempts by the refugee community—through "Feuilleton" among others—to refine the urban landscape of New Orleans, and it illustrates the influence that refugees coming from a more developed society could exert on what was still largely a frontier society, despite the improvements that had been made under Spanish rule.

The refugees were also involved in repeated attempts to promote improvements or alterations in Louisianan politics. Several refugees, including Pierre David Bidet Renoulleau, signed the petition to Claiborne of 17 September 1804, asking for a less strict policy in matters of slave trade.[90] Moreau Lislet, for instance, was part of the committee of lawyers who sent a petition to Congress, asking for an increase in the salary of the justices of the Superior Court of the Territory of Orleans. Other examples can be found that attest to the refugees' presence and power, like the role of Moreau Lislet in inflecting Derbigny's decision to withdraw from the gubernatorial election of 1820 (despite a quasi-certainty of being elected) in favor of his adversary Robertson, who had obtained more popular votes.[91]

The refugees also played a definite political role by their mere support. For instance, Claiborne's election as first governor of the newly created state of Louisiana in 1812 may be partly attributed to his sympathy for the refugees, who, in gratitude, supported him electorally.[92] When Louisiana became American, the Creoles also used the refugees to reinforce their own political power against the Americans. The refugees' vote was important, and it may be contended that Creole political weight was thus reinforced by this numerical addition. This strengthened influence was all the more perceptible as the Americans, who came in larger numbers as time went on, did not immediately fulfill the property tax prerequisite to franchise that had been set in 1812. Their inability to vote, together with the early nineteenth-century refugee addition, gave more relative political power to the francophone community. It is necessary to slightly mitigate this assertion, however, since, despite their importance to the Creoles and their tendency to ally with them locally, the refugees did not necessarily oppose the early American policies. They were often strongly anti-French, which led them to warn the Louisianans against Napoleon and to readily accept the rule of the United States.[93] They sometimes even took sides in the national debates. Moreau Lilet, for instance, strongly supported Jackson against Calhoun during the Nullification Crisis of the 1830s. The refugees' influence, at any rate, was not lost on Louisianans, as exemplified by an excerpt from the 9 September 1825 *Louisiana Gazette*: "This faction is composed of foreign Frenchmen and refugees of Saint-Domingue, together with a few active recruits of the city. It is sowing seeds of discord and dissention in the city. It has three presses in the City, well organized for their purposes, some of them high in office and in our councils."

Beyond the polemical aspect of the opinion expressed in the *Louisiana Gazette*, it raises the question of the press, which was indeed the refugees' uncontested realm until well into the 1820s. From Louis Duclos and Jean-Baptiste Lesueur Fontaine, who founded in 1794 *Le Moniteur de la Louisiane*, the first newspaper in Louisiana, which remained the sole press organ until the Louisiana Purchase, all the main founders and editors of Louisiana newspapers were refugees. Claudius Beleurgey created *Le Télégraphe*, which ran from 1803 to 1812; *L'Ami des Lois* was directed by Hilaire Leclerc, then Arnold Du Bourg, from 1809 to the early 1820s; *L'Abeille* was François Delaup's creation in 1827. Louis Placide Canonge and his role in *Le Propagateur Catholique* and *La Lorgnette* should not be forgotten, no more than the existence of *Le Courrier de la Louisiane*, directed by J. B. Thierry and Dacqueny, in which J. C. de St. Romes, another refugee, played an important part. To this list should be added *La Lanterne Magique* (Daudet) and numerous individual contributions by refugees to various organs of the press.[94] What varies from one contemporary source to another, however, is the assessment of the involvement of the newspapers in local and national politics. The excerpt quoted above of the *Louisiana Gazette* is an example of a certain critical vision of the refugees' excessive power. In November 1809, however, when Claiborne sent to Secretary Robert Smith a list of the various newspaper editors who could become the official printers of the laws of the United States, he insisted on the unbiased positions of many of them. He defended J. B. Thierry of the *Courrier de la Louisiane*—who had been, until then, the official printer—mentioning that he had "hitherto evidenced a disposition to support the measures of the government" and had "manifested a friendly disposition toward the American government." Of Fontaine of the *Moniteur de la Louisiane*, the official printer of the Laws of the Territory, he wrote that he took "no part in the politicks of the United States."[95]

Claiborne made it clear, however, that they often had strong positions on international politics (either pro-Bonaparte or pro-English), and that some of the refugees' newspapers, although they were not actively involved in local or national politics, could be seen as opposition papers (Beleurgey's *Télégraphe* and Daudet's *Lanterne Magique*).[96] In several cases, the refugee journalists were accused of being too closely involved in political opposition. At the time of the Batture controversy of September 1807,[97] J. B. Thierry was accused of taking sides in the debate and even of being a Burrite, to which he replied that he had always remained faithful to the interests of the Louisianans and that he supported the government who had rallied to his ideas.[98] *L'Abeille* supported the Whigs and John Quincy Adams, then defended Van Buren against Clay, thus proving a constant interest not only in local matters but also in national politics. This newspaper was nonetheless "the official journal of the state and of the city of New Orleans" from 1833 to 1836.[99] Whatever the reputation they had for intervening in politics and taking sides, the Louisiana newspapers, all in the hand of the refugees for at least one generation, could not help but influence politics. Whether they were very vocal or not, the newspapermen's main task was to express opinions for Louisianans to read, which means that they influenced their readers through the topics they chose to discuss and the positions they adopted.

By the monopoly they had on the press, by their appointments to important political positions, and by their vote and local alliance with the Creole population against the Americans, the white refugees had a definite impact on Louisiana's politics in the first decades after their arrival. They played an essential part in favoring the prevalence of Roman Law over Common Law in Louisiana, an exception that still sets Louisiana apart from the rest of the United States. They managed to maintain that Latin exception despite Jackson's attempts at imposing on Louisiana an American system of organization, following the precepts that had been set by the land ordinances of 1787. Their political experience, reinforced by a dynamism resulting from the very traumatic experience of flight and estrangement, made the white refugees a force that counted in Louisiana. They used their experience and their adaptability to fit in politically, but also to leave their mark on the political life of the state and beyond. Through the refugees' numerical reinforcement, the French-speaking community managed to retain control of the state and local governments for almost four decades after the Americanization of Louisiana. In early American New Orleans, the city was divided into three municipalities. They kept control of two of the three, enacting their own legislation in French to prevent any American takeover of those two municipalities. Refugees were obviously present in many fields, which at times infuriated the Americans. James Brown, for instance, repeatedly complained in very strong terms about the presence of too many refugees on the police force of New Orleans.[100]

Representing 63.3 percent of the free community of color in 1810, refugees could also influence the actions of this community and launch a fifty-year crusade for the equality of rights. They again left their imprint on Louisiana political life during Reconstruction. Their renewed 1867 campaign against segregation succeeded in securing equality in New Orleans public transport. They also managed, through the actions of Desdunes' Citizens' Committee, to influence the terms of the 1867 state constitution. This constitution was profoundly different from those of the other states, as it went further than any other along the path of equality for black Louisianans. It granted them equal treatment in public transportation and public accommodation, and it ensured political equality of all men, whatever their color. In short, this constitution put Louisiana ahead of all the other southern states by about 100 years. Without the free refugees of color and their offspring, the Roudanez, the Trevignes, the Desdunes, this would never have happened. They also favored the passage of the 1868 Civil Rights Bill in Louisiana. In 1870, they obtained the desegregation of public schools, which was effective for nineteen Louisiana schools by 1874. Even though this legislation was short-lived and was superseded by national measures, it breathed an air of freedom and modernity over New Orleans. The next action attempted by Desdunes and his committee, the attempt at suppressing segregation beyond the boundaries of Louisiana through the Homer Plessy case was unfortunately unsuccessful and sent Louisiana back into the nineteenth century. It was not the last fight of the Louisiana free Creoles of color of Saint-Domingan descent, however. They went on fighting for their rights, they went on militating, in particular in interracial labor organizations, and they returned to court in the 1920s to attempt to achieve the long awaited racial equality.[101]

Saint-Domingan refugees, black and white, thus not only promoted nineteenth-century political activism in Louisiana but also actively participated in the shaping of the state's politics and policies for several decades. Their role was essential in the development of ideologies, since the largest influence the refugees—from Louisiana and elsewhere—exerted was probably on the debate over slavery. The presence, narrations, and messages of both the white victims of the revolution in Saint-Domingue and the proud slaves and free refugees of color left a deep imprint on American minds and inflected both proslavery and antislavery ideologies. They deeply influenced the attitude of the Americans toward slavery and, this affected both sides of the debate in ways that were both similar and diametrically opposed.

## Shaping the Ideologies of Nineteenth-Century America

The white refugees' narratives insisted on the savagery of the insurgents and the faithfulness of certain slaves who helped their masters flee from the island. From these narrations originated a depiction of African slaves as both potential savages and tamed protectors of their masters. The dual representation had a twofold effect: it favored the passage of very strict slave codes in the South, but it also spurred the development of southern paternalism. Both sides of the narrations were largely exaggerated, however. The stress that lay on the savagery of the slaves was too heavy and tended toward overgeneralization. On the other hand, since many escape stories included the episode of the master's children hidden by a faithful slave in a basket, there was probably, here also, a slight exaggeration. Playing on the dual representation of the slaves became prototypical of the refugees' narratives.[102] The Manichean representation of the slaves conveyed by the narratives necessarily influenced the sectional debate, and this "myth is formative of the residual lore of the Haitian Revolution in the Lower Mississippi Delta," and more largely in the American South.[103] By insisting both on the idealized representation of the faithful slave and on the horrors that could arise when those faithful savages became unleashed, the narratives led proslavery advocates to prove the necessity of enslavement in the aim to favor the development of the potentialities of the slaves and to check their natural tendencies toward cruelty and disorder.

The refugees' narratives abounded in the southern press. Pamphlets, articles, and stories were also published in the refugee press.[104] Hundreds of narratives were published at the turn of the nineteenth century. *De Bow's Review* contained many such examples.[105] The eastern press was also full of such narratives.[106] French speakers of Louisiana also had access to the narratives of Moreau de Saint-Méry or Pamphile de Lacroix and many others. These narratives fueled the dread of the southerners that they might become the powerless witnesses to a similar uprising, and they used them to prove the impossibility of abolishing slavery. In all the asylums reached by the refugees, the same use was made of the narratives. In Cuba, for instance, the *Junta Cubana* organized by the planters after independence was still using the horrors of Saint-Domingue in their proslavery tracts.[107] When dealing with slave conspiracies, both in the Anglo-Saxon South and in Louisiana, proslavery ideologues always established a link between these rebellious fits and the revolution in Saint-Domingue. This made them conclude on the necessity of maintaining, reinforcing, and strictly codifying slavery. Even during the Nullification Crisis, the role of France in triggering the Saint-Domingan revolution was evoked to try to undermine the arguments of the defenders of what came to be known as the Tariff of Abominations, southerners foreboding a slave revolt as one of the potential consequences of the chaos that would ensue if the tariffs were maintained and southern rights were negated. In Saint-Domingue, after all, the slaves had used the tensions between the white Creoles and the French government to launch their own movement.

The Saint-Domingan example was often used by the most vocal proslavery advocates. From Dew and Calhoun to Taylor, Fitzhugh, De Bow, Cartwright, and Harper, all relied on the Haitian example to oppose emancipation, support the colonization of free blacks, and advocate the reinforcement of the slave codes.[108] Protecting slavery was, for them all, the only means to guard the United States against racial war. The argument pervaded all fields of southern response to abolitionism, from politicians to poets.[109] It invaded southern political rhetoric. It was alluded to in all the main debates in Congress at the time of the Missouri Compromise and during the Nullification crisis. It recurred in all the local oppositions, as during the debate in the Virginia legislature at the turn of the 1830s. It came back persistently in all occasions, at the time of Harpers Ferry, or during the Civil War.[110] It remained so strongly implanted in southern minds that it was still alluded to after the Civil War, when white supremacists were pushing southerners toward the Ku Klux Klan and other such organizations. When Lothrop Stoddard wrote his *Rising Tide of Color* in 1920, his defense of white supremacists still included references to the foundation of Haiti.[111] Although there is only rare scientific evidence of the refugees' direct role in influencing the proslavery debate, there is no doubt that their presence, with the narrations of their personal stories that were circulated both as oral history and in published form, did influence the southern rhetoric in the defense of slavery. It was a powerful tool to dramatize the risks of replication of the revolution in Saint-Domingue and was thus quite useful to both the ideology and rhetoric of the southerners.

It is fascinating that the opponents of slavery, both white and black, used the same allegories and the same references to defend opposite beliefs. Here again, the narratives by protagonists or witnesses of the Saint-Domingan revolution played an important part. In 1854, for instance, the *Memoir of Pierre Toussaint Born a Slave in St. Domingo* gave a good testimony of what had occurred on the French island. It also included a laudatory biography of Toussaint Louverture, all terms used to describe the Saint-Domingan leader being positively connoted: from the "power of his intellect," to the "respect and deference" he inspired, to his "magnanimity that equals the records of ancient history." The island under his rule was "peaceable and tranquil," and "his measures were mild and prudent."[112] Pierre Toussaint was not the only one to provide such a narrative, and all of them were echoed by the abolitionist politicians and ideologues. Some even devoted entire lectures or essays to the study of the revolution in Saint-Domingue, as did W. W. Brown in his "St. Domingo: Its Revolution and Its Patriots," a lecture he delivered in London and Philadelphia in 1854 and which was published in Boston in December of the same year.[113] All the writings of the time echoed this interest in the Haitian experiment. In the 1830s, Wendell Phillips used Haiti and Toussaint to prove that the black race was not inferior; William Lloyd Garrison used this example to show that the security of the country depended on abolition and that it was a way to prevent a holocaust. References to Haiti are found in the writings of David Walker (in his 1829 "Appeal to the Colored Citizens of the world," for instance), Lydia Maria Child, Henry Highland Garnet, Angelina Grimké, and many others.[114] Abraham Lincoln also used the example of Haiti in his prenomination speech in New York. References are so numerous as to suggest that "events in St. Domingo made an indelible impression upon those concerned with black history in the antebellum America," as well as the postwar nation.[115]

References to Haiti indeed persisted long after the termination of slavery and were used by all the defenders of the advancement of blacks in America. During the Civil War, it was used to promote the enlistment of blacks in the Union army. It also pervaded the late-nineteenth-century debates on the advancement of the black race. While W.E.B. Du Bois declared in the 1890s that Haiti and Toussaint were models that had affected his whole life, Desdunes, in his pamphlet against Dubois, insisted that Toussaint should not be considered the hero of the Saint-Domingan revolution, because of his acceptance of French domination, but that the status of hero was to be attributed to Dessalines, who symbolically and physically destroyed everything that was white in the new Haitian republic. The comparison between Saint-Domingue and the United States was further enhanced by Desdunes's identification of Toussaint Louverture as the Booker T. Washington of Haiti. Haiti was so central to his indefatigable fight for black rights that he launched plans for immigration to Haiti.[116] James Redpath's founding, in the late 1850s, of the newspaper *Pine and Palm*, to promote the creation of a big black nation from the Caribbean (palm) to the North (pine), was also related to this movement. Like Desdunes in Louisiana, he promoted immigration of the eastern free blacks to Haiti and founded the Haytian [*sic*] Bureau of Immigration in Boston. All leaders of color, in Louisiana as in the rest of the country, took the Haitian rebels as their role models. All the fights were fought in the name of the brotherhood of all men with the Haitian rebels. The front page of the first issue of *L'Union* printed a letter from Victor Hugo, the famous French author, to Heurtelou, a Haitian journalist, in which he insisted on this brotherhood: "We are brothers! It is for this truth that John Brown is dead. It is for this truth that I struggle," Hugo wrote, before adding that Haiti served "as a good example" that would "help them to destroy slavery."[117] The editors of the Louisiana newspaper clearly claimed Haitian leaders André Rigaud, Louis Jacques Beauvais, Jean-Baptiste Villate, and Jean-Baptiste Belley as their forebears.[118] This persisted much longer and throughout the United States, since the Haitian example recurred, for instance, in the writings of Benjamin Brawley and Marcus Garvey in the 1920s. Brawley took pride in the Haitian revolution as the first example of Negro freedom in the Americas, while Garvey insisted on Toussaint as proof of Negro superiority. Later still, black Marxist intellectuals, such as C.L.R. James or the French poet Aimé Césaire, revived the symbolic origins of the Haitian fight by writing hagiographic biographies of Toussaint.[119]

The Saint-Domingan experience, publicized in the United States through the arrival of the black and white refugees, thus widely fueled the abolitionist argument. The white abolitionists thought that emancipation was indispensable to avoid a blood bath. Black leaders, both in antebellum America and during Reconstruction and segregation, referred to their Saint-Domingan brothers to foster black pride and promote black nationalism. White southerners used Haiti as proof that slavery should be maintained and reinforced. It is thus clear that the refugees' political and ideological influence, although it might be considered indirect, was felt far beyond the limits of Louisiana. It is also clear that it pervaded the American political and intellectual life long after the refugees themselves had died.[120] Their testimonies and the legacy they passed down to their descendants long survived them, a tradition most obvious in New Orleans among the free refugees of color.

The refugees broadly influenced the Louisiana political scene. Their arrival first induced increased repression against the expansion of republican ideals and against migration of black refugees, both slave and free. Their presence triggered the development of sometimes paranoid fears of slave rebellion and thus heavily influenced the psyche of the Louisianans, whatever group they belonged to. The refugees directly participated in Louisiana political life through their appointments—either by nomination or election—to high positions. They also shaped political activism in Louisiana throughout the nineteenth century. Their experience and education made them easy leaders in all three racial categories, although this is more difficult to prove in the case of the slaves for lack of objective documentary evidence. They and their offspring are found among the great white and free black leaders of nineteenth-century Louisiana. The refugees' numerical addition also ensured a much longer resistance of the Louisiana Creole community to Americanization. Directly or indirectly, they influenced the legal and political decisions of the state. They shaped local, state, and even national policies for many decades after their forced migration to Louisiana, both through direct action and political and intellectual tutelage. This intellectual prominence also had many more effects on their Louisiana asylum, particularly in the cultural sphere, the area that probably bears the clearest imprint of the Saint-Domingan legacy.

# 7

# A Still Unfathomed Cultural Legacy

## Refugees in Creole New Orleans

In previous chapters, many areas of the refugees' influence were seen to pertain to the cultural field. The role of the white refugees in the fields of education, entertainment, or journalism undoubtedly verges on cultural influence, as do the literary ventures of the offspring of the free refugees of color. These areas of the refugees' legacy require reexamination in a different light, together with many other areas of cultural influence, such as architecture, language, or vernacular culture. All the "unfathomed" legacies, great and small, of the Saint-Domingan refugee community in Louisiana remain largely unexplored.

Many monographs have been written by twentieth-century historians acknowledging the role of the refugees in specific fields.[1] Even though the necessity of examining the invaluable cultural role of the refugees has often been evoked, no historical work has really focused on this legacy as a whole.[2] Even though one group may have added more than the other two to some specific area, it now appears that it was the refugees' existence as a community that really enabled them to influence Louisiana culture. Because they were, beyond the racial and social divisions, a community, their influence was stronger. It is the cultural continuum created by their common origins that strengthened the visibility and significance of their influence. For this reason, the three groups will not be separated in this final chapter, although the preeminence of one group over the other two will be stressed in some areas.

The difficulty facing this study is that it is sometimes impossible to document the refugees' influential role. In many fields, like voodoo, for example, the cultural features that seemed to follow their arrival already existed in trace form in Louisiana culture. In other fields, like the Creole language, Louisiana already displayed similar cultural features, although later influences by the refugee group might be traced. In a certain number of other areas, where the refugees seem to have had obvious influences, these influences can hardly be dated with perfect accuracy. Whether the refugees created an influence or simply reinforced existing trends can be difficult to determine precisely. This is the case of architecture, where West Indian influences seem to have predated the arrival of the refugees. In other fields, the emergence of some cultural features occurred in the 1790s, but there is no proof it would not have, even without the refugees' arrival. Freemasonry, for instance, became extremely widespread and influential in Louisiana after the refugees' arrival. Although this input surely boosted its development in the years that followed, there is no way to prove it would not have known the same development without them.

Ascertaining their influence is thus sometimes difficult, since the appearance of cultural traits in Louisiana at the time of their arrival could be purely fortuitous. It might be contended that these evolutions were part of a larger movement spreading to the whole Western Hemisphere or even involving the developed societies of Europe and America in a global transatlantic perspective. The study of the refugees' cultural legacy may seem exaggerated in some areas. But what remains is that, whether the refugees were the initiators of certain cultural trends or they simply gave these trends visibility through their numerical importance and dynamism, they were responsible for giving momentum to certain cultural traits that subsequently became specific to Louisiana and survived the integration of the territory within the United States. Voodoo, for instance, may have existed residually in Louisiana and may have taken the form of some traditions of magic without a strongly organized cult, but with the St. Domingans' arrival, it became a popular and popularized Louisiana cultural trend, and Louisiana voodoo was assuredly shaped along the Haitian tradition. This chapter will attempt to examine as exhaustively as possible the cultural influences the refugees exerted by importing new features or by simply altering those already in existence. The study will first bear on the general cultural improvements consecutive to their arrival, before focusing on the development of certain cultural specificities, in particular in matters of folk culture, and concluding on their contribution to the creation of a French-Creole culture unique in the United States.

## A New Cultural Environment

The best possible introductory assessment of the extent of the refugees' influence in the Louisiana cultural sphere is probably the list established by Jacques de Cauna in the conclusive chapter of his book on the Haitian revolution. After mentioning refugee diaspora, he adds that a study of their cultural influences, in particular of the refinement they brought to the mores of societies which had remained rustic until their arrival, remains to be conducted. He mentions the creation of newspapers, schools, theaters, Masonic lodges, clubs, and societies; he alludes to fashions, both in clothes and architecture; he cites customs, religion, and languages (Creole and French).[3] Although some fields could be added, his conclusion engulfs the extent of the immigrants' cultural contribution and paves the way for a global study of the refugees' cultural continuum, a continuum which usually displayed no division between the various racial groups.

The refugees' first influential role bore on the development of culture in general. Although the Spanish regime had left the mark of some improvements in society, Louisiana was lagging in most cultural fields.[4] This belated development was particularly palpable when Louisiana was compared to Saint-Domingue. The first thing the refugees did in Louisiana was attempt to draw the society and culture of their new homeland closer to that of their birthplace. The press was unknown to New Orleanians; the refugees founded newspapers.[5] As in most other refuges, from Charleston to New York, their commitment to journalism was immediate. In 1794, at a time when the first few refugees were arriving at a very slow pace, New Orleans had its first newspaper, *Le Moniteur de la Louisiane*. Many refugees immediately found their place in this new venture. When Jean-Baptiste Lesueur Fontaine became *Moniteur*'s editor in 1797, he had been in New Orleans less than a year. This journalistic revolution had many consequences. It accustomed the Creoles to regular inputs of information and culture. It opened their minds to the world outside Louisiana by giving them world news. It exercised their ability to think by providing food for thought. It enabled advertising of cultural events. It also ensured the persistence of the French language and Franco-Creole culture in the face of the overpowering Anglo-American wave that streamed into New Orleans in the early nineteenth century. Those French newspapers may be qualified as "instruments of cultural cohesion," for they helped to "preserve the language pattern so fundamental to the Creoles' cultural identity" and "they kept Creole traditions alive in the face of an American cultural onslaught that absorbed all but the most tenacious subcultures."[6] This was possibly less noticeable in Louisiana, where the environment was still strongly francophone. In the English-speaking northern United States, for instance, they constituted "regular French *quartiers* with French pensions and shops, teachers of French, music, and dancing, French schools, French lodges, French newspapers and much French spirit."[7] In Louisiana, they melted into the French-speaking environment, but infused the moribund Gallicism of New Orleans with new vitality, making it the stronghold of the French language and culture in the United States. Beyond ensuring the persistence of Franco-

Creole cultural dominance, the refugee press also inflected this Franco-Creole culture by introducing the refugees' customs and topics of interest to the Louisiana readers.

Refugee schools also contributed to the state's general cultural level. Schools had been scarce until the 1790s.[8] The refugees' role in opening institutions of general or specific education, at all levels, and for all publics has already been detailed. Their legacy remains to be assessed. First, they made education accessible to many. Refugees also influenced Louisianans into believing that education should not be open only to whites. Either through individual ventures or through larger-scale enterprises (the managing of the Couvent legacy, for instance), the refugees gave people of African descent—free and even slave—easier access to culture. In 1850, almost 80 percent of the city's Creoles of color were literate, which was a very high figure for the mid-nineteenth century, even if white people sometimes reached this proportion in other regions of the United States. Over 1,000 free black children attended school in New Orleans at the time.[9] Refugees also made Louisianans conscious of the importance of education by opening colleges locally to avoid seeing only the richest educate their sons, in the North or abroad. The system of scholarships organized at the Collège d'Orléans, founded as early as 1805, thus opened higher education to greater numbers of Louisianans. As in the world of the press, refugees raised the educational level of the Louisianans, but probably also influenced them. It seems clear that any teacher is influenced by what he or she has seen, lived, or learned. Refugee teachers could not shed their past when entering a Louisiana school or academy. They were thus bound to exert a definite influence on their students, and the world of education "provided St. Domingans another opportunity to exert a continuing influence upon several generations of young Southerners." Louisiana historian Charles Gayarré always testified to the influence that his Saint-Domingan professors exerted on him, citing Davezac and especially Rochefort, his mentor, who, on his deathbed, is said to have told his pupil, "You are my work—never forget it." Beyond a formal education, those Saint-Domingan professors and, later, their students had a significant impact on a "sense of distinctiveness of Creole culture."[10] Gayarré, for instance, was essential in fostering historical interest for Louisiana and its culture, through his personal research and publications, but also by the founding of the Louisiana Historical Society, which he presided over for twenty-eight years. There is no doubt as to this essential legacy of the refugee educators in Louisiana, who "fostered a sense of community, giving the Creoles a base from which to develop culturally in Louisiana," and preserving the Creoles' "cultured upbringing and character, the last vestiges of French life in Saint-Domingue."[11]

Beyond newspapers and schools, the refugees pursued their cultural transmission to the Louisiana society by introducing all forms of cultural entertainment into New Orleans. They were directly involved in the foundation of places where Louisianans could attend theatrical performances and listen to classical music and opera. The cultural places they opened were among the first in the country where regular seasons were held. The New Orleans Opera House was "the first place in the country where grand opera was heard" and where an annual opera season was programmed.[12] The first integral performance of *Il barbiere di Siviglia* was given in New Orleans on 4 March 1823, three years before it was performed in New York.[13] Although there is a controversy about who founded the first theater in New Orleans, it is clear that the first professional actors of New Orleans had been trained in Saint-Domingue. There are many indications, however, that the Henry brothers from Paris, who are now granted paternity of the first theater of New Orleans, may have been connected with the refugee community.[14] Whether the founders were refugees or not, the first theatrical performances are attributed by all historians to a troop of refugee actors. As early as 1793, the theater was ruled by Madame Durosier, a relative (or wife) of a famous Saint-Domingan actor. The rest of the theatrical tradition in New Orleans is but an uninterrupted list of Saint-Domingan names: Jean-Baptist Lesueur Fontaine, Madame Marsan, Jean-Baptiste Fournier, Joseph Destinval, Jeanne-Marie Chapiteau, Louis-François Clairville, Scholastique Labbé, Madame Delaure, François de Saint-Just, and many more.[15] This influential role expanded largely beyond the first decade of the New Orleans theater. Both the founder of the Spectacle de la rue St. Pierre, Louis Tabary, and his successor at the head of the theater in 1808, François de Saint-Just, were refugees. In 1807, Tabary became the director of the Théâtre Saint-Philippe, which for one year had been directed by Auguste Tessier, who had previously been director of the theater in Kingston. He initiated the project of the theater on Orleans Street, which opened in 1809 and was the center for French theater and opera throughout the nineteenth century. The theater was destroyed by fire, but, like the phoenix, it was reborn in 1817 by yet another refugee, John Davis. It was open seven nights a week, three evenings being dedicated to opera performances. It harbored the French opera until 1859 and is often considered "the center for opera in the South."[16] It was, for a time, directed by Louis Placide Canonge, a playwright and the son of famous refugee parents. John Davis's son succeeded his father. The predominance of the refugees in the field of theater is thus undeniable. With them, the traditions of Saint-Domingue could spread to Louisiana, such as allowing quadroon actresses to perform, for instance, one of the specificities of Louisiana in the nineteenth century.

The opera and theaters were the main cultural ventures launched or expanded by the refugees. Refugees also played in orchestras and gave Louisianans the infrastructure necessary to the development of the arts, for instance, by opening music stores and bookstores and by expanding the book trade.[17] They also developed less visible fields of cultural expression, such as dancing, where they also prevailed. Jean-Baptiste Francis, for instance, a refugee, was a ballet dancer, choreographer, and teacher.[18] In short, their old artistic tradition permeated Louisiana society. As in all their American refuges (Baltimore, Norfolk, Richmond, Charleston, and Savannah), the refugees animated the cultural entertainment of their new city. Contrary to the other asylums, however, where the French language was obviously a barrier to their cultural expansion, these entertainments thrived in New Orleans. Not only did the refugees build the theaters, write the plays, direct, and perform theatrical and musical pieces, they also transmitted their love for the theater and opera to the Louisianans. As with the newspapers and educational activities, they influenced the Louisiana public and tinted southern culture with Gallic traces. They "introduced a distinctively French element to American fine arts" and made "a definite contribution to the culture of Southern cities."[19]

With cultural entertainments, the refugees also developed other forms of connected—although less cultural—entertainment, mainly balls and gambling. The "quadroon balls" had been in fashion in Saint-Domingue, where, as Moreau de Saint-Méry reports, they had been called *Redoutes*.[20] The practice of *plaçage* and quadroon balls was undoubtedly known in Louisiana before the refugees' arrival. They vitalized these practices, however, granting them both visibility and persistence in Louisiana. In the early 1800s, fifteen ballrooms were opened, together with the ballrooms that systematically went with the theaters. The Bal du Cordon Bleu, also known as the Quadroon Ball, was probably the most famous of those events, gathering the finest women of color and the richest whites. It was first held on Condé Street, then at the St. Philip Theater. Dupuy, a refugee who purchased the theater, added a gambling room to the theater and ballroom, as he had already done at the corner of Orléans and Bourbon, and as did Davis later at the Theâtre d'Orleans.[21] Those were traditional activities both in Saint-Domingue and among the refugees of Louisiana. Even such a respectable institution as the College d'Orléans requested—and was granted—permission to organize lotteries to fund the college activities and scholarships. This gambling activity, which had been highly developed in Saint-Domingue, thus spread to New Orleans. The refugees, as they had in Saint-Domingue and in all their refuges (Jamaica, Cuba, Charleston, and the northeastern cities, as is of common knowledge), also largely favored socialization in New Orleans by opening small drinking places (such as the Café des Réfugiés) and coffeehouses, a convivial tradition that has persisted to this day in the Crescent City.

The refugees also strongly influenced many other areas of the cultural and intellectual life of their new homeland. Freemasonry flourished in New Orleans after their arrival, as it did in all their other refuges.[22] Freemasons had been both numerous and well organized in Saint-Domingue. There were lodges in each of the main towns of the island: Port-au-Prince, Cap Français, Petit Goave, Les Cayes, and Saint-Marc.[23] Many influential Saint-Domingans were Masons. After their exodus, affiliated lodges were found in North America and the Caribbean (la Loge de la Vérité at Baltimore, for instance, and several at Charleston and in Jamaica).[24] There is no definite proof that they initiated the Masonic movement in Louisiana. As in the field of the theater, however, whether they initiated the first such experiment or simply added so tremendously to a barely launched tradition, their role was immense. The first lodges were created in the 1790s, exactly when the first refugees started reaching New Orleans. The beginnings are difficult to detail, since the first lodges were organized secretly. The Spanish authorities maintained a ban on Freemasonry, in accordance with the Papal Bull condemning the practice. The first traceable lodges, La Parfaite Union and L'Etoile Polaire, asked for recognition by lodges in Charleston and Paris in 1793 and 1794.[25] The American authorities were much more lenient toward Freemasonry, which bloomed in early-nineteenth-century New Orleans, aided by the tolerance of Father Antoine de Sedella and the rest of the Catholic clergy. The clergy never refused to welcome Masons into the Catholic Church or to grant them the sacraments. Sedella went so far as to invite the famous Mason Jean-François Canonge to deliver the commemorative address at the memorial mass for Napoleon Bonaparte in 1821.[26]

Refugees not only helped found the lodges. They were both rank and file and leaders of these lodges, since they had had a longer membership in Freemasonry than any other Louisianan. Many refugees were indeed Freemasons and are referred to in the literature: Canonge, Doctor Christian Miltenberger, the surgeons Yves and René Lemonier, and Dominique You, among others.[27]

Most family papers of famous refugees display proofs that they were involved in Freemasonry. The Prevost Family Papers contain a certificate guaranteeing that Guillaume Majastre was a Mason. The Lambert Family Papers display a certificate that Lambert was a Mason at the Loge du Grand Orient. Judge Augustin also belonged to a lodge, as shown by the Augustin-Wogan-Labranche Family Papers.[28] Some refugees have remained famous for occupying leadership positions in the Louisiana Freemasonry. Aimable Barthélémy Charbonnet was secretary-treasurer of L'Etoile Polaire.[29] Pierre François Du Bourg was Worshipful Grand Master of the Loge de la Parfaite Union.[30] In 1812, he formed a Grand Lodge combining all the others (including L'Etoile Polaire) and served for three years as Grand Master.[31] Moreau-Lislet was most certainly the leader in Louisiana Freemasonry. An article of the *Louisiana Free Mason* reads that "probably no other man contributed more to the early history of Masonry in this State than Moreau-Lislet." His Masonic story was long and went back to Saint-Domingue, where he had been Worshipful Master of the Loge La Réunion Désirée no. 3013, organized in April 1783. He was Grand Master in Louisiana, and his portrait was placed in the Grand Lodge office of the Parish of Orleans.[32] This Saint-Domingan influence did not stop after the first generation, as many refugees' children also became Freemasons.[33]

Refugees were involved in the foundation of the lodges and were members of them, often even in leading positions, and thus imprinted their vision of Freemasonry in Louisiana. By their influence, the lodges became the center of political agitation. They also led the Louisiana lodges toward multiethnic patterns, and many free refugees of color were also members and, sometimes, leaders. As early as 1820, Pierre Roup, a free refugee of color, played an essential part in the foundation of the Loge de la Persévérance. He was, for years, a high-ranking officer of the lodge with many of his white fellow refugees.[34] One of the desegregation fights fought by the late-nineteenth-century free Louisianans of mixed African ancestry concerned the Masonic Lodges, under the lead of Paul Trévigne, a descendant of refugees and chief editor of *La Tribune*. Freemasonry, placed under their intellectual tutelage, was thus another bastion of Creole culture and French language in nineteenth-century Louisiana. It was also a focal point of the fight against the biracial order that the Americans were trying to impose on the Louisiana society. By their presence and influence, refugees sustained Louisiana's exception in Anglo-Saxon America.

Although the influences examined might seem to benefit the white community, it is already obvious that the cultural legacy of the refugees is not to be solely attributed to one or the other racial group. Free refugees of color were involved, although slightly less than their white counterparts, in the press, the development of education and cultural entertainments, and in Freemasonry. The presence of people of African descent among actors, musicians, or Freemasons was one of the typical features of the Saint-Domingan Creole world, and it persisted in Louisiana once the refugees had transmitted it to their host society. The arts in general and folk culture were areas where the refugees, black and white, free or slave, found the best vehicles for the expression and transmission of their differences. Many fields bear their mark, a combination of white and black influences, the result of a cultural continuum that had started in Saint-Domingue and had been reinforced by the vicissitudes they had shared during flight and relocation. These fields of the arts, where Creole and folk cultures blended thoroughly, are best studied without differentiating the communities, although some fields will bear a clearer mark from one or the other group, the other(s) merely serving as adjuvant to the development and long-term implantation of the cultural features.

## Creole and Folk Cultures

It is not often that the legacy of the refugees is considered as a one-piece legacy, most historians having focused on one specific contribution by one peculiar group. The idea of a certain syncretism, however, might exceptionally be found in the literature, in general through the enumeration of the refugees' contributions in endless lists of fields where white and black influences mix. Charles R. Wilson, for instance, writes that "this migration introduced many of the central cultural customs and institutions of Southern Louisiana," before enumerating some of these contributions in a list that seems to mix all influences, the significant as the most anecdotal, the obvious as the most allusive, in a disorder which seems to privilege none of the three groups. His list gives "Voodoo, gumbo, jambalaya, zydeco music, street dancing to Afro-Latin rhythms, shotgun houses, Creole cottages, the prevalence of festivals, and a Creole language."[35]

The artistic fields indeed display a mixture of influences, in which all refugees had a part to play. Many historians and specialists of architecture, for instance, have attributed to the refugees architectural influences on lower Louisiana. The white refugees, by having their houses built in a certain way, by giving Louisiana several famous architects, most certainly exerted a strong influence. The free artisans of color and slave laborers also had their parts to play. As in other fields of cultural influence, it is all too natural that all of them went on using the techniques they had been taught and that they kept reproducing the building habits that they had known from childhood, techniques and patterns which had progressively developed in colonial Saint-Domingue over the decades of French colonization. That there are West Indian influences in the architecture of Louisiana leaves no doubt. That they were consecutive to the refugees' arrival is much more difficult to prove and is, at times, even doubtful. In many cases, premigration constructions display clear West Indian features and may be the result of influences by prior individual movements between the two areas, both of whites and of slaves—who were sometimes imported to Louisiana by way of the West Indies. There is no doubt, however, that the refugees reinforced these influences, as many Louisiana buildings show.

The refugees' influence is most undisputable in terms of industrial architecture and spatial organization of the sugar plantations. The sugar industry developed only after their arrival and in a large part thanks to them. It was a multiethnic process, as technicians who could be whites or free blacks worked side by side with black slaves. An examination of the sugar plantations of lower Louisiana attests to the West Indian influences. The industrial architecture is a first obvious element. Because sugar cane required special treatment, the industrial buildings developed, closely following the West Indian pattern. The sugar mills, sugar houses—with their typical chimney visible throughout the cane-growing Caribbean—as well as the barns closely resembled the traditional West Indian sugar plantation. The plantations were turned to the Mississippi River as they had been to the sea in Saint-Domingue, and the Louisiana planters started building private railroads to carry the sugar products to the river, as had been the case in the Caribbean (to carry the plantation production to the sea where it could be shipped directly). The correspondence went much further and was visible in what John Michael Vlach calls the plantation "landscape" or what John B. Rehder calls "cultural geography," that is, the spatial organization of the plantation. Studying the plan of the Uncle Sam Plantation in Convent, and following the conclusions of the geographer Rehder, Vlach shows that the sugar plantations of Louisiana, as those in Saint-Domingue, but contrary to the plantations in the rest of the South, followed a linear model, from the mansion to the sugar house (and other industrial buildings), and to the slave houses arranged in two parallel lines, as in the French Caribbean. He—together with Rehder—attributes this to the refugees' influence, adding that the Uncle Sam Plantation he studies, partly linear but L-shaped, is "a synthesis of traditions born of decades of cross-cultural contact," an allusion to a process of creolization that occurred in Louisiana as in the European colonies of the circum-Caribbean basin.[36]

Adding to this industrial and spatial organization, certain Louisiana architectural patterns are also often attributed to the refugees. The building tradition of the shotgun house is one of those, although it is a disputed topic among specialists. Some attribute it to a direct African tradition, others to a creolization that occurred in Saint-Domingue between African and Amerindian traditions. Shotgun houses may derive from the traditional habitat of the Taïnos Indians called *Bohío*, adapted by the Spanish homesteaders, with very strong African influences.[37] The appearance of the shotgun house in Louisiana is generally dated to the early 1800s, which may attest to the refugees' influence, but there are several theses in existence concerning its origin, one of them being "the arrival of black Creoles from the Caribbean (who brought African-derived influences)."[38] The refugees' influence on vernacular architecture may be described as "significant," and those shotgun houses are often found to be identical "even down to the dimensions" to houses found throughout Haiti, a feature generally attributed to the influence of free artisans of color from Saint-Domingue.[39]

The Creole cottage, found throughout southern Louisiana, may be another of their architectural influences. Many specialists defend the thesis that it was a syncretic adaptation of European styles to West Indian climates and customs and that "it was this adapted house which French West Indian planters brought to Louisiana."[40] Its most common features are the circular gallery supported by light wooden *colonnettes*, an asymmetrical arrangement of rooms, without interior hallways, French doors with louvered windows, broad-spreading roofs with dormers for ventilation, and small bricks between poles (*briquettes entre poteaux*) as the main construction technique.[41] The West Indian refugees were also often credited with the habit of raising the houses to avoid the consequences of flooding and other natural catastrophes. In short, they brought architectural techniques adapted to the climate, in particular to the scorching summer heat. Many examples of such houses may be seen in lower Louisiana, although some of them were built before the refugees' arrival. Ormond, Parlange, Rosedown, the Lacour House, Destrehan (built in the 1790s), with its West Indian style hip roof, or the Pitot House on Moss Street in New Orleans are definitely houses that might be seen in the Caribbean.[42] This is probably what led a traveler to Louisiana, in 1818, to comment on his visit to Pointe Coupée as follows: "One almost supposes himself in the West Indies."[43] There were already houses similar to those in late-eighteenth-century Louisiana.[44] Prior West Indian influences clearly existed, but they were reinforced by the refugees' arrival, and this West Indian style gained momentum in Louisiana, becoming one of the most obvious differences between this area of encounters and blending and the rest of the South.[45] Many Louisianans nowadays acknowledge the refugees' clear influences, which the development of tourism has tended to publicize. The Evangeline Commemorative Area Park in St. Martinsville, for instance, taking the example of Pierre Olivier du Clozel de Vezin in Evangeline in 1815, has a whole poster on French Creole architecture, detailing the various influences, especially the Caribbean one, which is listed as such: use of the first level for storage, second level for living space; placement of doors, windows for cross-ventilation; galleries; pier foundations; external stairways.

The origin of the Louisiana townhouse is another debated topic, although many specialists attribute it to the refugees.[46] The famous iron railings, of Spanish inspiration, are often said to have been built by skilled Saint-Domingan slaves, and Laffite's blacksmith shop is mentioned as one of the places where they were made.[47] Quite obviously, considering the occupational pattern of most of the free refugees of color and of some of the slaves from Saint-Domingue, they participated in the construction of those edifices and implemented the techniques they knew. Moreover, some famous Louisiana architects were originally from Saint-Domingue, like Arsène Lacarrière-Latour, who settled in New Orleans in 1808 and designed the project for the St. Philip Theater,[48] and the most famous of all, Joseph Pilié, who came from Saint-Domingue in the early nineteenth century (since he was a draftsman in New Orleans in 1808). He became the city surveyor of New Orleans, in which position he drew a tremendous number of maps, and he also designed and built several edifices in New Orleans.[49] He is even said to have designed the mansion of Oak Alley for his daughter, although the official credit is given to George Swaney. His son, Louis Henri, assisted his father and then became city surveyor. He is credited with building the iron gates of the Cabildo. The Pilié family even gave a third generation of town surveyors to New Orleans in the person of Edgar Germain Pilié, grandson and son of the two previous Piliés. That all those Saint-Domingans had means of transmitting their traditions and culture is indubitable. That there are clear traces of West Indian influence in the architecture of Louisiana is also obvious. It is, however, difficult to give absolute proof that they were the initiators of the trend, due to the anteriority of West Indian–style houses to the refugee movement, as proven by the ex-

Figure 5. Destrehan Plantation, Destrehan, La.

Figure 6. Pitot House, Moss Street, New Orleans.

amples of the Parlange plantation or Magnolia Mound in Baton Rouge. There are fields, however, where the prominence of the refugees and their influence are still more patent and easier to pinpoint.

The field of literature is one of those influenced by the refugees. Although the white refugees were slightly less dynamic in the literary field than in others, the free refugees of color were clearly more so. As for the slaves, they left their imprint on the oral literature of Louisiana, or what Antilleans call "oraliture."[50] Several refugees or refugee offspring contributed to nineteenth-century Louisianan literature. The poet Tullius St. Céran, for instance, was born in Jamaica of refugee parents in 1802 and came to New Orleans in 1805.[51] In his *Histoire Littéraire de l'Amérique Française* (Paris, 1954), Auguste Vialatte also attributes to the Saint-Domingan refugees the publication of the first book in Louisiana, a history of Louisiana written by Guy Soniat du Fossat. Louis Placide Canonge is another famous nineteenth-century Louisiana writer, the author of comedies as well as proverbs in verse and prose, which were performed under his direction in the literary salons of New Orleans. Besides being a leading collaborator of *L'Abeille*, he was "for half a century, the bright light of literature in New Orleans."[52] Other names are cited, like those of Edouard de Rossignol des Dunes de Poincy, Jean-Baptiste Sel, and François Mathurnin Guérin.[53] The free Creoles of color contributed still much more to Louisiana literature, including Louis Victor Séjour, Michel Séligny, Camille Thierry, and Armand Lanusse—who displayed uncommon dynamism in launching and coordinating the publication of *Les Cénelles* in 1845. No one questions their contribution, and they might indeed be classified among "the city's most celebrated Romantic literary artists."[54] Beyond the works they have left, they can be credited with a number of first-rate contributions to Louisiana culture. They launched the tradition of protest literature and spread both republican spirit and romanticism in Louisiana.[55] Their literature was definitely a committed one, and they contributed much to the tradition of interracial collaborations, for instance, in starting the literary magazine *L'Album littéraire: Journal des jeunes-gens, amateurs de littérature* in 1843. Armand Lanusse was among the creators of the journal and one of its most frequent contributors, together with Camille Thierry. The tradition of referring to a Saint-Domingan background was also one of their common features. To take but a single example, Séjour's most famous short story, "Le Mulâtre," published in 1837 by Cyril Bissette in his *Revue des Colonies*, takes place in Saint-Domingue and studies the complexities of the Saint-Domingan society. These artists and many others (for instance, Joseph Rousseau, who married one of

Colonel Savary's granddaughters and finally exiled himself to Haiti) deeply influenced the nineteenth-century New Orleans literary tradition.[56]

Slave oral literature, in the form of tales, is another area that requires more attention. Although there is a clear common substratum in all the French Creole areas, a closer proximity might be traced between Haiti and Louisiana. Chaudenson and Relouzat have worked much on comparative studies of Creole tales. Both conclude that some tales may be found in all the Creole societies. All of these tales display clear French origins (narrative process, stereotyped initial, interactive, and final formulas), to which were added traditional African tales and motives, as well as adaptations to the local context. In short, they represent perfect examples of the creolization process. By comparing tales in the West Indies, Louisiana, and Canada, Relouzat attempts to trace influences. And indeed he finds some common points between Saint-Domingue and Louisiana, which he attributes to the refugees' slaves. Among the common features is the hero's name, since Bouki (*Compère Bouki*) is found only in Haiti and Louisiana. Chaudenson notes the same feature, adding that in the rest of the French Caribbean, the same hero appears in the same tales under the names of Zamba or Léfau.[57] Studying the processes of stratification that occur in those tales, Relouzat concludes that this syncretism developed through a creolization that occurred in Haiti between French, Amerindian, and Fon cultures, thus attesting to the later importation of those tales into Louisiana by the slaves from Saint-Domingue. There is still much to do in oral literature, as well as in the fields of proverbs, of which some insights are given in Lafcadio Hearn's *"Gombo Zhèbes."* There appears to be a clear community of Creole proverbs, with proverbs that are often common to the whole circum-Caribbean and, most of the time, to France, although Hearn mostly disregards this proximity with the metropolitan culture. Some derive their similarity from the French tradition, others from African culture, but Hearn notes some proverbs that seem to be shared solely between Haiti and Louisiana.[58] He also shows that some Louisiana proverbs seem to refer to a geographical reality that is Haitian rather than Louisianan. Quoting, for instance, the proverb "Ratté mange canne, zanzoli mouri innocent," he writes that this proverb (which means "the rat eats the cane, the lizard dies innocent") clearly refers to the Saint-Domingan technique of burning the sugar cane before collecting it, to destroy the pests.[59] There was thus an obvious cultural continuum established between Saint-Domingue and lower Louisiana in the nineteenth century, in all the literary manifestations of the three racial groups of the Louisiana community.

A constant of the various refugee white and free people of color groups is also an unusual vitality, mixed with an uncommon degree of education. This is especially true for the free group of color in the South. If literature is a field strongly influenced by the refugees, music indeed seems another of their strongholds. And here again, the three communities gave musicians or made musical legacies to Louisiana, sometimes establishing links between black and white music. Haitian influences seem to have been very strong in the slaves' music, and the best laboratory that historians have found for the study of these influences is doubtlessly Congo Square, celebrated by all, from Cable to Hearn, as the best representation of slave music in nineteenth-century Louisiana. The square, which had existed for a long time and had served mainly as a marketplace in the eighteenth century, was revived in the nineteenth century, first by the presence of a circus, then progressively as the center for slave dancing. It became still more important after 1821, when the American authorities, in a vain attempt to prevent the expansion of voodoo, forbade slaves to gather and dance except in authorized open spaces on Sundays. Congo Square, at the intersection of the Vieux Carré and the Faubourg Trémé, thus became the vital core of slaves' musical tradition. When comparing the narrations that were made by the visitors and historians of Congo Square with what could be seen in Saint-Domingue before the revolution, it is obvious that many features are similar. Certain types of dances witnessed in Congo Square definitely had a Saint-Domingan background; the Calinda, the Chica, and the Bamboula are described in both geographical areas. Musical instruments also manifestly had come by way of the refugees, in particular the banza, the bamboula—a small drum made from bamboos in Saint-Domingue—and the marimba, described by Cable, derived from Saint-Domingue's Marimbula.[60] The dances on Congo Square are systematically associated with the influences of the Saint-Domingan slaves in Louisiana.[61] The cultural continuum between the West Indies and Louisiana becomes perceptible with the multiplication of narrations made by the Americans in the early American era. Until then, the visitors had not been shocked by what they saw there, since "most French and Spanish visitors to colonial New Orleans came by way of the Caribbean islands and would have viewed such dances . . . as too commonplace to deserve note."[62] In the early nineteenth century, the American visitors had a different background and were stunned by what they saw. Creolization, the process of mixing the various cultures (sometimes called *métissage*), shows that the blending of European, African, and West Indian traditions that was found in Congo Square made the Afro-Creole culture of New Orleans as unique

Figure 7. E. W. Kemble, "The Bamboula at Congo Square," from *Century*, April 1886. Courtesy of the Historic New Orleans Collection.

as later musical genres such as jazz music.[63] When studies are conducted on the words of some of the songs performed in Congo Square, clear references to Saint-Domingan folk songs appear.[64] In "Creole Slave Songs," Cable notes that the reference to high mountains in a song entitled "A Suzette" evokes the geography and topography of Saint-Domingue, not that of Louisiana, as was the case of the proverb noted by Hearn. Cable also explains "Calalou" with reference to Saint-Domingue (where Calalou was a ragout), before explaining its relexification in Louisiana as a term applying to the "quadroon" women who swarmed into New Orleans in 1809.[65]

Although it does not appear clearly in the rhythms and melodies, the link between slave and white music was established by Louis Moreau Gottschalk, the most famous nineteenth-century Louisiana composer. He was a descendant of refugees and the nephew of Louis Moreau Lislet, after whom he was named. Gottschalk's wish was to record the tradition of the Afro-Creole dances and music of Congo Square. His best known composition, released in Paris in 1848, was entitled "Bamboula." Although, contrary to what he proclaimed, the presence in his composition of the African rhythms he heard in Congo Square in his childhood is far from obvious, what is important to the present discussion is that it was his intention to record and spread them through his music. His "Danse des Nègres" is known for having "recorded the music of the West Indians."[66] He was also said to be "sensitive to the evidence and influence of Caribbean culture in his regions."[67] It is true that most of his compositions bear evocative titles: "Bamboula, Danse des Nègres," "La Vavanne, Ballade Créole," "Le Bananier, Chanson Nègre," or "Le Mancenillier, Ballade Créole." The last title, in particular, refers to a definite West Indian context, the tree mentioned (the manchineel) being alien to the Louisiana environment. As for his "Bananier," it is also said to have been inspired by a Creole song, "En avant Grenadier." In his *Notes of a Pianist*, Gottschalk himself narrates childhood memories of his grandmother telling him about Saint-Domingue and the revolution that sent her away from her native island. There is no doubt that he knew about Saint-Domingue and that these family records were essential to his intellectual formation. And eventually he established a link between white and black music through his Saint-Domingan connection.

Other Louisiana musicians and composers are also related to the refugee community, although not all of them connected black and white music in the way Gottschalk did or tried to do. Henri Fournier, although he was less renowned than Gottschalk, did integrate Haitian rhythms and sounds into his compositions.[68] Among the other famous musicians with Saint-Domingan origins was Gustave d'Aquin, a composer and flutist, who conducted at the French Opera House and was the music director of the Cotton Exposition in New Orleans in 1884. He composed orchestral pieces, masses, and even a symphony.[69] Louisiana could also take pride in having a number of free Creoles of color with Saint-Domingan connections among its musicians. The most famous was probably Edmond Dédé, born in 1827 of refugees of the 1809 wave, whose father had been a music director in the militia. He played the clarinet and was a violin prodigy. His compositions gained wide recognition in the musical world. There were other less known free composers of color. Desdunes dedicates a few pages to those musicians.[70] Constant Debergue, the conductor of the Philharmonic Society, may be cited here, as well as his son Eugene Arcade and also Samuel Snaër, whose family emigrated from Saint-Domingue to Cuba and then to Louisiana.[71] Surprisingly, the connection between their pieces and Saint-Domingan traditions is much less obvious than in the cases of Gottschalk and Fournier, to the point that Desdunes wonders why, "compared to the white Gottschalk, New Orleans black composers made so little use of local color."[72] In short, Louisiana music was marked in the nineteenth century by the Saint-Domingan immigrants, whites, free people of color, and slaves, whose obvious love for music transmitted West Indian cultural patterns to Louisiana. The originality of these musicians, beyond the West Indian rhythms and melodies they introduced, was the cultural continuum they created between black and white musical traditions, making New Orleans "the first American urban area to blend white and black art forms into a hybrid, one that subsequently engendered the most distinctive genre of American vernacular music and dance."[73]

There are other artistic forms where Saint-Domingan contributions—although more minor—can be found.[74] More important, the refugees, white and black, also left traces on the vernacular culture of lower Louisiana. Although the people of African descent apparently brought more specific Saint-Domingan traits to this vernacular culture, whites also played a significant part in the implantation and persistence of these traits. The fields of folk medicine, cookery, and clothing proved "osmotic," to use the notion Chaudenson applies to intercommunitarian features.[75] Although the slaves' folk medicine was originally African, Creole folk medicine, according to Chaudenson's study, later started following European modes of preparation and using local pharmacopeias. What the slaves from Saint-Domingue knew when they left the Caribbean island was the result of this long process of creolization, and there is little doubt that they introduced practices and remedies unknown to the Louisiana slaves.[76] Despite the same original African basis, creolization implies a mutation through adaptation to the environment, which means different inputs according to where the mutation occurred. This may be illustrated by the tradition of *ouanga* (sometimes spelled *Wanga*), the habit of wearing a pouch containing healing ingredients, a tradition of Dahomean origin used throughout the Caribbean, which partly entered directly with the importation of slaves from Dahomey, but which also came into Louisiana with the West Indian slaves.[77] Cookery is another closely related field, since it follows the same syncretic principle, where the African and European practices mix, borrowing from the local products.[78] In the case of cooking, all three racial groups were equally involved, since slaves, whites, and free Creoles of color cooked and since the tastes of all three communities had evolved in parallel in Saint-Domingue. The African cooks had adapted their traditions to the Caribbean environment (products, climatic conditions) and to the whites' tastes, which, in turn, evolved throughout the colonial period in Saint-Domingue. All categories of population took on the habit of consuming exotic, mostly spicy, and even hot food, a mix of imported and local products, prepared in specific ways.[79] Creole cuisine, defined as a mixing of influences, had been "created from the cultural memory of cooking in Africa combined with the acculturated tastes and ingredients from indigenous peoples in the Caribbean."[80] The refugees are credited with introducing into Louisiana a "new emphasis on the culinary arts," as they did on other forms of less prosaic arts.[81] What is certain is that many of them became pastry chefs when they reached Louisiana, and some opened restaurants (as did John Davis, where Creole food was served).[82] The Saint-Domingan community is said to have influenced the Louisianans into using certain spices unknown until then. Jambalaya and Mirliton are often said to be Louisiana dishes with clear Afro-Caribbean roots as are desserts containing bananas. The *filé* made from ground sassafras was popularized by white and black Saint-Domingans.[83] In cookery as in folk medicine, the refugees introduced elements that had emerged through creolization in Saint-Domingue.

Another topic of interest in matters of Louisiana vernacular culture is to determine whether the arrival of the Saint-Domingan refugees of all colors influenced the practices of Carnival, as was the case in other refuges.[84] Little has been written on this, except that the arrival of the refugees coincided with the expansion of masked balls and Carnival processions, which until then had been forbidden by the *Cabildo*. Under the Spanish regime, blacks were forbidden to wear masks and attend night balls. Although the first reference to a Carnival in Louisiana dates back to 1781, the practice gained momentum when the refugees reached Louisiana.[85] The definite part they played in this development remains to be fully assessed. In general, however, the *métissage* that the manifestations of Carnival display along the Gulf Coast is acknowledged. It is said to represent "a syncretism of French/Spanish, Native American, and African/Afro-Caribbean performance style and structures."[86] As in many of the specific Louisiana cultural manifestations, this Afro-Caribbean influence is thus underlined and undoubtedly comes from the numerous Saint-Domingan immigrants. Specific studies of New Orleans's pre-Lenten Carnival conclude that its "celebrations are variations of Afro-Caribbean festivals that underwent further creolization in North America. Mardi Gras combines the European, African, and Caribbean influences of West Indian festivals and their variants and, like a tasty Callaloo, adds more spicy ingredients from another continent."[87] The black Indian parades performed in New Orleans obviously borrow from Native mythology, although "their performance style is essentially Afro-Caribbean, as expressed in competitive dance and song and the call-and-response chants that mark their foot parades."[88] There is also a clear proximity between the Cajun and Black Creole Mardi Gras songs, but the latter follow the call-and-response pattern, typical of Afro-Caribbean influences. The Carnival thus seems to display, in a similarly creolized way, strong links with the Caribbean traditions.[89]

The refugees also seem to have strongly influenced clothing fashions. According to all accounts, they dressed differently, often more elaborately and luxuriously, using embroidery, lace, and finer material.[90] Because many of them worked as tailors, seamstresses, or embroiderers, they passed their fashions onto Louisiana society. The refugees of color actively participated in this movement. They were also said to dress elaborately. As in most other areas examined until now, a clear creolization seems to have occurred in Saint-Domingue, where the inhabitants had mixed European, African, even Amerindian fashions and adapted their clothing to the climate by choosing lighter materials. They were dressed in bright colors, as all the descriptions by foreign travelers attest, they usually superposed layers of clothes, and their hair was often tied up in a handkerchief of bright colors, often in Madras.[91] What they called "*coiffe calendée*" was one of those *tignons* of Madras, in which yellow color had been applied manually. It is found in many descriptions of both late-eighteenth-century Saint-Domingue and early-nineteenth-century Louisiana.[92] Even white women sometimes took to wearing the colorful *tignons*. It has become common to acknowledge these influences. To give but a single example, the catalog of a 2003 exhibition dedicated to the Louisiana Purchase bicentennial, commenting on the painting of a free woman of color by François Fleischbein in 1837, reads that her hairdo is in the Caribbean fashion, which means that she is free.[93] More research remains to be conducted on the influence of the refugees in the field of fashion, furniture, or objects useful for the Louisianans' daily life.[94]

There is little doubt that many aspects of the vernacular culture of early-nineteenth-century Louisiana bore the mark of the refugees, as did, for instance, the religious environment of Louisiana. The refugees reinforced the Catholic community at a time when Anglo-Saxon Protestantism was threatening to supplant it. The refugees' influence inflected the racial practices of the Church toward a better integration of the racial communities, and Church records display an equal treatment of whites and free people of color in matters of sacraments. The Louisiana Catholic Church also adopted a lenient policy toward Freemasonry. Beyond this official religion which they did influence, the communities of African descent—free or slave—are also credited with introducing the voodoo cult in Louisiana. This field is much more extensively documented than any of the others mentioned in this chapter. Voodoo, as it existed in Saint-Domingue, was a syncretic religion, born from the mixture of African (especially Dahomean) and Catholic religions. Both in the beliefs (with correspondences, for instance, between the African Loas and the Catholic saints, and influences from Fon or Congo beliefs) and in the practices (African trances, animal sacrifices as in the Fon culture, but also minuets borrowed from the French court, military marches, and Catholic prayers), voodoo was an experiment in creolization in Saint-Domingue.[95] There are several explanations for the swift development of voodoo in Saint-Domingue. The relative leniency of the French Catholic masters and clergy, the wide disproportion of the slaves to whites, which prevented the masters from exerting tight control over their slaves, the adaptability of the Bantou slaves who had understood that cultural resistance would be detrimental and thus tried to conform to the Catholic model, and the easy adaptation of the Bantou cult of ancestors to the Catholic rites, among many other reasons, account for the emergence of voodoo that Herskovits calls "reinterpretation," that is, an interpretation by the slaves of Catholicism through their own practices and traditions.[96] No one contests that voodoo really bloomed in Louisiana thanks to the presence of the refugees of African descent, free and slave.[97] Even the historians who support the thesis of a natural development of voodoo in Louisiana with direct African influences, before the arrival of the refugees, recognize that the arrival of Saint-Domingan slaves reinforced the cult and introduced Saint-Domingan elements into Louisiana practices.[98] What might be asserted as a middle term between this thesis and that of the refugees' predominant role is that there were African beliefs and religious manifestations before the refugees' arrival but that the organized large-scale Afro-Catholic cult is imputable to the Saint-Domingan people of pure or mixed African descent.[99]

A study of voodoo in Louisiana clearly shows numerous connections with the Saint-Domingan community. Most of the important figures of New Orleans voodoo had refugee origins, like Dr. John.[100] The most celebrated voodoo queens, for example, Sanité Dédé and the two Marie Laveaus (mother and daughter), were connected with Saint-Domingue. In the case of Sanité Dédé, the origins are direct and doubtless.[101] In the case of Marie Laveau, the lineage is slightly more complex. Some historians have given her Saint-Domingan origins.[102] This is not proved for the first Marie Laveau, but is obviously true for her daughter. Since history has blurred the line between the two (the substitution of one for the other having occurred in an unpublicized way, detectable only through the age granted to Marie Laveau in descriptions posterior to 1850), there tends to be, in many people's minds, only one queen who reigned over New Orleans for more than eighty years.[103] What remains is that if the first Marie Laveau had no proven blood connections with Saint-Domingue, her husband, Jacques Paris, is said to have been born in Jérémie in Saint-Domingue.[104] Once widowed, she had fifteen children with her companion (some say husband), Louis Christophe Duminy de Glapion, also a *quarteron* from Saint-Domingue and a veteran of the d'Aquin/Savary battalion during the Battle of New Orleans.[105] Their daughter Marie, born in 1827, was thus indisputably of Saint-Domingan origins, even if her mother was not, which is not yet absolutely proved. The connections between Saint-Domingue and New Orleans's voodoo leaders are—whether true or slightly exaggerated—indubitable.

When comparing the voodoo cult as it was described by eyewitnesses in Saint-Domingue and New Orleans, there are also many common features.[106] The cult of the dead and the worshipping of the snake are common to Saint-Domingue and Louisiana voodoo. The dances described in Saint-Domingan ceremonies as in Congo Square (later Bayou Road, then on Lake Pontchartrain) are the same: Calenda, Chica, Danse à Don Pedre, to the sound of banzas and bamboulas. Although most historians insist on the originality of the matriarchal structure of Louisiana voodoo (with queens always in the forefront, present at all ceremonies and at Congo Square every Sunday), many testimonies of voodoo ceremonies in Saint-Domingue acknowledge the same prominent presence of priestesses.[107] The invocations and incantations described by Moreau de Saint-Méry for Saint-Domingue and by Henry Castellanos for New Orleans are the same: "L'appé vini, le gran Zombi, L'appé vini pou fai gri-gri" as well as the song "Eh Bomba! Heu! Heu! Canga Bafie te, Danga moune de le, Canga do ki la, Canga li" are common to the two cults and were probably imported.[108] The main difference undergone by voodoo when it crossed the Gulf of Mexico is that it became a transcommunity feature, a characteristic most certainly due to the very specific conditions of the migration and relocation.[109] Voodoo had been a cult reserved for the slaves in Saint-Domingue. In Louisiana, both slaves and free Creoles of color actively practiced it. The voodoo queens were free women of color, and the free community of color was present at the ceremonies, whether at Congo Square, on Bayou Road, or on the shore of Lake Pontchartrain. The salient feature of Louisiana voodoo, however, is that most descriptions of ceremonies there refer to the presence of white women. Moreover, the white Creole society had, from the start, been involved in voodoo magic, and it is said that the first Marie Laveau started practicing voodoo magic when she went to white people's houses as a hairdresser, long before she became voodoo queen. This is in total opposition to the Saint-Domingan voodoo, which was clearly reserved for slaves and from which whites were obviously excluded. This involvement of whites in Louisiana voodoo gives "further evidence of the enormous impact of the Afro-Creole folk religion on the Creolized culture of New Orleans,"[110] as well as of the tendency displayed by the Saint-Domingan refugee community to develop common cultural features. The Saint-Domingan refugees, as in many other cultural areas, thus vitalized the practice of voodoo in New Orleans, widely influenced it, and made it a common cross-ethnic cultural feature. They strongly influenced the creolization process that gave Louisiana distinctive features in nineteenth-century America, features that have persisted, to a certain extent, to the present.

## Linguistic and Cultural Heritage

The cultural legacy of the refugee community was indeed very strong both in the maintenance of French culture and in the creolization of Louisiana culture, starting with the languages spoken in nineteenth-century Louisiana. By an input of a few thousand French speakers, at a time when both the migration to Louisiana of numerous English speakers and the inclusion of the territory within the United States jeopardized the survival of the French language, the migration from Saint-Domingue favored the persistence of French for at least two generations. French remained the language of the proceedings of two of the three municipalities of New Orleans, legal documents of New Orleans (as shown by the precedent of the Civil Code), the Catholic Church, and most of the life in downtown New Orleans. The newspapers and schools founded by the refugees undoubtedly favored the transmission of the language. Without this input, the struggle against Americanization fought by the Creole community would have been lost very rapidly.

The Saint-Domingan migration also reinforced the use of the Creole language. Although some historians have attributed to the refugees the development of the Creole language in Louisiana, there seems to be no doubt nowadays that this is wrong and that a specific Creole language predated the arrival of the refugees.[111] Current theses maintain (as in the case of voodoo) that some middle term might be considered, and that Louisiana records prior to 1790 display "a pidginized form of French rather than a proper Creole."[112] The refugees then might have contributed to the completion of the elaborate form of Creole language in existence in Louisiana in the nineteenth century.

Whatever the general assessment might be, there are clear signs that the arrival of several thousand Creole speakers, slaves, free people of color, and whites indeed vitalized the practice of Creole and also influenced specific areas of its lexicon and syntax.

The refugees' legacy in this field leaves no doubt. The pioneer historians in matters of Creole language—Cable, Mercier, Fortier, and Harrison—wrote in the 1880s that there was no doubt that the refugees had created Louisiana Creole.[113] Showing both an absolute certitude in the refugees' founding role and rudimentary notions of creolistics, Cable wrote, "The African slave in Louisiana—or, it may be more correct to say, in St. Domingo before coming to Louisiana—corrupted the French tongue . . . grossly."[114] Present-day historians studying the community of the Creoles of color sometimes forget to acknowledge the presence of the Saint-Domingan refugees. They never forget, however, to mention their role in ensuring the development of the Creole language.[115] If there is no doubt about the role they played, at least numerically, it is more difficult to ascertain their legacy on the structures of the language itself. To do so, it is necessary to compare the two languages in the forms they had at the time. It is not possible to use present forms of the languages, since they have experienced significantly opposed altering processes. While Louisiana Creole has been de-creolized through prolonged contact with French, Cajun, and English, the Haitian Creole has re-creolized for lack of strong contacts with new inputs of population. To compare, it is thus necessary to use transcriptions of early-nineteenth-century Creole languages, which are naturally rare.[116] Moreover, creolistics is a recent discipline, and there are still controversies regarding the origins and development of Creole languages, which means that similarities in the Saint-Domingue and Louisiana Creoles might derive from a parallel evolution, without necessarily involving direct influences.[117] Taking into account, however, the fact that several thousand speakers of the Creole language were added to the Louisiana population, an absence of reciprocal influences between the two Creole-speaking populations seems unimaginable. And there are, indeed, traces of the Saint-Domingan Creole language in Louisiana.

The syntax and conjugation used in Saint-Domingue and Louisiana manifestly contain similarities which the two languages share with no other Creole language of the French-speaking Caribbean area. The two languages share a preverbal anterior marker *te,* used when anteriority cannot be deduced from the context. They also have in common a prospective marker *ava* (displayed by no other Antillean Creole, which use only *a* or *va*) which is an emphatic form generally used after a contraction, as well as a continuous form *ap* or *apé* (*ka* in the rest of the French Caribbean). Thus *m'ap manjé* means "I am eating" in Saint-Domingue, and *l'ap dansé* means "he is dancing" in Louisiana, to cite the most often used example. Similarly, *l'ava manjé* in Saint-Domingan Creole means "he will eat" and *m'ava protégé toi* means "I will protect you" in Louisiana. Combinations of these markers can also be found, *te* combined with *a* (short form from *ava*). In this case, anterior and prospective markers are used to express a conditional form in both Creoles. Finally, the particles *fin* and *fek* seem to be common to the two Creoles, introducing a nuance of completion.[118] Alcée Fortier, quoting Alfred Mercier, also ascribes to the refugees the introduction of a dative form, although its usage seems to be rare in Louisiana, the two most often quoted examples of it being *zié a moin* (my eyes) and *tchor a li* (his heart).[119] Finally, the two Creole languages share a possessive form *ken/kin,* which some linguists explain by the influence of the Spanish *quien*. These similar forms, unknown to the other Caribbean Creoles, seem to attest to a clear influence from the Saint-Domingan refugees on the Louisiana Creole. There are also sounds and words that may have transited through Saint-Domingue before reaching Louisiana, although there are some dissensions on the topic.

Some creolists, for instance, indicate the absence, in the two Creoles considered, of two affricates found in all the other Creoles of the French West Indies (c and j).[120] Many words connected to voodoo are common to the two languages: *bamboula, Calinda, Candjo* (a Creole black considered a leader by the slave community), *koujail* (dance), *gri-gri* (or its equivalent, *conja*), *wanga*, and *zombi*.[121] The same is true of words linked with food—*cala* (a rice cake), *tafia, jambalaya, gombo,* and *couche-couche*. The debate, however, is whether these words of African origin came directly to Saint-Domingue and Louisiana or if they transited by Saint-Domingue before reaching Louisiana. There is no scientific evidence to support either thesis, except for the occurrence of the word *gri-gri* noted by Gwendolyn Hall in judicial records in 1773. Nothing proves that the word might not have been introduced in Louisiana by slaves purchased from the West Indies. What appears is that the regular use of these words (as the development of voodoo and Creole cuisine) is concomitant with the arrival of the Saint-Domingan refugees.[122] Whatever the degree of influence exerted by the Saint-Domingan white and black refugees on the Creole language of Louisiana, they added to the number of creolophones and most certainly transmitted words, sounds, and structures to their Louisiana peers. They also, as in the other fields, tended to spread the tradition of using the Creole language on a multiethnic basis.

The whole community seems to have influenced the culture of its host society in many ways, introducing new elements, altering current practices, and blurring the racial limits in matters of culture, religion, and language. The refugees permitted a stronger implantation of the French-Creole culture and enabled this French-Creole continuum to persist at least until the late nineteenth century (as the literary and political achievements of the descendants of free refugee of color show). Their legacy was both to the French cultural tradition of Louisiana and to the Creole culture of Louisiana.[123] They ensured the persistence of the French language and culture (through the newspapers, schools, and theaters, for instance) and that of a Creole culture that became specific to Louisiana (through the Creole language, voodoo, and all the various aspects of vernacular culture), recalling that the refugee boats were shared by those who introduced French opera and those who introduced voodoo into the United States.[124] This is why it is much more appropriate not to differentiate the various inputs and to consider the role that the refugees community as a whole played in the cultural construction of nineteenth-century Louisiana. When discussing the use of the word *Creole*—sometimes used to designate the whites born in the colonies (West Indian tradition), sometimes used to designate the people of color—Chaudenson shows that, in New Orleans, the two meanings have always coexisted. For him, the tradition of calling the free people of color Creole originated in Louisiana, while its use to designate the white community was imported to Louisiana by the refugees.[125] This obviously denotes persisting Caribbean and Afro-Caribbean traditions in Louisiana.

The notion that probably applies best to the kind of cultural continuum the refugees bequeathed to Louisiana is that of creolization. A simplistic definition of this process would be that of a cultural confrontation between various populations, followed by a syncretization accompanied by an adaptation to the milieu in which this confrontation/mixture occurs. It generally involves "linguistic, religious, cultural, culinary, architectural, medical, etc., practices of the different people in question."[126] Brathwaite and Hall have given slightly more restrictive definitions considering that it was "a sociocultural continuum radiating outward from the slave community and affecting the entire culture in varying degrees."[127] This definition is relatively more specific than those given by most historians of Creole cultures—notably those of the Caribbean—because it makes the slaves the center, but it introduces the notions of cultural continuum and of large-scale influence on the society. The result of creolization, whatever the definition considered, is the creation of a new cultural identity that, in the end, has little to do with each of the original ones, and displays obvious differences from other parallel creolizations occurring in different places. There is no doubt that a creolization process had started long before the arrival of the refugee community in lower Louisiana, with the prolonged confrontation and adaptations of Native American, African, French, and Spanish cultures. The refugees, however, carried with them a whole new process of creolization that had occurred in their West Indian home, involving similar cultural bases, with variations due to the specificity of the Caribbean natives and to the confrontation with a different milieu. What the refugees brought with them thus displayed a different mode of adaptation, what might be called "their Caribbean brand of French culture."[128] The two Creole cultures mixed, as has been amply demonstrated in matters of language, religion, cookery, clothing, music, and vernacular culture in general. The refugee input thus revitalized the creolization process and introduced new elements into it. This second creolization, the sum of two anterior ones, conferred features that still give New Orleans a distinctively different flavor within the mainstream American culture.

It is difficult to assess the long-term legacy of the Saint-Domingan community, since the cultural continuum has never ceased to blur the different influences that have interplayed in Louisiana. In the late nineteenth century, Cable was still mentioning "the West Indian softness that had crept into" the New Orleans Creoles' pronunciation.[129] Desdunes, speaking of Emile Desdunes, wrote that "he had been born in New Orleans and was Haitian by education and custom," although he does not explain what this means exactly.[130] New Orleans gained the status of "Creole capital," a status which had much to do with the role of the refugees, white and black, free and slave, who came to Louisiana at the turn of the nineteenth century.[131] By mixing, through intermarriage, with the Creole population of New Orleans, they spread their cultural traits to the whole society. By having a still more relaxed position on interracial relationships, by including members of the other racial groups in their ventures, they participated in the creation of this strong continuum that characterizes the Louisiana culture. There were whites who practiced voodoo, there were black Freemasons, there were Freemasons in the Catholic Church, and architectural creation was a common enterprise. All these features that are very specific to Louisiana in nineteenth-century America may be in large part attributed to the refugees.

The notion of community is essential in the discussion. In many fields, all the members of the Saint-Domingan community had a part to play. Even in voodoo, which is generally considered a single-community feature (that is to say, not transcultural), Louisiana mingled the racial groups in a cultural continuum hardly found anywhere else. Religion, the field which Chaudenson describes as "non-osmotic" became "osmotic" (common to all the groups) in Louisiana after the arrival of the refugees. The tradition might come from the refugees themselves, who identified culturally with each other because of the circumstances of their flight and settlement; it might come from the porosity of the Louisiana society itself; or it might come from both. What remains is that a definitely original culture was then created, in which the Caribbean elements are still perceptible today. The celebration of Mardi Gras displays obvious signs of this persistence of Afro-Creole signs in Louisiana. The Creole speakers of today are often associated with the Saint-Domingan community. The various forms of original music that have emerged in Louisiana, from Congo Square to jazz music and zydeco, are always strongly related to the Caribbean influences brought from Saint-Domingue. Historians often make the dances at Congo Square the ancestors of jazz, some even asserting that "the influence of refugee descendants in the prosography of jazz is unmistakable."[132] Zydeco is always described as a mixture of Cajun, Afro-American, and Afro-Caribbean influences, the latter expressed more particularly in the rhythmic complexity of this musical style.[133] Zydeco might well be the best illustration of creolization in Louisiana, since it was born from a very specific contact and has absolutely no equivalent elsewhere.

The arrival of the Saint-Domingan community thus had a threefold effect on the Louisiana culture. The mere numerical increase the refugees made to the Gallic population ensured the persistence of the French culture and language. Their situation had given them more obstinacy in protecting their own cultural origins. Their arrival was also essential to the preservation of Gallic culture in New Orleans because they were culturally more "French" than the Louisianans who had probably already started acculturating after several years of contact with the Spaniards and the Americans.[134] Newspapers, schools, legislation, social groupings—all those fields to which the refugees contributed or which they initiated—ensured that persistence. They undoubtedly delayed the de-culturation process inaugurated by the Louisiana Purchase. They also revitalized the Creole culture of Louisiana, re-creolizing such fields as music, language, and vernacular culture in general. Finally they marked Louisiana in a special way, enabling the Louisiana culture to remain different for over two centuries after their arrival. The Saint-Domingan immigrants are said to have introduced into Louisiana a "romantic touch," as well as specific linguistic, culinary, religious, musical, literary influences still perceptible today. There is no doubt that they participated in the shaping of Louisiana's exceptionalism in today's America.

# Conclusion

Historiography has long neglected the migration that led several thousands of whites, free people of color, and slaves from French Saint-Domingue to Louisiana at the turn of the nineteenth century. Due to attention given to the Louisiana Purchase, this historical fact has long been buried in oblivion. Because more important events were occurring in Louisiana, because the Creoles were starting the longest and hardest fight in their history against acculturation, because the refugees integrated quite well into the Louisiana community, there have been few reasons for any special interest in the migrants. Because the history of migrations has experienced renewed interest in the twentieth century, however, and because relationships in the transatlantic world have aroused interest in population movements, the Saint-Domingan migration has recently surfaced. There is no doubt that the bicentennials of the Louisiana Purchase and of Haitian independence have also contributed to this renewed interest.

The present volume is still a work in progress. It is aimed at global assessment of all the various influences of the Saint-Domingan refugee community on Louisiana. I hope that this work will fuel the interest of historians. The work that remains to be done is tremendous, but there is now evidence of the importance of the migration. Its unprecedented magnitude in a short period is the first interesting feature that emerges from the previous study. The peculiar conditions of departure, migration, and relocation of the group are another. The exceptional vitality of Saint-Domingue in the late eighteenth century gave the migrants a powerful background economically, politically, and culturally. The difficult conditions under which they all migrated as well as the feeling of relative estrangement they had when they reached Louisiana led them to weave intricate links among themselves, regardless of social or racial status. That they were a community in certain specific ways reinforced their potential for exerting strong influences. That they found, on reaching their new home, a society that was close to theirs, permitted their easier integration into Louisiana life. That they, together with the Louisiana Creoles of all colors, built a Gallic stronghold against the indefatigable attempts of the new American owners at imposing their own social, racial, political, legal, economic, and cultural patterns was another factor in their assimilation within the French-speaking community and their development of vital integration strategies.

They undoubtedly contributed to the shaping of nineteenth-century Louisiana. They participated in the reinforcement of certain sectors and launched new economic trends. They contributed to the development of the sugar industry. They inaugurated new fields, such as education, the press, or cultural entertainments. They added to the artisan class in New Orleans. They brought much to medical science, clothes and furniture making, and architecture.

Their social contributions were numerous. They reinforced the numerical proportion of free people of color in New Orleans as well as the Catholic community at a time when it could have been overwhelmed by the Protestant Anglo-American immigration. Their political role in Louisiana was also essential. They contributed to the organization of the institutions, legal system, and political life of the early American era. They shaped activism and provided active leaders to the white and free Creole communities. Either by direct influence or through the indirect testimonies they provided of their past, the slaves from Saint-Domingue participated in several rebellious movements aimed at destroying the institution of slavery. The presence of the flesh and blood victims of the revolution in Saint-Domingue, as well as the narratives of their misfortunes, inflected the pro-slavery argument in Louisiana and in the South at large. The feats of the revolutionary heroes, as well as the testimonies of the free people of color, fueled the abolitionist theses. St. Domingue refugees were to be found in all areas of Louisiana politics, and their Saint-Domingan influence spread throughout the United States. Long after the refugees themselves had died, their offspring still obviously shaped Louisiana political life, as the uncommon vitality of the Creoles of color of refugee descent proves in the fight against segregation, both during and after Reconstruction. They were active and often successful, although their successes were sometimes shattered by national politics.

The refugees did much to develop the cultural level of Louisiana, through the importation of the press, the opera, the theater, and through the invaluable contributions they made to the educational structures in Louisiana in addition to opening the first college there. They also brought many specific Afro-Caribbean features to Louisiana. From literature to music, dancing, architecture, and language, they contributed new elements. They also left their mark on vernacular culture in general, introducing new fashions in cooking and clothing, new medicines, new traditions. They gave birth to an organized voodoo cult, influenced the Creole language, and introduced new practices in the Carnival celebrations. They enabled the persistence of French culture for much longer by actively participating in the fight against Americanization alongside Louisiana Creoles of all colors. Some say that this influence only lasted until the mid-nineteenth century, but there is clear evidence that the Creoles of color, for instance, still wrote in French until well after the end of the Reconstruction, as the example of Desdunes proves. Saint-Domingan refugees also ensured the vitality of the Creole culture, earning New Orleans the title of Creole capital. They inflected this Creole culture in ways that are traceable to the present, as proved by the clear Afro-Caribbean influences perceptible in the Mardi Gras processions and in original musical genres such as zydeco. The influences are probably still farther ranging. A recent commentary written about Ulrick Jean-Pierre, a Haitian-born painter who lives in Louisiana and pictures in his work the Haitian and Louisianan histories in symbiosis, reads that "the creolization of Indian, African, Spanish and French cultural traditions emerged in part as a result of the influence of the free African Haitians in Louisiana," thus acknowledging the Saint-Domingan/Haiti legacy on the Louisiana cultural vitality.[1]

What has emerged from this study, beyond the recording of the refugees' various areas of influence and assessment of those influences, is the cultural continuum that existed in the refugee community as well as evidence of the creolization that occurred in nineteenth-century Louisiana. Ever since they began to deal with Louisiana culture, historians have displayed an obvious tendency to study the racial groups separately. Nineteenth-century historians had a linear interest that lay with the white community, as amply demonstrated by the violent reactions of Charles Gayarré or Grace King to George Washington Cable's new interest in the free community of color.[2] Since Cable's attempt to restore a certain balance by granting attention to what had remained until then a secondary community in the history of New Orleans, the twentieth-century tendency has been to conduct equal but separate historical studies of the three racial groups.[3] This has largely affected the reflection of the historians on the refugees from Saint-Domingue. The slaves' influences are present in Gwendolyn Hall's studies, for instance, whereas Caryn Cossé Bell's focus is almost solely on the free community of color.[4] It seems that examining the various influences of the three groups together is new in the studies bearing on this community. The interest of this method is that it gives more comprehensive results and a better view of the extent of the influences the migration had in Louisiana. It is true that some fields were more influenced by one group. The white refugees were undoubtedly more involved in the press or in cultural entertainment. The Creoles of color did more in late-nineteenth-century politics or in literature. The slaves were more influential in revitalizing the Creole language. The people of African descent—free and slave—brought more to the development of voodoo in Louisiana. Free people of color, however, were actors and musicians as well and wrote for the newspapers of the early nineteenth century. White people participated in voodoo celebrations and went to voodoo doctors or queens for medicine and magic. All three communities spoke Creole. In some fields, like clothing, cooking, architecture, and medicine, all three communities participated. In others, like music, for instance, the refugees attempted to bridge the cultural gaps between the various racial communities. To quote but one, Gottschalk purposefully created a continuum by trying to include the tunes and words of Congo Square in his compositions. Whether this was a pious wish or a reality, the very fact that he claimed this heritage is a sign of the uncommon cultural symbiosis that existed between all the refugees, much more so than in the Louisiana Creole society. Considering the three groups together also gives a much better view of what each of them brought to Louisiana and what incredible influence they had when taken together.

If there is doubt as to their large-scale and long-ranging influence, it is because this influence is sometimes difficult to document. While their visibility in some fields is easily seen, the detail of the influences is sometimes harder to establish. It is, for instance, almost impossible to prove (or disprove) that some parallel influences were not exerted by slaves directly imported from Africa or by slaves imported earlier—during the colonial period—by way of the Caribbean. In matters of folk culture, cooking, or vernacular medicine, in matters of Creole language and voodoo, for instance, original influences seem difficult to pinpoint with absolute certainty.[5] The same could be said about architecture, where different theses arise concerning the origins of the shotgun house and where Caribbean-style Creole cottages seem to have slightly predated the arrival of the refugees.

Documentation is rare in certain areas of society. Not enough is known about the slaves, for instance, and there are few direct testimonies by slaves. Except at trials and through oral literature, it is difficult to find a source on the slave community that is not white. There is also still much to discover in the huge archival material available in Louisiana. The notarial files and books of wills still hold many treasures. Moreover, the Saint-Domingan origins of Louisianans are difficult to assess in many cases, especially after the second generation. The genealogical checking is painstaking and does not necessarily give convincing results. For these reasons, many suppositions still require documentary evidence. In several cases, although there is, among the small team of researchers interested in the topic, a general feeling that some persons might be descended from refugees, especially among the free people of color, names have been left out of this study for lack of documentation of their origins. Research progresses constantly, and new findings may bring novel elements to our perception of the way the creolization process occurred and of the direct input each community brought to this process.[6] Finally, the historiographical gap is difficult to fill, since so much has been written about these refugees without any mention of their origins. The ignorance of their origins, based on the original obliteration by the first historians of Louisiana, is still common. Many articles or books discuss the importance of some artistic figures without noting their link with the refugee community.[7] There is still reluctance in the official versions of Louisiana's history to "map the past connections between the Gulf Coast and the adjacent islands or the common populations, cultures, traditions—the civilization—they share."

It might be believed that "Louisiana's history awaits a general reinterpretation that transcends the confines of national boundaries."[8] This is what all scholars interested in the refugee movement are trying to do. A way to improve our knowledge of this migration—and of Louisiana—would be to conduct a wide-ranging comparative study of the different territories where the refugees settled. It could partly confirm some assumptions that have been made concerning the influences of the Saint-Domingan refugees on Louisiana. Finding certain common features introduced in several refuges would verify their participation. The common features would also permit firmer conclusions on the integration strategies of the refugees, on the specific features of the group, on what they carried with them as opposed to what they created when confronted with a new environment. On the other hand, manifest differences would teach much about the Louisiana society at the time of their arrival, about its capacity for absorption, about the osmotic character of its cultural features, as well as the porosity it displayed. What makes the study still more challenging is the wide diversity of situations encountered by the refugee diaspora. A broad comparative study would include a totally French culture (for those who returned to metropolitan France); an Anglo-Saxon, Protestant environment, free of the institution of slavery (for those who settled in the northeastern United States); a Catholic, English-speaking environment with slavery for Maryland; a Protestant, English-speaking slave society (in Virginia, the Carolinas, or Georgia, despite the delusory presence of a potentially francophone Huguenot community in Charleston); Spanish Caribbean societies, in other words Creole societies with slavery and Catholicism but a different linguistic environment (Cuba and Puerto Rico); Dutch or English colonial societies, where the only common features with Saint-Domingue were a high degree of creolization and the existence of slavery, but where language, religion, and culture were different (Jamaica, Trinidad, or Curaçao). Such a study would probably teach much about the creolization processes in general, about the way the refugees had been creolized by their life in their Saint-Domingue and about the consequences of contact with other differently creolized (or noncreolized) societies. It would enable interesting conclusions about two-way acculturation (that is, when the host society and the migrant community influence each other). It would probably also yield stimulating conclusions about migratory processes in general, in particular the respective roles of the society the migrants come from, of the conditions of migration, and of the role of the host society and culture. This comparative study, which requires much work from many, remains to be conducted.

# Notes

## Introduction

1. Brasseaux and Conrad in *The Road to Louisiana*, x. These figures will be clarified in chapter 2.

2. François-Xavier Martin, e.g., dedicated five lines to the migration in his 1882 *History of Louisiana from the Earliest Period* (346). Henry E. Chambers did not even mention it in his 1925 *History of Louisiana*, while Alcée Fortier, in his comprehensive five-volume 1904 *History of Louisiana*, devoted a single page to the migration (3:60). Even as late as 1957, when Albert E. Fossier wrote *The New Orleans Glamour Period*, he only mentioned the refugees when dealing with the creation of the College d'Orléans. He devoted one paragraph, full of historical imprecision, to the 1908 Cuban migration of Cubans, but mentioned them in none of the fields they heavily influenced, such as the theater and the press. See chapters entitled "Theatre" (467–85), "The Judiciary and the Bar" (143–60), "The Fourth Estate" (175–92), and "Slaves and Free Persons of Color" (366–80) as evidence of total neglect of the main protagonists' origins. Two brief mentions are to be found in "The Heterogeneous Population of New Orleans" (257) and "The Progress of Education in Louisiana" (230).

3. French historians also neglected this significant historical event, an omission that may be attributed partly to their diminished interest in a territory that was no longer a French possession. As for historians whose interest lay in Saint-Domingue, they were more attracted to the tragic events on the island than to the fate of those who fled from it. Among many others, see Haitian historians Thomas Madiou and Gérard Laurent.

4. In 1901, George Washington Cable, in his *Creoles of Louisiana*, devoted chapter 23 to the refugees, but he simply stated some facts of their arrival (156–60). In 1905, Luis M. Perez dedicated a short article to the 1809 migration, calling attention to the refugee movement and giving excerpts from the abundant official primary sources, especially W.C.C. Claiborne's correspondence at the time of the influx. Perez himself concludes that his article "will supplement the account and the documents quoted in Gayarré's History of Louisiana 214–219," adding that "there appears to be nothing else written on the subject" (296).

5. See, e.g., Cable's *Old Creole Days*, "Café des Exilés," 85–117.

6. Debien and Le Gardeur studied official documents and personal correspondence from the refugees, yielding a profuse series of publications. Le Gardeur did much of the pioneering work on the Saint-Domingue refugees in Louisiana. As for Debien, he thoroughly researched the refugees' routes, following them in most of their asylums. See Debien's "Réfugiés de Saint-Domingue aux Etats-Unis" and "The Saint-Domingue Refugees in Cuba, 1793–1815"; Debien and Wright's "Les Colons de Saint-Domingue passés à la Jamaïque (1792–1835)"; and Debien and Le Gardeur's "Saint-Domingue

Refugees in Louisiana, 1792–1804." Also see manuscript letter from René Le Gardeur to Gabriel Debien, 2 November 1970 (Tulane University, New Orleans, Louisiana Collection, M 561).

7. In 1950, Gabriel Debien indicated that he was exploring an immense field of research but that his intention was merely to call the attention of American (and more specifically Louisianan) historians to the topic. Debien, "Réfugiés de Saint-Domingue aux Etats-Unis," 4.

8. To use Fiehrer's expression in "From La Tortue to La Louisiane: An Unfathomed Legacy." See also Fiehrer, "The African Presence in Colonial Louisiana," as well as Paul Lachance's "The 1809 Immigration," "Intermarriage and French Cultural Persistence," and "Were Saint-Domingue Refugees a Distinctive Cultural Group in Antebellum New Orleans?"

9. Brasseaux and Conrad, *Road to Louisiana*, vii. This book contains Fiehrer's "From La Tortue to La Louisiane," Lachance's "The 1809 Immigration," Debien's "The Saint-Domingue Refugees in Cuba, 1793–1815," and Debien and Le Gardeur's "The Saint-Domingue Refugees in Louisiana, 1792–1804," the last two essays being translations by David Cheramie.

10. Fiehrer, "From La Tortue to La Louisiane," 2.

11. Augusta Elmwood's Saint-Domingue Special Interest Group has a rich Web site at http://freepages.genealogy.rootsweb.com.

12. Historians recently have been fighting over Jean Laffite's supposed Saint-Domingue ancestry, but Louisianans remain certain that the famous pirate could only be from Saint-Domingue. See, e.g., Christine Levet Gerbel, "Information from the Family of Jean Lafitte, Buccaneer." The latest attempt to disprove the Laffites' Saint-Domingue origins is that of William C. Davis. The first chapter of Davis's 2005 *The Pirates Laffite* places them in southwestern France, but the expressions of uncertainty seem far too numerous to make the source entirely reliable. More research will be needed before Davis's theses are acceptable. But that is not the purpose of the present work, which considers as equally interesting the fact that legends (if those are indeed legends) have been so widely circulated for so long.

13. Legends even make a Saint-Domingue refugee the inventor of the cocktail, both the word and the beverage. The Lonely Planet's *Louisiana and the Deep South* states: "It all begins with a man named Peychaud, who settled in New Orleans after fleeing the eighteenth-century slave uprisings in Hispaniola. He opened an apothecary on Royal Street, where, we are told, he developed a penchant for drinking brandy in an eggcup. The concept appealed to the people of New Orleans, and Peychaud began serving drinks in this fashion in his shop. . . . The eggcup, of course, was not called an eggcup in French-speaking New Orleans. It was called a *coquetier*. It was called that until Peychaud's inebriated patrons began mispronouncing it. The term evolved—much as Acadian turned into Cajun—from *coquetier* to *cocktay* to *cocktail*" (199). This story is also found in Stanley C. Arthur, *Old New Orleans*, 48.

14. In *Haïti: l'éternelle révolution*, Jacques de Cauna wrote: "Reste à étudier l'affinement des moeurs qu'ils provoquent autour d'eux, dans des mondes restés rus-

tiques, par la création de journaux, de théâtres, d'écoles, l'ouverture de loges maçonniques, de clubs, de sociétés, l'introduction de modes vestimentaires et architecturales différentes, la propagation de leurs coutumes, de leur religion catholique et de leurs langues, créole et français, diffusées également par les gens de couleur et les esclaves qui les accompagnent" [Remains to be studied the refinement in mores that they provoked around them, in areas that had remained rustic, by the foundation of newspapers, theaters, and schools, the creation of Masonic lodges, clubs, and societies, the introduction of different clothing and architectural fashions, the propagation of their customs, of their Catholic religion, and of their languages, Creole and French, also spread by the people of color and the slaves they brought with them] (297).

15. For an interesting survey of notions related to ethnicity and migrations, see Werner Sollors's *Theories of Ethnicity*.

16. The notion of "symbolic ethnicity" was developed by Herbert J. Gans in 1979. See Sollors, ed., *Theories of Ethnicity*, 425–59.

17. The reason for this neglect was sometimes merely a question of focus. To understand this, compare two articles dealing with the same writers, all Creoles of color of New Orleans in the second half of the nineteenth century: Michel Fabre's "'Une émulation sans envie': la presse et la littérature des Créoles de Couleur de la Nouvelle Orléans au dix-neuvième siècle" and Caryn Cossé Bell's "Haitian Immigration to Louisiana in the Eighteenth and Nineteenth Centuries." They discuss the same intellectuals, but while Fabre considers them Louisiana Creoles, without giving any further precision, Cossé Bell traces their common link of Saint-Domingue ancestry. Another telling example is Fossier's *New Orleans Glamour Period*, in which there is almost no mention of the refugees, although he deals with all the areas in which they were dynamic, including the theater, the press, education, the bar, or the militia. About the first actors of New Orleans, e.g., Fossier simply says, "A small troupe of comedians arrived in New Orleans," without mentioning their origins (467).

## Chapter 1

1. The title of this chapter was borrowed from Elizabeth Sullivan-Holleman and Isabel Hillery Cobb's invaluable contribution to the topic. Their painstaking genealogical research on the Rossignol des Dunes family perfectly illustrates the epic history of Saint-Domingue. In chapters with such evocative titles as "The Golden Years" or "Chronicle of the Dead," they show how the colony expanded and how this expansion was abruptly put to a halt in the late eighteenth century. See *The Saint-Domingue Epic*, 79–279.

2. A detailed presentation of Louisiana will be made in chapter 2. The few references to it in this chapter are aimed at highlighting the most obvious differences between the society that the refugees left and the one that they found upon reaching Louisiana.

3. Louisiana totaled only about 400 French colonists in 1717. Hall, *Africans in Colonial Louisiana*, 5.

4. The design of this book is not to dwell on the history of the French colony of Saint-Domingue. The bibliography, however, lists many references for further read-

ing. Devèze, *Antilles, Guyanes, La Mer de Caraïbes de 1492 à 1789*, and Laurent-Ropa, *Haïti: Une colonie française*, contain many details on the island in the seventeenth and eighteenth centuries. Philip Boucher offers a very good survey of prerevolutionary Saint-Domingue in *Les Nouvelles Frances* (85–96), as does Knight, *The Caribbean: The Genesis of a Fragmented Nationalism* (203–10). There are also numerous accounts left by travelers or residents on the island, e.g., those of Wimpffen, Malenfant, Malouet, de Laujon, Dubuisson, Hilliard d'Auberteuil, and Labat as well as Moreau de Saint-Méry's invaluable *Description topographique, physique, civile, politique et historique de la partie française de l'isle de Saint-Domingue*. Much can be learned from monographs of Saint-Domingue plantations, including Gabriel Debien's studies of the Guiton de Maulevrier coffee plantation and the Foäche sugar plantation (*Etudes Antillaises*, vol. 11) or Jacques de Cauna's monograph of the Fleuriau sugar plantation (*Au temps des isles à sucre)*. These detailed studies, relying on letters, plantation records, invoices, property titles, marriage contracts, and wills, offer reliable information that can often be extrapolated to give a better representation of colonial society in Saint-Domingue.

5. Census of 1789 cited by Pluchon in his annotated edition of Wimpffen, *Haïti au XVIIIe siècle*, 203. Also see Pamphile de Lacroix, *La Révolution de Haïti*, 393–95. The figures vary from one historian to the next, since the figures of the official census are said to be erroneous for various reasons. Moreau de Saint-Méry gives almost 40,000 whites because of the undervaluation of the population of Cap Français (by some 850 persons, according to him) and because he adds 7,850 soldiers and sailors (both military and commercial) and between 1,000 and 2,000 unsettled whites (*Description topographique*, 1:84–85). Similar reflections can be made concerning the free population of color, although most historians confirm a figure of around 28,000 for *gens de couleur libres* (e.g., Girod, *Une fortune coloniale*, 12; Pluchon, *Vaudou, sorciers, empoisonneurs*, 203; Moreau de Saint-Méry, *Description topographique*, 1:84–85; Adelaïde-Merlande, *Histoire Générale*, 120). As in the case of white people, however, the exact number of free people of color can be considered higher because, in the late eighteenth century, masters tended to grant some of their slaves unofficial manumission, making them *nègres de savane* (literally "Savannah negroes") and thus avoiding the fees that had to be paid to emancipate a slave. Altogether, it may be concluded that the white population and the free population of color (comprising people of mixed ancestry and manumitted slaves) were of roughly equal proportions. The figures concerning the slave population vary in similar proportions: 434,429 according to Pluchon (in Wimpffen, *Haïti au XVIIIe siècle*, 203), 450,000 for Adelaïde-Merlande (*Histoire Générale*, 120), 452,000 for Moreau de Saint-Méry (*Description topographique*, 1:45) and Girod (*Une fortune coloniale*, 12), and even 480,000 for Knight (*Caribbean*, 115). For figures of the Louisiana population, see Hall, *Africans*, or Berlin, *Many Thousands Gone*, among many other works cited in the bibliography.

6. To give but one element of comparison, the total population of the Spanish side of the island, Santo Domingo (almost twice the size of the French part) was 125,000, with only 30,000 slaves. Fiehrer, quoting Humbolt, mentions the single exception

of Jamaica, where the slave population represented a large majority. Fiehrer, "Saint-Domingue/Haiti," 422.

7. Hall, *Africans*, 278.

8. Saint-Domingue, e.g., was said to be twenty times more productive than its Spanish counterpart, Santo Domingo. On the eve of the French Revolution, the French colony accounted for three-fourths of the world's total sugar production and had a revenue of 137 million livres; that is to say, it represented 70 percent of the French colonial revenue and one-third of France's international commerce. One in eight French persons directly or indirectly lived off the colony. The ports of the French part of the island harbored 1,500 vessels a year, with a total tonnage of 220,000. It was visited by 80,000 sailors and an average of 750 great vessels per year (see, e.g., Lacroix, *La Révolution de Haïti*, 395–99, and Laurent-Ropa, *Haïti*, 161–62). According to Barbé de Marbois, the *intendant* of the colony, in 1789, 793 plantations produced sugar, 54 cocoa, 3,151 indigo, 789 cotton, 3,117 coffee, and 182 rum. There were also 370 lime kilns, 26 brickyards, and 29 potteries. The livestock included 40,000 horses, 50,000 mules, and 250,000 head of cattle (Cauna, *Au temps des isles à sucre*, 12–13).

9. Among the 700 French ships that left the West Indian harbors in 1789, 350 set sail from Saint-Domingue. Among the 200 million livres of annual exports of colonial goods from the American colonies, 116 came from Saint-Domingue (Girod, *Une fortune coloniale*, 10). Many markers of Saint-Domingue's increasing predominance could be mentioned. A single one will suffice: in 1728, 38 ships left Nantes for Saint-Domingue and 37 for Martinique; in 1743, 60 left for Saint-Domingue, only 17 for Martinique, and 2 for Guadeloupe (Devèze, *Antilles*, 259).

10. The fertility of the island was one factor explaining this rapid surge, together with the diversification of the economy, as shown by the varied production of the colony: 50 percent sugar, 24 percent coffee, 14 percent indigo, and 8 percent cotton (Adélaïde-Merlande, *Histoire Générale*, 125–26; Knight, *Caribbean*, 116). Among other reasons cited to account for the vitality of the island was the higher proportion of resident planters compared with the other West Indian colonies (e.g., the British ones) and the fact that the French colonists could deal directly with Santo Domingo and thus with Spain (see, e.g., Mr. Long, absentee Jamaican planter, answering a 1790 question of the British government as to why Saint-Domingue was producing three-fourths of the French sugar, in Augier et al., *Making of the West Indies*, 118–19). Finally, the stability of the colony during the Seven Years' War enabled a real development of interlope trade with England and Holland, as well as with the newborn United States, especially the northern states, from Pennsylvania to Massachusetts. The French colony traded sugar, molasses, and rum with the new nation for wheat, fish, lumber, candles, and soap.

11. Girod, *Une fortune coloniale*, 202. All accounts and studies of Saint-Domingue in the eighteenth century are full of examples of wealthy members of the free class of color. Debien quotes the case of Charles Delair, a small planter, who granted, through his will of March 14, 1757, to his—not yet free—two illegitimate sons, his two plan-

tations (*habitations* in the French colonial societies) of Port-à-Piment and who, in a codicil added to the will on September 17, *in extremis* manumitted them, before bequeathing to them, in communal estate with their mother, one of his concessions in Mattheux (Debien, *Etudes Antillaises*, 32). The notarial files of Marc Lafitte, a refugee notary in New Orleans, give examples of free mulattoes, legally recognized by their white Saint-Domingue father who declares that they are entitled to their share of inheritance, mentioning the property upon which they have rights in Saint-Domingue. See, e.g., Marc Lafitte notarial files, New Orleans Notarial Archives, 8:75, 321.

12. Fearing the increasing number and economic power of free blacks, the planters managed to persuade the government of the necessity of limiting their rights. From 1766 on, free blacks could no longer be officers in the militia, they were not allowed to carry firearms, and some garments were prescribed for them. In 1779, for fear they might join slaves in rebellions, a curfew was imposed on free blacks after midnight.

13. As in the rest of the slave societies, they were treated unequally, according to whether they were field slaves or house servants, rural or urban slaves, and they saw their fate vary according to the size of the plantation and the personality of the master. The deepest division among them was related to their origins: the slave population comprised a majority of *bossales*, i.e., individuals imported from Africa, and a minority—albeit increasingly numerous in the prerevolutionary decades—of Creole slaves. The Creole slaves filled the higher positions in the slave hierarchical order and were often found among the skilled workers. Toward the end of the prerevolutionary period, there was also an increasingly larger category of unofficially freed slaves, the *nègres de savanne*, who were considered free by their masters but were not acknowledged as such by the authorities. See, e.g., Devèze, *Antilles*, 289–90.

14. See Labat's description (*Voyage aux Isles*, 329–31) or Wimpffen's (*Voyage à Saint-Domingue*, 92).

15. For a very detailed account of life in the colony, see Moreau de Saint-Méry, *Voyage aux Etats-Unis de l'Amérique*, Wimpffen, *Voyage à Saint-Domingue*, or Laussat, *Memoirs*, among the most valuable primary sources. Also see Fouchard (*Plaisirs de Saint-Domingue*, *Le théâtre à Saint-Domingue*, and *Artistes et répertoires*) as well as Girod (*Une fortune coloniale*, 97–104) for good secondary sources.

16. For very exhaustive studies of the colonists' autonomist ideals, see Debien, *Esprit colon et esprit d'autonomie*, and Cauna, *Haïti: l'éternelle révolution*. For a very good summary of this trend and its manifestations, see Girod, *Une fortune coloniale*, 26–28, 204–26.

17. For more details on the revolution in Saint-Domingue, see Pamphile de Lacroix's account or such secondary sources cited in the bibliography, such as Adélaïde-Merlande (*Histoire Générale*), Bruley (*Les Antilles pendant la Révolution Française)*, Cauna (*Haïti: l'éternelle revolution*), Debien ("Esprit colon et esprit d'autonomie"), Devèze, Fick, Gaspar and Geggus, Geggus, Hernández Guerrero, Hurbon, ed., *L'insurrection des esclaves de Saint-Domingue;* Laurent-Ropa, Madiou, Martin and Yacou eds., Maurel, Ott, *Haitian Revolution*, or Stoddard, *French Revolution in San Domingo*, among

many others. For a more synthetic presentation of the Haitian revolution, see Philip Boucher, who situates quite well the events that caused the loss of the colony, giving an excellent summary of the different internal forces and external alliances taken in the turmoil of the revolutionary period (97–104).

18. Knight explains: "In the unconscious assumptions of the superordinate groups of literate whites and free persons of color in Saint-Domingue in 1789, liberty and equality meant relaxation of metropolitan controls and the removal of political and legal disabilities of the wealthy *gens de couleur* (people of color). To the slaves of Saint-Domingue—unschooled as they were in eighteenth-century rational thought—liberty and equality meant complete freedom from bondage and nothing less. In the social context of exploitation, the two connotations of liberty were irreconcilable." Knight, *Caribbean*, 83–84.

19. Boucher gives an excellent synthesis of the internal oppositions and foreign alliances. Boucher, 97–104.

20. Testimony cited in Cauna, *Au temps des isles à sucre*, 212.

21. Ibid., 228.

22. Declaration of the French Assembly of February 4, 1794: "Déclare que l'esclavage des Nègres dans toutes les colonies est aboli. En conséquence, elle décrète que tous les hommes, sans distinction de couleur, domiciliés dans les colonies sont citoyens français et jouissent de tous les droits assurés par la Constitution."

23. The July 8, 1801, constitution of Saint-Domingue reads: "Une colonie faisant partie de l'empire français" [A colony belonging to the French empire].

24. Historians cite the terrifying figure of 8,000 survivors out of a total 60,000 sent to Saint-Domingue from 1789 to 1803. See, e.g., Laurent-Ropa, *Haïti*, 323.

25. For instance, the Fleuriau plantation studied by Cauna in *Au temps des isles à sucre* was destroyed in June.

26. This ordinance is essential to the later fate of the refugees, since it imposed on Haiti a financial compensation that was used by the French authorities to indemnify the refugees.

27. A full measure of these horrors is found in the *Mémoires pour servir à l'histoire de la Révolution de Saint-Domingue* by Général Pamphile de Lacroix, an officer of Leclerc's expeditionary corps (see, e.g., 86–88). His narration of the events that occurred in Saint-Domingue between 1789 and 1803 covers some 435 pages and contains the texts of all the important decrees and laws, as well as the mention of all the political and military actions. It also gives many pages of horrendous descriptions of exactions committed on both sides. More slaves were killed than free people of whatever color. During the first rebellion in the northern region, in 1791, the estimations give 2,000 whites and 10,000 slaves killed in two months (Augier et al., *Making of the West Indies*, 113). The narration by Lacroix is very interestingly annotated, completed, and sometimes disproved by historian Pierre Pluchon in the 1995 Karthala edition of *La Révolution de Haïti*. Also see Parham, ed., *My Odyssey*, 28–30, 60–62, 92–93, 132–35, for a detailed account of the horrors in Saint-Domingue. Sullivan-Holleman and Hillery

Cobb give numerous instances of horrors committed on colonists and refer to many members of the Rossignol family who perished in revolutionary Saint-Domingue. See, e.g., *Saint-Domingue Epic*, 256–81. Also see Parham, *My Odyssey*, 28–35, 132–35.

28. The death toll of the Haitian Revolution, from the first troubles in 1789 until the 1804 independence, may be estimated around 52,000 soldiers, about 20,000 white colonists, and between 100,000 and 150,000 black men, women, and children. See, e.g., Laurent-Ropas, *Haïti*, 323.

29. In "Les registres d'état civil anciens des Archives Nationales d'Haïti," Jacques de Cauna, however, studying the 1819 death records in Haiti, mentions the instances of a few rare whites (Citoyen Lacoste, Louis Morisset, François Ducas) who manifestly remained there after independence (13).

30. The racially mixed free people were the enemies of the new power. Although he tried to reestablish a certain degree of order within the colony, Toussaint did not hesitate to kill some 10,000 of them. Augier et al., *Making of the West Indies*, 115.

31. The migration, indeed, often took the form of a flight, and emergency departures resulted in a total absence of records: some flights were individual, depending upon whatever boat was available, and thus were never recorded; even when the flights were more massive (as after the fire at Cap Français), no precise passenger list was established, due to the emergency. The only precise records available are those concerning individuals who planned their departure from or return to the colony, either in the very early months of unrest or later, during Toussaint's rule, in which case lists of passport deliveries are sometimes available. Return passports issued for people sailing to Saint-Domingue, e.g., are recorded in the legal and fiscal records of the National Archives. Compilations of lists made by Alice D. Forsyth were published in *New Orleans Genesis* 20, nos. 78, 79, 80, as well as 21, nos. 81 and 82. They prove that there was much movement between the various refuges and that many refugees attempted to return to their homeland. Between June 1799 and October 1801, 266 passport requests for Saint-Domingue were recorded in the United States for individuals or whole families. Some refugees justified their request by the fact that they had been granted proxy to manage plantations and others by the fact that they wanted to become overseers there. The lists indicate that some of these refugees in the United States had been naturalized since 1793.

32. Both primary and secondary sources mention individual or massive departures from the island. In the very early days, departures appear anecdotal (Lacroix, *Mémoires*, 136, Madiou, *Histoire d'Haïti*, 150). In their seminal article, "Saint-Domingue Refugees in Louisiana," Debien and Le Gardeur indicate that there were departures from the very beginning of revolutionary activity but that these departures were sparse and might be described as occurring on an individual scale. They subsequently allude to the many deportations of counterrevolutionary colonists by the civil commissioners Sonthonax and Polverel in the years 1793 and 1794 (115).

33. Lacroix, *Mémoires*, 165. Debien and Le Gardeur say that the burning of Cap Français "increased the departures ten-fold." "Refugees in Louisiana," 115. This large flux cannot remain unnoticed, due to its size and concentration, since all those refu-

gees were taken away by a fleet led by Galbaud, composed of 137 vessels, supposedly bound for France but finally unloading all the refugees in Hampton, Virginia. See, e.g., Childs, *French Refugee Life*, 15.

34. Lacroix, *Mémoires*, 181.

35. See, e.g., Folder History 1803–15 Territorial Saint-Domingue, 1992 NSG Conference in the States, doc. 1, Louisiana Collection, Howard-Tilton Memorial Library, Tulane University, New Orleans.

36. I have not been able to locate any general study of returns to metropolitan France in French historiography, and such a study still has to be undertaken. Several individual examples are found in the literature, however. Concerning people who had family interests, examples may be cited such as Henri de Sainte-Gême, who returned to southwestern France where his family roots were—after a stop in New Orleans, where he left a plantation and several items of property, but also his free companion of color and their offspring. Henri de Sainte-Gême Papers, MSS 100, Historic New Orleans Collection. As for other cases exemplifying those colonists involved in the French army or administration, the Goguet family might be evoked. Marie Renault-Goguet's family had had a long residence and possessed many interests in Saint-Domingue, but her husband, Antoine Goguet, was in the French army. Although they both remained in various refuges in the Americas well into the early nineteenth century, they were ultimately repatriated to metropolitan France. See Goguet, *Lettres d'amour créoles*. It is extremely difficult to assess the proportion of colonists who went back to France, since it generally takes memoirs and other personal narratives to find mentions of them. Historians, however, acknowledge the fact that the metropolitan destination was far from being the norm. See, e.g., Cauna, *Haïti: l'éternelle révolution*, 295. The figures of the Comité des Colons in Paris give a total of 6,000 persons having returned to metropolitan France from the Caribbean by July 1810, 400 from Saint-Domingue, 5,000 from Cuba, 400 from Puerto Rico, and 400 from Martinique, Guadeloupe, and Guyane. These figures may be found at the Archives Nationales, Section d'Outre-Mer, Dépôt des Papiers publics des Colonies, in Paris.

37. This is exemplified by Henri de Sainte-Gême, who remained in the Americas until 1819 and only returned to France once he had settled his family of color in New Orleans and married a white Louisianan heiress.

38. In March 1825, through a royal ordinance, Charles X finally acknowledged the loss of Saint-Domingue and independence of the island, provided that a sum of 150 million Francs be paid to the colonists as compensation for their lost property. The sum was to be paid in five installments, beginning in December 1825. The debt was eventually reduced in 1838 (Haiti had already paid 30 million Francs, and the balance was reduced to 60 million Francs payable in thirty years).

39. Even non-Creole inhabitants of Saint-Domingue sought refuge in the Americas instead of returning to their native region of France. Debien and Le Gardeur cite the example of Jean Leclerc, born in France in 1770, who owned a coffee and indigo plantation in Baynet estimated at 200,000 livres in the 1832 *Etat de l'Indemnité* and who, with his wife, Elisabeth Carrière, settled in New Orleans ("Refugees in Louisiana," 220).

Rodríguez Demorizi gives the figure of 1,500 to 2,000 to Santo Domingo (*La era de Francia en Santo Domingo*, 70).

40. Deive gives precise figures, details about how the subsidies were granted, about individuals who obtained them. He often refers to the transient status of these refugees, some of whom left for Cuba when Spain gave over the control of the colony in late 1795 and early 1796 and went on being subsidized (this was the case of Madame Tremais). Deive, *Los refugiados franceses*, 107–8.

41. See Deive, *Los refugiados franceses*, for a detailed study of those refugees. Deive gives very few figures (see, e.g., 150), but he includes lists of refugees and indicates the significance of the movement by speaking of "current" (*corriente*).

42. Deive shows that they were not as successful economically as their counterparts who had settled in Cuba, which probably did not encourage them to stay (*Las emigraciones*, 129). Moreover, Toussaint's invasion of Santo Domingo in 1801 sent more refugees from Santo Domingo to Cuba—for the most part—or to other Spanish colonies such as Venezuela. Deive gives several specific examples of individuals who went to Cuba at that moment. Haiti's rule over Santo Domingo lasted until July 1809, when forces from Puerto Rico and Jamaica helped the colonists rebel against Haitian forces and restored Santo Domingo to Spain, which ruled over it again until 1821. Deive, *Los refugiados*, 159–60.

43. Deive, *Los refugiados*, 9.

44. On Cuba, see Yacou, "L'émigration à Cuba des colons français de Saint-Domingue au cours de la révolution." Also see Debien, "De Saint-Domingue a Cuba avec une famille de réfugiés, les Tornézy (1800–1809)" as well as "Refugees in Cuba, 1793–1815."

45. Fiehrer gives 25,000 in "From La Tortue to La Louisiane," 22. In his article "Saint-Domingue/Haiti: Louisiana's Caribbean Connection," he quotes Irene Wright, who gives 27,000 (434). Deive gives 30,000 in *Las emigraciones* (132).

46. Laussat, *Memoirs*, 55. For examples of migrations to Cuba, see Sullivan-Holleman and Hillery Cobb, *Saint-Domingue Epic*, 283–308.

47. In his *Memoirs*, Pierre Clément Laussat writes: "The governor, a Spanish officer of Irish birth, received them very well and offered them at low cost small land grants on which they planted coffee" (56). Deive, in his studies of the migrants from Santo Domingo to Cuba after the Treaty of Basle, also mentions the existence of very cheap land sold to the French refugees. He gives the example of the Santa Catalina plantation, property of Manuel Justiz, first offered by the governor of Cuba to the Spanish migrants and refused by them, and which was sold after 1802 at the price of 20 pesos for one *Caballería*. It was subsequently settled by French refugees (see Francisco Pérez, *El Café*, 21–31). Fieher, however, indicates that some Cubans gave them a more mitigated welcome, for fear of a propagation of the French revolutionary ideals, despite the usual political conservatism of the refugees. He adds that the refugees also often had a military formation and thus could not be considered as defenseless (some of them had belonged to the French army, and some had even provided assistance to the American

revolutionaries). Finally, their very quick economic success also created resentment among the Cubans (Fiehrer, "Saint-Domingue/Haiti," 430).

48. On Jamaica, see Debien and Wright, "Les colons de Saint-Domingue passés à la Jamaïque (1792–1835)"; Cauna, "La diaspora des colons de Saint-Domingue et le monde créole: le cas de la Jamaïque"; Bryan, "Émigrés Conflicts and Reconciliations."

49. Deive, *Los refugiados*, 181.

50. Ibid., 102. For those who settled in Jamaica, see Cauna, *Haïti*, l'éternelle revolution, 297. Also see Patrick Bryan, who gives examples of planters still in Jamaica in 1816 and 1817 (16) or even in the 1820s (17). He even mentions those who had to resort to relief after the fire that destroyed part of Kingston in 1843 (15).

51. Debien and Le Gardeur give several examples of those who moved. Also see Debien and Wright for a more general survey, or chapter 11 of Sullivan-Holleman and Hillery Cobb, 363–404.

52. Other Antillean destinations must also be mentioned, although very briefly, due to their secondary importance in the migration. Of course, individual moves led some colonists to the Lesser Antilles, in more important proportions to the Leeward than to the Windward Islands. Although some went to Martinique or Guadeloupe, they did so in very small numbers, for fear that the revolution might expand to those colonies and, after 1794, because the abolition of slavery had been generalized to all the French colonies. Other cited destinations included Puerto Rico, where 200 refugees contributed to the defense of the Spanish colony during England's failed invasion attempt in 1797, and Trinidad. See Laguerre, "Haitians," in *Encyclopedia of Southern Culture*, ed. Wilson and Ferris, 433. Dutch St. Thomas and Danish St. Eustatius also welcomed some refugees (Debien and Le Gardeur, "Refugees in Louisiana," 115). Although more distant, the Dutch colony of Curacao was another refuge for St. Domingans. This is a rarely mentioned area, but we understand, from the letters written by Marie Goguet to her husband from Curacao (where she had found temporary shelter), that there was, in this island, a small colony of refugees whose members she keeps mentioning (32). Other destinations are mentioned anecdotally through the various memoirs and correspondences, the Goguets exchanging, e.g., letters with a refugee in St. Barthélémy.

53. On refugees in the United States, see Debien's "Réfugiés de Saint-Domingue aux Etats-Unis." Also see Babb, "French Refugees"; Hunt, *Haiti's Influence on Antebellum America*; and Childs, *French Refugee Life*.

54. Adélaïde-Merlande, *Histoire Générale*, 113. Also see Logan, *The Diplomatic Relations of the United States with Haiti*, 1776–1891, and the index of important names in de Lacroix, *Mémoires*.

55. For example, Logan, *Diplomatic Relations*. This may be easily confirmed by the fact that roughly 10,000 left Cap Français for the United States at the time the city was burned down in 1793.

56. Alfred Hunt quotes many newspaper articles published in the *Virginia Chronicle*, the Aurora *General Advertiser*, and the Norfolk and Portsmouth *General Adver-*

*tiser* in 1791 and 1793, calling for the Americans' sympathy toward the refugees. He also mentions the March 1794 appropriation by the federal government of $15,000 as emergency relief funds, as well as the "remission of the duties arising on the tonnage of sundry French vessels which had taken refuge in ports of the United States." Hunt, *Haiti's Influence*, 42–43. Many pages are also dedicated by Babb to the question of emergency relief to the refugees in the United States. See esp. Babb, "French Refugees," 54–88.

57. See Sullivan-Holleman and Hillery Cobb, *Saint-Domingue Epic*, 309–62.

58. Moreau de Saint-Méry, *Voyage aux Etats-Unis*, 55.

59. Laguerre, "Haitians," 433. The burial records (as well as the many tombstones still visible at the Charleston St. Mary of the Annunciation cemetery) indicate that many of these refugees came from Môle St. Nicolas, which suggests that they came together on one or several boats.

60. The urgency of the flight (as in the case of Galbaud's fleet) did not enable the establishment of accurate passenger lists and the significant number of refugees reaching the northern United States at once did not make it easy to record the arrivals in a precise way. Moreover, as mentioned by Frances Sergeant Childs, "vital statistics were not kept by states or municipalities," only by churches (as will be seen in New Orleans). Childs adds that misfortune made the so precious registers of some of those churches unusable: those of St. Mary's Catholic Church in Philadelphia, e.g., which was attended by many refugees, were destroyed by fire. Childs, *French Refugee Life*, 138.

61. Ibid., 65–67.

62. This summary does not do justice to the diversity and complexity of the population movements. To give but a few instances of migrants who ended in Louisiana, Louis Marie Elisabeth Moreau-Lislet, who later became one of the leading public figures in Louisiana first found refuge in Philadelphia in 1794 before returning to Cap Français in 1802–1803 and migrating to New Orleans through Santiago de Cuba in 1804 (Debien and Le Gardeur, "Refugees in Louisiana," 205). Louis Guillaume Valentin Dubourg, who was to become the bishop of New Orleans, was born at Cap Français in 1766 and educated in metropolitan France. He later moved to Spain, then to the United States in 1802 and to Cuba before reaching New Orleans ("Refugees in Louisiana," 189). His family settled in Louisiana, and his brothers became affluent and influent members of the Louisiana society.

63. Moreau de Saint-Méry, *Description topographique*, e.g., in 1798.

64. A good picture of the many movements between the various American asylums may be found in the thorough genealogical study of the Rossignol des Dunes family in *The Saint-Domingue Epic* (e.g., 292, 296, 297, and 398). Sullivan-Holleman and Hillery Cobb conclude: "During those years of turmoil, the survivors were moving from one colony to another or to the United States and back to France or from Cuba to Jamaica. In tracing their paths back and forth across the Atlantic, or through the Caribbean, and because of the confusion and mass transition of this period, it is nearly impossible to fix their final destination before 1828" (299).

65. The letters exchanged by Antoine and Marie Goguet between Santo Domingo

(where Antoine was) and Curaçao (where Marie had found temporary refuge) show that people moved back and forth between the two islands, visited each other, and shared news from other refugees, and correspondence often moved back and forth with passing visitors to one or the other colony.

66. Lambert Family Papers, 244 (four folders).

67. Eliza Gould's Memoirs, in Marshall (Maria Chotard and Family) Papers #3256.

## Chapter 2

1. See, e.g., a few instances of direct arrivals, including that of the Le Gardeur de Tilly family (ancestors of René Le Gardeur) in Sullivan-Holleman and Hillery Cobb, *Saint-Domingue Epic*, 296.

2. Although some figures apparently include the slaves brought over by their masters, others only take into account the white migrants. Jacques Houdaille, for example, clearly considers only the white refugee community because, when he discusses figures, he writes that 15,000–25,000 refugees would not materially have come to the United States, since the white community in Saint-Domingue had comprised only about 30,000 whites, many of whom had been killed and many were known to have emigrated elsewhere. "French Refugees in the United States, 1790–1810," 213. The only thing that makes the figures plausible is the knowledge that the wave was multiracial.

3. Debien and Le Gardeur, "Refugees in Louisiana," 141.

4. Ibid., 141–62.

5. Debien and Le Gardeur do not give precise figures (although they seem to estimate the numbers at around 200) but they detail the biographies of some of those refugees coming, again, mainly from the south of the Caribbean island. Ibid., 164–74. Some historians give surprisingly high figures, going up to 4,000. Logan cites the figure of "some four thousand refugees—whites, *gens de couleur* and slaves—[who] landed at the [New Orleans] port." *Diplomatic Relations*, 47.

6. Volumes 5, 6, and 7 of the *Archdiocese of New Orleans Sacramental Records* cover 1791–95, 1796–99, and 1800–1803, respectively. There may be some omissions or errors in the counting of entries concerning the Saint-Domingue refugees, but they do not significantly alter the proportion if the numbers of entries per volume are considered: 2,950 for volume 5, 2,381 for volume 6, and 2,570 for volume 7.

7. See Lachance, "The 1809 Immigration," 246, or Debien and Le Gardeur, "Refugees in Louisiana," 150–62, for precise examples, including that of Jacques-François Pitot, who was to become mayor of New Orleans in 1804.

8. Debien and Le Gardeur, "Refugees in Louisiana," 224. The two historians, stressing the difficulty in giving accurate figures, modalize the assertion by adding "most probably."

9. Ibid., 225. The sources used by Debien and Le Gardeur include baptismal records for children born in Jamaica in 1802 and baptized at St. Louis Cathedral in New Orleans in 1804.

10. Michel Laguerre gives a total figure of "more than 15,000 immigrants, including French planters, people of color, and slaves [who] settled in Louisiana" between 1791

and 1803. He probably meant 1791–1810, however, the figure of over 15,000 being much too high for the first ten years of the migration. Laguerre, "Haitians," in *Encyclopedia of Southern Culture*, ed. Wilson and Ferris, 433.

11. See Lachance, "Repercussion of the Haitian Revolution." For Lachance, many refugees died or moved forward. This ceaseless movement is also clearly perceptible in Debien and Le Gardeur, who give several precise examples of such movements.

12. Debien and Le Gardeur, "Refugees in Louisiana," 192, 216.

13. Debien, "Refugees in Cuba," 94, 97. This is confirmed by Paul Lachance, who demonstrates that most refugees were in no hurry to leave Louisiana. Lachance, "The 1809 Immigration," 260.

14. The hostilities were started by France, which felt that England had not respected the terms of the 1802 Treaty of Amiens.

15. Lachance "The 1809 Immigration," 246.

16. Rowland, ed., *Official Letter Books of W.C.C. Claiborne*, 1:388, 2:95–96.

17. Debien and Le Gardeur, "Refugees in Louisiana," 199.

18. For instance, the children of Damoiselle Piemont and Jean-Baptiste de Rossignol des Dunes Le Clere. Among their seven children, the two eldest were born in Saint-Domingue. Sullivan-Holleman and Hillery Cobb, *Saint-Domingue Epic*, 436. The same book cites many other examples in the Rossignol family, e.g., 234–35, 434–36, 441.

19. Louise Peychaud (born in Jamaica of Mathias Peychaud and Henriette Morel, former planters from Saint-Domingue) married, at St. Louis Cathedral on April 2, 1815, Henri Duvivier Peire, who had come from Cuba. Ibid., *Saint-Domingue Epic*, 293.

20. Volume 7 of the *Archdiocese of New Orleans Sacramental Records* covers 1804–6. Here again, there might be errors and omissions in the counting, but they do not alter the proportion.

21. A few lists of passengers exist (see, e.g., Sullivan-Holleman and Hillery Cobb, *Saint-Domingue Epic*, 374), but they are neither systematic nor sufficiently thorough to allow accurate conclusions.

22. There may have been a clear intent behind this silence, the refugee press not wanting to draw excessive attention onto the massive arrivals.

23. For examples, see Debien and Le Gardeur, "Refugees in Louisiana," 199.

24. Ibid., 228.

25. All these examples and more are given in ibid., 220–24.

26. See Parham, trans., *My Odyssey*.

27. Lachance, "The 1809 Immigration," 246.

28. Volume 9 of the Nolan, *Sacramental Records*, 1807–9. Considering that there are six or seven entries per page, it gives a proportion of over 10 percent.

29. "Extracts from the Lists of Passengers Reported at the Mayor's Office by the Captains of Vessels Who Have Come to This Port from the Island of Cuba," July 18 and August 7, 1809, in *Official Letter Books*, ed. Rowland, 1:381–82, 409. The two reports of the mayor, dated July 18 and August 7, give the names of forty ships: thirty-five from

Santiago, four from Baracoa, and one from Havana. Also see figures in Debien, "Refugees in Cuba," 93.

30. Report of the mayor of New Orleans to Governor Claiborne of January 18, 1810, published in the *Moniteur de la Louisiane*, January 27, 1810.

31. *Moniteur de la Louisiane*, January 27, 1810. Indeed, there were some refugees who were detained in Jamaica on their way from Cuba to Louisiana. Debien adds that the refugees occasioned a large increase of the population of New Orleans, "something in the neighborhood of 30 to 40 percent." "Refugees in Cuba," 93.

32. Debien and Le Gardeur, "Refugees in Louisiana," 114.

33. Lachance, "The 1809 Immigration," 248.

34. See Lambert papers (Louisiana Collection, Howard-Tilton Memorial Library, Tulane University), especially folders 3 and 4. Many illustrations of this pattern may also be found in Sullivan-Holleman and Hillery Cobb, *Saint-Domingue Epic*, 405–60. Refugees from the Rossignol des Dunes family are shown to have migrated to Louisiana from Cuba.

35. Debien and Le Gardeur, "Refugees in Louisiana," 117.

36. Sullivan-Holleman and Hillery Cobb, *Saint-Domingue Epic*, 375

37. Ibid., 391, 399, 402, and 388, respectively.

38. Ibid., 389.

39. Nolan, *Sacramental Records*, vol. 10.

40. This estimate is in accordance with Fiehrer's assertion that "by 1815, well over 11,000 refugees [that we know of] had regrouped [to New Orleans] from disparate points in Europe and the Americas." Fiehrer, "From La Tortue to La Louisiane," 4.

41. A good example of these incessant displacements may be given by the case of François Bocquet, who went from Saint-Domingue to Cuba, then to New Orleans, then back to Cuba, and finally back to New Orleans. Debien and Le Gardeur, "Refugees in Louisiana," 228. Elisabeth Labat, a Saint-Domingue Creole, was married at New Orleans in 1804. She went to Cuba in 1819 and returned to New Orleans as a widow, where she died in 1827. Ibid., 232.

42. Ibid., 165–66.

43. Fiehrer, "From La Tortue to La Louisiane," 6, 11. Fiehrer mentions that "families in the island and in Louisiana shared numerous kin and business networks for a century and a half."

44. Debien and Le Gardeur, "Refugees in Louisiana," 218, 226.

45. Ibid., 126.

46. Ibid., 126–27.

47. Ibid., 130.

48. Ibid., 131.

49. Debien and Le Gardeur mention the 29,407 *gourdes* that were sent from Saint-Domingue to assist victims of the great fire that destroyed New Orleans in March 1788. Ibid., 141.

50. Cited in Sullivan-Holleman and Hillery Cobb, *Saint-Domingue Epic*, 375.

51. Laussat, *Memoirs*, 157.

52. Sullivan-Holleman and Hillery Cobb, *Saint-Domingue Epic*, 436.

53. Gary Mills mentions several free family of color from Saint-Domingue settling on the Isle, intermarrying with the Creoles of color, and "becoming integral parts of the Colony." He also gives the example of Balthazar Monet, who had fought with Toussaint Louverture. Mills, *Forgotten People*, xxviii, 79, 89.

54. See West, *An Atlas of Louisiana Surnames of French and Spanish Origins*, or Fiehrer, "From La Tortue to La Louisiane," 23.

55. The proportion of 90 percent is often found. See, e.g., Brasseaux and Conrad, *Road to Louisiana*, x.

56. Hall describes a situation of chaos, consecutive to the French Revolution, in New Orleans (*Africans*, 317), but Louisiana was doubtlessly much less affected than if the colony had been French.

57. For more details on French and Spanish Louisiana, however, see Kimberly Hanger, Gwendolyn Hall, Ira Berlin, Thomas Ingersoll, Daniel H. Usner, Acosta Rodriguez, and John C. Clark.

58. *Récapitulation Générale des Recensements*, Colonies de la Louisiane, Papeles de Cuba, Legajo 2357, Archivo General de Indias (Sevilla), available in microfilm at the Historic New Orleans Collection (ed. 145, reel 40).

59. Hall gives 2,600–3,000 Acadians and 2,000 Canary Islanders. Hall, *Africans*, 277.

60. Ibid., 278.

61. Eccles, 188.

62. Hanger, *Bounded Lives*, 22.

63. Fiehrer says that the population of New Orleans was "scarcely larger than the refugee movement itself." "Saint-Domingue/Haiti," 432.

64. Wall, *Louisiana: A History*, 60; Ingersoll, *Mammon and Manon*, 149. Hall mentions that Spanish migrations exerted little cultural influence upon the more numerous inhabitants who spoke French, Acadian, and Creole. Hall, *Africans*, 277.

65. Ingersoll, e.g., writes that "the town's basic social structure remained unchanged and its culture retained its local traditional character." *Mammon and Manon*, 150.

66. Hall, *Africans*, 60.

67. For instance, three of the Spanish governors, Unzaga, Galvez, and Miró, married French Creoles. Babb, "French Refugees," 396.

68. A very famous anecdote very well illustrates this. Following the Louisiana Purchase, a conflict opposed the Creoles to the new rulers of the territory concerning the dances that had to be performed in ballrooms. When they protested against the inclusion of American dances, the Creoles based their arguments on the fact that the Spaniards had ruled the colony for over thirty years without obliging the New Orleans population to dance the Fandango. See, e.g., Crété, *La vie quotidienne en Louisiane*, 38.

69. Ingersoll goes so far as to say that "the society remained composed of Francophones, white and black, who mostly rejected Spanish culture." *Mammon and Manon*,

149. Although this assertion may be slightly exaggerated, it undoubtedly contains some truth.

70. Or, as Hall puts it, "outside the capital, Spanish Louisiana remained French, Acadian, and Creole in language and culture." Hall, *Africans*, 302, 317.

71. Ibid., 276–315.

72. There is, however, a debate between historians of French colonial Louisiana as to the importance of the free population of mixed African ancestry. While most historians (Hall, Hanger, and Lachance, among others) argue that the Louisiana society was extremely fluid racially, Ingersoll disagrees. For a better view of the controversy, see the works by these Louisiana historians cited in the bibliography (e.g., Hall, *Africans*, 239–42). There are, however, indications that there was, at times, a large proportion of people among the enslaved who purchased their own or their family's or friends' liberty. For the 1769–1803 period in New Orleans, Berlin cites the figure of 1,500 blacks who came out of enslavement (*Slaves without Masters*, 333).

73. Fiehrer, "Saint-Domingue/Haiti," 133.

74. Ingersoll, *Mammon and Manon*, 123. Although some of his theses are at odds with the conclusions of most of the Louisiana historians on the question of race fluidity, his book contains a very interesting comparative study of Saint-Domingue and Louisiana at the eve of the Revolution (123–43), where he shows that despite the booming economy of Saint-Domingue and the possibility of making "quick fortunes" (123), the best future prospects were undoubtedly to be found in Louisiana.

75. Ingersoll says that the free black population of the New Orleans parish was very small at the beginning of Spanish rule, adding that "when O'Reilly ordered the men of that group to swear an oath of allegiance on September 20, 1769, just thirty were counted." Ingersoll, *Mammon and Manon*, 214. Hall confirms the scarcity of the free people of color, since she says that the Spanish census of 1769 records 165 free people of African descent, among whom 80 percent were of mixed African and European ancestry in the whole of Louisiana. Hall, *Africans*, 239.

76. From the 165 free blacks in the whole of Louisiana in 1769, the figure rose to 1,175 in 1785, with 563 for New Orleans alone. The census of 1788 gives a total of 1701 free blacks, among whom 820 were in New Orleans. Sterkx, *Free Negro*, 33, 85. When Louisiana was purchased by the United States, the free population of color was up to 1566. *Appendix to an Account of Louisiana*, cited in Sterkx, *Free Negro*, 95. Berlin confirms that the free black population in New Orleans doubled between 1777 and 1791. *Slaves without Masters*, 333.

77. Figures given for 1805 by Berlin, *Slaves without Masters*, 333. Hanger, for the same year, gives 1,566, representing 19 percent of the total New Orleans population, 30 percent of the free population, and 33.5 percent of the nonwhite population. Hanger, *Bounded Lives*, 18, 22.

78. According to Hall, the degree of fluidity was very high, whereas Ingersoll writes that "mixture between white colonists and blacks was not exceptionally high in New Orleans" and "race relations were not more relaxed than they were elsewhere." Ingersoll, *Mammon and Manon*, 141.

79. For a detailed study of the free black society in colonial New Orleans, see Hanger, *Bounded Lives*.

80. Hall, *Africans*, 238–39; Ingersoll, *Mammon and Manon*, 53.

81. See Hall, *Africans;* Usner, *Indians, Settlers, and Slaves*; and Zitomersky, "Race, esclavage et emancipation," among others, on this question of social fluidity.

82. Wall, *Louisiana: A History*, 75.

83. This notion will be discussed more fully in the last chapter, but there is an interesting discussion of it in Hall, *Africans*, 156–58. For another presentation, see Ingersoll, *Mammon and Manon*, 94–95, 106.

84. Hall, *Africans*, 276.

85. Ingersoll, *Mammon and Manon*, 179.

86. For a detailed presentation of the responses in the North-American refugees, see Hunt, *Haiti's Influence*, chap. 2, esp. 42–44. Also see Babb, "French Refugees," 54–88.

87. In the Spanish possession of Santo Domingo, e.g., they were subsidized by the government (see Deive, *Los Refugiados*, 107–8). In Cuba, very cheap land was sold to them (Deive, *Las emigraciones*, 157). In the United States, the refugees were also supported by the authorities. The towns of Hampton, Portsmouth, and Williamsburg offered $1,075 to the refugees, while the State of Virginia, e.g., granted $2,000 to the mayor of Norfolk for relief to the refugees (Moreau de Saint-Méry, *Voyage aux Etats-Unis*, 55 and 56, respectively). For more examples, see Hunt, *Haiti's Influence*, 43; Debien and Le Gardeur, "Refugees in Louisiana," 168; Parnham ed., 79 and 99. On their reception in Charleston, see Klein, *Unification of a Slave State*, 234; Hunt, *Haiti's Influence*, 43. On the Northern States, see, e.g., Hunt mentioning the granting of $2,000 by John Jay, the governor of New York (*Haiti's Influence*, 43).

88. In Santo Domingo, the "auxiliary negroes" were often deported to other destinations (see Deive, *Las emigraciones*, 31, 32, 126–28). In South Carolina, many fears were expressed in relation to the arrival of slaves contaminated by revolutionary ideals. Throughout the 1790s, the South Carolina legislature attempted to restrict the influx of persons of color, either free or slave, into the state. In 1797, the free people of color of French origin who had arrived after 1790 were asked to leave the state and, in 1798, Governor Charles Pinckney warned of "the danger of suffering either free persons of colour or slaves to be introduced from these islands," and urged immediate passage of a law inflicting severe penalties upon any captain or ship owner importing "any slave or person of colour from any island in which an insurrection had taken place" (Klein, *Unification of a Slave State*, 234).

89. This was also true in Cuba, e.g., where the colonists and authorities feared a propagation of the French revolutionary ideals, despite the usual political conservatism of the refugees. See, e.g., Fiehrer, "Saint-Domingue/Haiti," 430.

90. See Berquin-Duvallon and Alliot quoted in Debien and Le Gardeur, "Refugees in Louisiana," 168, 172.

91. This was done first through a secret royal order on May 11, 1790, with an addendum a few days later ordering the deportation of those who had already entered the territory.

92. See, e.g., Robertson, ed., *Louisiana under the Rule of Spain, France, and the United States*, 194, and Debien and Le Gardeur, "Refugees in Louisiana," 175.

93. The reactions to the arrival of the last waves, in 1803–4 and 1809–10, have been very well presented by Debien and Le Gardeur and Paul Lachance. See Brasseaux and Conrad, *Road to Louisiana*, 192–203, 244–84. Also see Lachance, "The Foreign French," footnote 13, 107.

94. See Lachance, "The 1809 Immigration," 251.

95. Rowland, ed., *Official Letter Books*, 4:402.

96. See Lachance, "The 1809 Immigration," 250.

97. Cable, *Creoles of Louisiana*, 157. Also see Hunt, *Haiti's Influence*, 45; Sullivan-Holleman and Hillery Cobb, *Saint-Domingue Epic*, 307; Fiehrer "Saint-Domingue/Haiti," 430, among others. This is a most widely accepted fact. Also see Rowland, ed., *Official Letter Books*, 4:302, 400.

98. Lachance, "The 1809 Immigration," 254.

99. Details will be given later on the Baratarians led by the Laffite brothers.

100. Proceedings of Council Meetings, City Archives, New Orleans Public Library, May 24, 1809, 2:65. Also see James Mather to Claiborne, July 18, 1809, in Rowland, ed., *Official Letter Books*, 4:387–93.

101. Letter from Madison to Claiborne asking him to welcome the refugees with courtesy and humanity, March 12, 1804, Rowland, ed., *Official Letter Books*, 2:93.

102. *Le Moniteur de la Louisiane*, June 14, 1809.

103. James Mather wrote to Claiborne in August 1809: "I have not had one single complaint lodged with me against any of them, since the first arrivals to this date,—Their conduct generally breathes respect for our Laws; and their industry and activity must be astonishing indeed, since it has till now afforded the most part of those who had no slaves, the means of lawfully getting a livelihood." Rowland, ed., *Official Letter Books*, 4:405.

104. Cable, *Creoles of Louisiana*, 157.

## Chapter 3

1. See, e.g., Lee, ed., *Memoir of Pierre Toussaint*. Toussaint's testimony details the life of the refugees in New York, and Toussaint clearly expresses his solidarity to his mistress (17) and to the rest of the (white) refugee community (21).

2. The committee of benevolence was created by decision of the city council. See resolution discussed in the *Louisiana Gazette*, June 6, 1809. Also see Bonnie Mathews and John Minor WISDOM collection, MC 230, Louisiana Collection, Tulane University, box 5, doc. 180. This was true in other refuges as well. In the northern United States, these advertisements were common. *Le Courrier de la France et des Colonies*, e.g., contained an abundant advertising section where "Moreau de St. Méry's books were advertised, land was offered for sale, balls and concerts noted and official regulations made public. Merchants and teachers and shoemakers made themselves known. Through the advertisements, the French refugees kept in touch with one another and

through them we are able to watch the daily round of refugee life, and their efforts to carry on in the New World" (Childs, *French Refugee Life*, 138).

3. Memoirs of Eliza Williams Chotard Gould, Marshall Papers # 328, Special Collections, Louisiana State University, Baton Rouge.

4. Henri de Sainte-Gême Papers, MS 100, Historic New Orleans Collection, New Orleans. Henri de Sainte-Gême had been a planter in Saint-Domingue. After evacuating to Cuba, he ended up at New Orleans in 1809 with his black lover and their children (folder 21). He became a planter at Gentilly, which he left (after marrying Marguerite Dreux) for southwestern France, in 1818, never to return. During his years in New Orleans, he was a member of the militia and commanded an elite corps, the Dragons à Pied. He fought as a major under Jackson during the Battle of New Orleans. He also financed privateering expeditions. Jean Boze, his friend from Saint-Domingue, followed him in his successive removals except the last. He had been a high officer of the harbor of Port Républicain, appointed in 1802 as head of all the harbor movements (*A Calendar of the Rochambeau Papers*, no. 200, an 10, 16 Germinal, April 6, 1802), before being temporarily appointed harbor captain (*Rochambeau Papers*, no. 362, an 10, 23 floréal, May 13, 1802). He remained on Sainte-Gême's plantation until his death in 1842. The episode of their arrival in New Orleans is evoked by Boze in his letter of November 1, 1818 (folder 24).

5. Folder 21, letter from Boze, April 20, 1818. Also see folder 283.

6. Folders 43 through 86.

7. On the attempts of Lambert's friends to settle the problem of his sequestered property in Cuba, see Lambert Family Papers, folders 3 and 4, 1810–18.

8. Again, few sources exist on Louisiana, but the memoirs of Toussaint, although he settled in the northeastern states, are a constant proof of this solidarity. Toussaint recounts how, when his mistress had to sell her jewels to survive, he pretended to sell them but gave her instead the little money he had. Lee, ed., *Memoir of Pierre Toussaint*, 17–21.

9. See correspondence to Sainte-Gême in Sainte-Gême Family Papers; also see several letters from Philadelphia to Lambert in St. Yago between September 1804 and July 1805 (folder 1), as well as numerous letters quoted by Debien in "Réfugiés de Saint-Domingue aux Etats-Unis." In "De Saint-Domingue à Cuba," Debien quotes a letter from C. Bredon to Tornézy (New York 1805): "Je pense toujours à notre Saint-Domingue et je me prépare à pouvoir y retourner avec fruit dès que la paix le permettra" [I still think of our Saint-Domingue and I am getting ready to go back there profitably as soon as peace permits it], 24. The use of the pronoun *our* shows that the refugees were indeed bound together by this common origin and had strong feelings about their community.

10. Several letters to Lambert reveal Lambert's attempts to have news of his mother. They narrate a failed attempt to rescue her from the island (September 19, 1804, folder 1), as well as her death (September 27, 1804, folder 1).

11. Pierre Toussaint says his mistress "believed—we all believed—that she would recover her property in the West Indies." Lee, *Memoir*, 17. De Borde's letters to Lambert

keep mentioning the day when they would meet again at Grande Rivière (September 19 and 27, 1804, folder 1).

12. Again, De Bordes, Lambert's correspondent, described his evenings with La Fraise, another refugee, and their plans for revenge and reconquest: "Nous avons conquis vingt fois Jérémie; tous les Brigands y ont été pendus ou brûlés, et réunis dans une tonnelle dans le Morne des Abricots tous nos amis y ont vidé plus de cent flacons" [Twenty times we conquered Jérémie; all the Brigands there were hanged or burned, and, gathered in an arbor on the Morne des Abricots, all our friends emptied more than 100 flasks.] Letter of July 22, 1805.

13. This was true in most of the refuges. Moreau de Saint-Méry's library, at the corner of Front and Walnut streets in Philadelphia, became one of these meeting places were the refugees could socialize. Some organizations, although they were more political in their aims, also gave them the opportunity to meet and exchange views, such as the Philadelphia Colons de Saint-Domingue réfugiés aux Etats-Unis.

14. Arthur, *Old New Orleans*, 86, 154. Arthur notes that this address was also sometimes recorded as "58 Levee Street" (153).

15. Cable, *Old Creole Days*, 90–94.

16. Congo Square was the place in New Orleans where the Americans allowed slave gatherings on Sundays, in a vain attempt to prevent illicit gathering and the consequent spreading of voodoo. More details will be given on Congo Square in chapter 7, since the place is a good laboratory to study the cultural continuum between the various categories of refugees and to apprehend the process of creolization.

17. Vol. 10 of the records published by the Archives of the Archdiocese, covering 1810–12, is very revealing in this respect, all the more so because the entries concerning refugees are innumerable.

18. Bryan, "Émigrés Conflicts and Reconciliations," 18. Bryan even describes them as "clannish and inter-dependent" (16), although the term *clannish* might be regarded as negatively connoted when describing a group so obviously distressed by forced migration and estrangement.

19. Of the fifty marriage contracts in the Lafitte files from 3:213 to 13:308, almost all concern Saint-Domingue refugees. From May 1814 to August 1816, e.g., seventeen out of twenty-four marriage contracts filed by Lafitte concern at least one refugee from Saint-Domingue. Notarial Archives, New Orleans.

20. See chapter 4 for more details.

21. See Maduell, *Marriage Contracts*, as well as Nolan, *Sacramental Records*, published by the Archdiocese of New Orleans Archives, especially vol. 10.

22. See, e.g., Paul Lachance, "Intermarriage and French Cultural Persistence," or "The 1809 Immigration," especially 264–65. However, in "Were Saint-Domingue Refugees a Distinctive Cultural Group in Antebellum New Orleans?" Paul Lachance also develops the thesis that the mere fact they signed marriage contracts was proof of their specificity and a clear sign that they were not "immediately absorbed into the Creole population" (192).

23. Notarial files of Marc Lafitte, February 19, 1816, 8:64, Notarial Archives, New Orleans.

24. Notarial files of Michel de Armas, December 7, 1815, 9–A:396. Notarial Archives, New Orleans.

25. Nolan, *Sacramental Records*, e.g., baptism of Marie-Françoise Auguste, 10:11.

26. For instance, burial of Antonio Baleau, 10:18; or Santiago Henrrique Bengham, 10:30. These are references to Nolan, *Sacramental Records*, vol. 10. The next references to this volume are included in the body of the text.

27. This slave group is, of course, more difficult to study, for lack of abundant documentation.

28. See, e.g., Notarial Files of Marc Lafitte, 3:227, 270, 4:12, 30, 183, 277, 290, and 5:138, Notarial Archives, New Orleans. Also see Will Books at the New Orleans Public Library, e.g., vol. 4, esp. between August 1825 (67) and January 1832 (346).

29. An example may be found on a tomb in the St. Mary of the Annunciation cemetery in Charleston, bearing indication of the residence in Saint-Domingue of a surgeon born in metropolitan France: Firmin LE ROY, Né à Baugenci, France, Chirurgien et habitant de Saint-Domingue, Mort le 30/04/1819, Agé de 76 ans [Firmin LE ROY, born at Baugenci, France, surgeon and inhabitant of Saint-Domingue, died April 30, 1819, at age 76].

30. Will Books, New Orleans Public Library. See, e.g., those concerning the 1820s and 1830s. Almost all those written in French are refugees' wills, while a survey conducted on those written in English proves that they included Creoles and "foreign" French.

31. For instance, "Mme ROYE, Françoise, née Félicité NOULLE A Lile Saint-Domingue" [*sic*], although she died in 1875.

32. Babb, "French Refugees," 383.

33. Lachance, "The 1809 Immigration," 264.

34. Ibid., 125–28. Also see Lachance's Index of Homogamy, 135–36, and his 1999 article, "Were Saint-Domingue Refugees a Distinctive Cultural Group in Antebellum New Orleans?"

35. Brasseaux and Conrad, eds., *Road to Louisiana*, xvi.

36. Augustin-Wogan-Labranche Family Papers 1803–1936 (MS 223, Louisiana Collection, Tulane University, New Orleans), folder 4. Also mentioned by Boze (box 6, letter 231, September 30 to November 7, 1833 in Sainte-Gême Papers).

37. Notarial files of Marc Lafitte, marriage contracts May 1814 to June 1818; notarial files of Michel de Armas, marriage contracts January 1810 to August 1817, Notarial Archives, New Orleans. See Maduell, New Orleans Marriage Contracts, 78–79, 94–103, for a short presentation of these contracts.

38. Debien, "Refugees in Cuba," 111. For more details on the refugees in Cuba, see 108–12. On refugees in Santo Domingo, Deive wrote "Optaron por quedarse, terminaron por mezclar su sangre con la de nuestros criollos y españoles. No son pocas las familias dominicanas que hoy ostentan apellidos heredados de los refugiados." [They chose to stay and eventually mixed their blood with that of our Creoles and Spaniards.

Numerous Dominican families today bear names inherited from the refugees.] *Los refugiados*, 9.

39. Lachance, "The 1809 Immigration," 278.

40. Ibid., 126.

41. Ibid., 135–36.

42. Babb, "French Refugees," 393, 391.

43. Fiehrer, "Saint-Domingue/Haiti," 433.

44. Cable, *Creoles of Louisiana*, 191.

45. Ronald Morazan's study of the veterans of the Battalion of New Orleans, cited by Lachance, "The 1809 Immigration," 280.

46. See Babb, "French Refugees," 398.

47. Brasseaux and Conrad, e.g., write that they "tended to blend into their new economic surroundings" (*Road to Louisiana*, xvi). In the late nineteenth century, Cable had already written that they "all too readily dissolv[ed] in the corresponding part of the native Creole community" (*Creoles of Louisiana*, 160).

48. Paul Lachance is the main defender of the thesis sustaining the disappearance of an ethnic feeling in the 1830s, although this conclusion might be mitigated. If it is true that they are not often mentioned as a community by later commentators or historians, it does not necessarily mean that their feeling of "symbolic ethnicity" disappeared altogether. If the main nineteenth-century intellectuals of the New Orleans free group of color are considered, they might attest to the persistence of strong ties among the second and even third generations of refugees. See chapters 6 and 7 for more details.

49. As Babb writes, "this decision would tend to curb their criticism and make for an easier assimilation," although this absence of critical attitude is by no means the only reason for their blending into the Louisiana society. Babb, "French Refugees," 392.

50. Cauna, *Haïti: l'éternelle révolution*, 295.

51. Tregle, *Louisiana in the Age of Jackson*, 199.

52. Certificate of naturalization of Jean Baptiste Donatien Augustin, a native of Port-au-Prince, New Orleans 1835. Augustin-Wogan-Labranche Family Papers, oversize folder.

53. Augustin-Wogan-Labranche Family Papers, folder 8.

54. Cable, "Creole Slave Songs," in *Creoles and Cajuns*, 403; *Creoles of Louisiana*, 315.

55. The references given here are to the version of Desdunes's book published in English (translated and edited by Sister Dorothea Olga McCants, Daughter of the Cross) in 2001 under the title *Our People and Our History: Fifty Creole Portraits*. Although the translation is not always entirely faithful to the original text, it seemed more convenient to include the English quotations in a text written in English. For people who can read French, however, a return to the 1911 original text is highly advisable.

56. Cossé Bell, "Haitian Immigration to Louisiana," 10.

57. Ibid., 11.

58. Ibid., 13.

59. Here, reference to the original is indispensable, since the translation loses several nuances of the French text. It reads: "Lanusse était d'abord Louisianais." "Et son instinct créole était encore plus prononcé chez lui que son attachement au titre de Louisianais ou au souvenir de son origine" (Desdunes, *Nos Hommes et Notre Histoire*, 1911 ed., 28). In McCant's translation, the quotation has lost some of its flavor, since a closer translation would be "Lanusse was first and foremost a Louisianan. And his Creole instinct was still more pronounced than his attachment to the title of Louisianan or to the memory of his origins" (Dessens translation). In the present discussion, the mention of the "memory of his origins" (which has become "everything pertaining to his origins" in McCant's translation) is, of course, crucial.

60. For instance, Meunier (145), Leroy (193), Dubergier (237), and Ely (291). All references are to the Will Books available at the New Orleans Public Library.

61. Allard (142), for instance.

62. Roiné (110), Allard (142), or Faunifs (162).

63. The exact quotation is "que ma fille soit indemnisée d'une partie de l'habitation," 162.

64. Pierre Dubourg de Ste. Colombe writes that his business in Saint-Domingue or Cuba has been settled (268). Jean-François Méance (296) shares the amount of the compensation among his heirs.

65. Marie Alexandrine Meunier (145), for example, was only twenty-six.

66. Marie Michel Sazin frees mulatto Zabeth who was born on her Saint-Domingue plantation in 1794 (239), but this is not the only example.

67. Boze to Sainte-Gême, Sainte-Gême Family Papers, esp. folders 134 to 268.

68. July and August 1829, folders 143 and 145, but also March 1830, folder 160, among others.

69. Docteur Lebeau, folder 152, for instance.

70. Folder 160, for example.

71. Folders 216 and 235, among others.

72. Folders 182 and 189.

73. See folder 216. Boze gives news of Mr. Marc Lafitte, notary, without mentioning his origins.

74. Hunt, *Haiti's Influence*, 46.

75. Brasseaux and Conrad, *Road to Louisiana*, xvii–xviii.

76. See, e.g., Sullivan-Holleman and Hillery Cobb's design in starting their genealogical research for *The Saint-Domingue Epic*. While doing research for this book, I met many residents of New Orleans who proudly referred to their Saint-Domingue ancestry or mentioned people they knew who were descended from Saint-Domingue refugees.

77. See Gans, "Symbolic Ethnicity: The Future of Ethnic Groups and Cultures in America." Although he only discusses contemporary migrations, his reflection is well adapted to the study of the Saint-Domingue group.

78. It may be recalled here that, although acculturation is more generally considered

the acquisition of cultural features peculiar to the host society by a group of migrants, it should be seen as a two-sided process. When defined by the Social Science Research Council in the mid-1930s, acculturation was said to comprehend "those phenomena which result when groups of individuals having different cultures come into continuous firsthand contact, with subsequent changes in the original cultural patterns of either or both groups." In the case of the refugees, there were some cultural differentials with the host society, continuous firsthand contact for many decades, and thus the possibility of reciprocal influences between the two groups.

79. In "Were Saint-Domingue Refugees a Distinctive Cultural Group in Antebellum New Orleans," Lachance, studying the marriage contracts, wonders about their degree of integration. Successively studying Tregle's inclusion of them into the group of the "foreign" French and Cable's description of their fusion into the Creole group, he concludes that the most adapted scenario is probably neither and that it is better to view them as a "distinctive cultural group" (173). To him, a close study of the marriage contracts proves that they were not immediately absorbed into the Louisiana society. He concludes that it would be better to substitute "the paradigm of a society stratified into culturally distinctive and competitive ethnic groups" with the "alternative paradigm of a cosmopolitan city in which individuals from various parts of the world collected, interacted, intermarried" (192). This new paradigm does not seem far from the definitions of the process of creolization.

80. Lachance insists on the progressive disappearance (through death or departure) of the refugees. He examines the numerous deaths entered in the burial records and mentions the "decline in the proportion of refugees in the White Catholic population due to the departure of some refugees, the arrival of other immigrants to replace them, and natural increase of the resident population." "The 1809 Immigration," 264.

81. "Nos colons de Saint-Domingue leur ont juré une haine implacable" [our St Domingue colonists have vowed them implacable hatred], folder 170.

82. Fiehrer, "From La Tortue to La Louisiane," 26.

83. This will be examined in detail in chapter 4.

84. See chapter 6. Recent historiographic trends, however, tend to downplay this role. In the second chapter of *Africans*, Hall insists that many features that were long attributed to the slaves from Saint-Domingue were direct importations from Africa. Whatever the origins of these influences, it is of deep interest that both primary sources and later historical works grant the refugees these influences. It is the best proof of their uncommon visibility.

85. Details will be given in chapter 5. Hall is clear about the fact that the Pointe Coupée rebellion had nothing to do with Saint-Domingue slaves directly, although the instigators of the rebellion were obviously influenced by news of the events in Saint-Domingue. Again, what is of interest to the present discussion is that, in the collective unconscious of the Louisianans, the Saint-Domingue refugees were so highly visible that they could not help but be at the origin of those events.

86. Cable, *Creoles of Louisiana*, 170, 172.

87. Cossé Bell writes, "Nowhere in North America, however, did the refugee movement exert as profound an influence as in South Louisiana." "Haitian Immigration," 2.

88. Cable, *Creoles of Louisiana*, 160.

89. Many historians, although with various interpretative lines, reach this conclusion, among them Fiehrer, Tregle, and Cossé Bell.

90. To Tregle, "it was a prize worth fighting for, and the Anglo-Americans soon felt the effectiveness of this leadership against them." *Louisiana in the Age of Jackson*, 53.

91. Tregle sustains the thesis that they became mere tools in the hands of the Creoles and that perhaps they were granted more visibility because they appeared as the Americans' most "potent enemy," which, according to Tregle, led the latter to do them "the honor never to underestimate their [the enemy's] skill or prowess" (53). This scenario is, however, challenged by Lachance in his "Were Saint-Domingue Refugees" (see esp. 172–73).

## Chapter 4

1. Rodríguez Demorizi cites several examples of their contributions to the society and economy of Santo Domingo, including the development of new food products *La era de Francia en Santo Domingo*, 66–70.

2. Adélaïde-Merlande, *Histoire Générale*, 176.

3. See Debien, "Refugees in Cuba," 73, 86, and 89; Perez, 191. On Puerto Rico, see Lugue de Sanchez, "Les Français réfugiés à Porto Rico."

4. See Le Riverand, 181–82; Deive, *Las emigraciones*, 132; Fiehrer, "Saint-Domingue/Haiti," 430.

5. Deive, *Las emigraciones*, 129.

6. Debien, "Refugees in Cuba," 53.

7. In a letter to the Association de Généalogie d'Haïti, Madame Geneviève Ruffier Landre reports that the roofs of colonial houses are still covered with tiles bearing the names, addresses, and logos of six tile factories from Marseilles. Letter available at http://www.agh.qc.ca/routecuba.htm.

8. Debien, "Refugees in Cuba," 68, 102–103.

9. Baur, "International Repercussions," 407; Bryan, "Émigrés Conflict and Reconciliation," 17.

10. De Cauna, "La diaspora," 348–51 and 355–57.

11. Baur, "International Repercussions," 407.

12. Bryan, "Émigrés Conflicts and Reconciliations," 17; Osborne, *History of the Catholic Church in Jamaica*.

13. Baur quoting Courtlander, "International Repercussions," 408.

14. Hunt, *Haiti's Influence*, 63.

15. See Gardien, "The Domingan Kettle: Philadelphian-Emigre Planters in Alabama," or Hunt, *Haiti's Influence*, 65.

16. In 1818, Madison said: "I have understood that the market of Baltimore has

been much benefited in dry seasons by the irrigation introduced by exiles from St. Domingo." Quoted in Baur, "International Repercussions," 399.

17. Baur, "International Repercussions," 397. Also see Gardien, "The Domingan Kettle," and Childs, *French Refugee Life*, 144–58. Garesché Holland, studying the refugee community in St. Louis, Missouri, also notes that they were well educated, had cultured tastes, and displayed uncommon dynamism. What is most noticeable to her is their readiness to turn to almost any activity to survive and their obvious will to make a new start "Saint-Louis Families from the French West Indies," 50.

18. Baur, "International Repercussions," 399. For occupational patterns in Philadelphia, New York, and in New Jersey, see Althéa de Puech, trans., *My Odyssey*, book 8, 180–81. For more details, see Babb, "French Refugees," 107–55. The refugees could be found in many areas of the job market. They became "pastry cooks, dancing and fencing masters, bakers, dressmakers, hairdressers, 'clearstarchers,' gardeners, teachers, botanists, physicians and surgeons." Logan, *The Diplomatic Relations of the United States with Haiti*, 48.

19. "For example, they were credited with introducing new fashions in jewelry, fresh modes of dancing and music, and a variety of confections. It was said that they induced their host country to use sweet oil and tomatoes, teaching Anglo-Saxons to prepare excellent soups, salads and ragouts, and fricassees." Baur, "International Repercussions," 397.

20. A leaflet mentions that Saint-Mary of the Annunciation was founded on August 24, 1789, that it was the first Catholic church in Georgia and the Carolinas, and that the "names of the trustees on the first deed of trust appear to have been Irish, owing to the early influx of Irish immigrants into the port of Charleston. French refugees from the West Indies greatly augmented this congregation. In 1793, the Marquis de Grasse with 100 white passengers and 14 servants, escaped from Santa Domingo during an insurrection and came to Charleston. The Marquis de Grasse had a noteworthy role in the American Revolution, having commanded naval forces of the Marquis de La Fayette's at the decisive British surrender at Yorktown on October 19, 1781. Two daughters of Admiral de Grasse were later interred in the churchyard. Other insurrections occurred in the West Indies, and ships brought more refugees, many descendants of whom currently attend St. Mary's. By Easter, 1819, there were 200 Communicants. The registers of the church were kept in French until 1822, when newly appointed Bishop John England directed that records were to be recorded in English. Bishop England was the seventh pastor of St. Mary's and the first Bishop of the new Diocese of Charleston (which encompassed the two Carolinas and Georgia)." Also see Baur, "International Repercussions," 399.

21. Among many others, Clark, *New Orleans*, 1718–1812, 276; Kendall, *History of New Orleans*, 86; Cable, *Creoles of Louisiana*, 157.

22. Ingersoll, *Mammon and Manon*, 257.

23. There are some instances, however, of refugees in a total state of destitution. Boze, for example, mentions one of Sainte-Gême's debtors who cannot be asked to pay

his debt, for his poverty can be truthfully compared to Job's ("On peut bien sans mentir le comparer à la pauvreté de Job"). Sainte-Gême Papers, folder 55. Also see *Louisiana Gazette*, June 6, 1809, for another example of a destitute refugee. There is a letter of February 18, 1812, from Widow Barpon to the mayor of New Orleans, in Bonnie Mathews and John Minor WISDOM Collection, MC 230, Louisiana Collection, Tulane University, box 6, doc. 219. These examples, however, are extremely rare when considering the enormous refugee population, and Lachance, studying the marriage contracts of New Orleans, shows that "white refugees were not quite so destitute." "Were Saint-Domingue Refugees," 191.

24. For instance, Hunt, *Haiti's Influence*, 83. Paul Lachance, who is presently researching the apprentice contracts, has found that the contracts demonstrate a much higher literacy rate among refugees than among other New Orleans residents.

25. James Mather to Claiborne, August 7, 1809, in Rowland, ed., *Official Letter Books*, 4:405.

26. Quoted by Fiehrer, "Saint-Domingue/Haiti," 354.

27. The New Orleans Public Library contains many of these sources: The indenture and apprentice contracts in the City Archives (Mayor's Office), issues of the *Louisiana Gazette* on microfilm, the New Orleans Books of Wills, and the *New Orleans Directory*. Marriage contracts (and other notarial archives) are available at the New Orleans Notarial Archives Research Center.

28. Fiehrer, "Saint-Domingue/Haiti," 432.

29. While corroborating Fiehrer's findings concerning the lower average income (even adding that no refugee could be found among the richest 10 percent signers of marriage contracts), Lachance studies both marriage contracts and newspaper advertisements, concluding that "in the short run at least, they reinforced the existing urban occupational structure by adding to all sectors proportionately." Lachance, "The 1809 Immigration," 269–70, 275. Also see Lachance, "The Foreign French," 123–25.

30. Sullivan-Holleman and Hillery Cobb, *The Saint-Domingue Epic*, 451. The social and political activities of Moreau-Lislet will be detailed in the next chapters.

31. King, *Creole Families of New Orleans*, 395. Among other references to the Canonge family, see King, 393–95, and Babb, "French Refugees," 174. Also see Maduell, *Marriage Contracts*, August 17, 1816, 9:362.

32. Babb, "French Refugees," 175.

33. See Villeré, "The Enterprising Career of Don Pablo Lanusse in Colonial New Orleans," 243–44. Also see Debien and Le Gardeur, "Refugees in Louisiana," 221.

34. All documents pertaining to this information are in the Augustin-Wogan-Labranche Family Papers (1830–1936), especially folders 4–6 (Special Collections, Tulane University). Also see Boze, folder 232, Sainte-Gême Family Papers, MS 100, Historic New Orleans Collection.

35. For a detailed picture of who and what Sainte-Gême was, see his Family Papers. He gave his house, located 1 rue Bourgogne, as well as several slaves to his children (folder 27). One of the rented houses was located in town, the other in the Faubourg (folder 41).

36. See King, *Creole Families of New Orleans*, chapter 33, 120; also see Debien and Le Gardeur, "Refugees in Louisiana," 224.

37. Among many others, see Babb, "French Refugees," 173.

38. Ibid., 172.

39. Ibid., 171.

40. Lambert Family Papers, 244, Louisiana Collection, Tulane University. Folder 6 contains all the official documents concerning Pierre-Alexandre (appointment as administrator of Charity Hospital by Governor White, appointment to the Eastern Medical Board, etc.).

41. Fiehrer, "Saint-Domingue/Haiti," 433, and King, *Creole Families of New Orleans*, 405. The archives give dozens of other cases.

42. Boze to Sainte-Gême, folder 152; Le Gardeur to Debien, MS 61, Louisiana Collection, Tulane University.

43. King, *Creole Families of New Orleans*, 398–99.

44. Melville, *Louis William DuBourg*, 303.

45. See Debien and Le Gardeur, "Refugees in Louisiana," 213 (quoting *Le Moniteur de la Louisiane*, January 3, 1806), and Boze to Sainte-Gême (MS 100, Historic New Orleans Collection), folders 182, 268, 213, 230, 228, 34. The example of John Davis could have been mentioned here, although his achievements will be considered in the last chapter dealing with cultural influences. About Davis, see Babb, "French Refugees," 184.

46. All these examples were taken from the archives of Marc Lafitte, 2:164, 3:227, and 6:438.

47. Cited in Debien and Le Gardeur, "Refugees in Louisiana," 217.

48. See Lachance's detailed study of the bakers' declarations in "The 1809 Immigration," 273.

49. Debien and Le Gardeur, "Refugees in Louisiana," 211 and 225; Le Gardeur to Debien, MS 561, Tulane's Special Collections, 61; Boze to Sainte-Gême, folder 252; Le Gardeur to Debien, MS 561, 62.

50. Boze to Sainte-Gême, folder 188; Debien and Le Gardeur, "Refugees in Louisiana," 206; Marriage Contracts, files of Marc Lafitte, 8:75.

51. Marriage Contracts, Files of Marc Lafitte, 3:213, 8:69.

52. For instance, André Daniel Chastart among goldsmiths (Debien and Le Gardeur, "Refugees in Louisiana," 153), Puech, who was an ironmonger on Levee (Boze to Sainte-Gême, folder 160), or Antoine Léon, a free man of color, who was a carpenter (Marriage Contracts, files of Marc Lafitte, 4:283).

53. See detailed study by Paul Lachance in "The 1809 Immigration," 270–72.

54. Boze to Sainte-Gême, folder 222, for Forcisi; *New Orleans Directory* 1822 for Charbonnet. As for Pilié, he is mentioned by Boze, folder 230.

55. Boze, folders 217 and 244; Debien and Le Gardeur, "Refugees in Louisiana," 222.

56. The exact words are "ébéniste et menuisier." Boze, folder 231.

57. King, *Creole Families of New Orleans*, 420.

58. Berlin, *Many Thousands Gone*, 337.

59. Hunt, *Haiti's Influence*, 51.

60. Ibid., 74.

61. Babb, "French Refugees," 195.

62. Advertisements in *Le Courrier de la Louisiane*, cited by Lachance in "The 1809 Immigration," 270–72.

63. Sainte-Gême Papers, folder 134.

64. Gayarré's manuscript quoted in Babb, "French Refugees," 197. Studying the marriage contracts and other notarized acts, Lachance shows that the women of color, among refugees, were often much better off than their Creole counterparts, adding that "female refugees of color arrived with more property than local free women of color had been able to accumulate." Lachance, "Were the Saint-Domingue Refugees," 191.

65. Mather to Claiborne, July 18, 1809, Rowland, ed., *Official Letter Books*, 4:388.

66. Desdunes, *Our People*, 92, 94. Also see Babb, "French Refugees," 196.

67. Mather to Claiborne, July 18, 1809, Rowland, ed., *Official Letter Books*, 4:387–88. On refugee slaves' occupations, see Debien and Le Gardeur, "Refugees in Louisiana," 173.

68. Sainte-Gême Papers, folder 229, for instance.

69. Ibid., folder 182.

70. Lachance, "The 1809 Immigration," 275, 278.

71. Letter of July 15, 1790, of the Terrien brothers, Navailles-Bonnas Papers, Archives départementales des Hautes-Pyrénées.

72. Debien, "Une plantation de Saint-Domingue," 127.

73. For more details about the sugar industry in Louisiana, see Conrad and Lucas, *White Gold*.

74. Sitterson writes that Josef Solís was "an emigrant from Santo Domingo." *Sugar Country*, 8. I have been unable to either prove or disprove this assertion.

75. Ibid.; Logan, *Diplomatic Relations*, 48; Conrad and Lucas, *White Gold*, 6; Babb, "French Refugees," 164; Berlin, *Many Thousands Gone*, 342.

76. Conrad and Lucas, *White Gold*, 8.

77. Ibid., 7.

78. Hunt, *Haiti's Influence*, 63.

79. Dunbar-Nelson, "People of Color in Louisiana," 15.

80. This was the case of James Pitot, although he chose to enter the political arena when he reached New Orleans. Debien and Le Gardeur, "Refugees in Louisiana," 153.

81. Sitterson, *Sugar Country*, 10.

82. Babb, "French Refugees," 164.

83. Dunbar-Nelson, "People of Color in Louisiana," 16. For such expressions of the refugees' indispensable expertise and dynamism, also see Berlin, *Many Thousands Gone*, 342; John B. Redder in *Encyclopedia of Southern Culture*, ed. Wilson and Ferris, 577; Cable in *Creoles of Louisiana*, 110; and Conrad and Lucas, *White Gold*, 10.

84. Berlin, *Many Thousands Gone*, 347.

85. Lachance, "The 1809 Immigration," 271.

86. Faust, "Slavery in the American Experience," 13.

87. De Cauna, *Haïti*, l'éternelle revolution, 297.

88. Wittler Ross, *Jean Lafitte*, 4; Remini, *Battle of New Orleans*, 28; Saxon, *Lafitte the Pirate*, 16; Cossé-Bell, "Haitian Immigration," 5. In *Jean Laffite, Prince of Pirates*, Ramsay is less assertive: "In the absence of any acceptable documentary proof, the parents of Jean and Pierre must have been, along with the others who bore similar surnames, a part of the Caribbean island colonial system known in the seventeenth century as Saint-Domingue" (10).

89. The birth of Marie Josephe Lafite [*sic*], the daughter of Pierre and Adelaïde Maseleri, "resident of the parish of St. Louis of Jeremie on Santo Domingo," is recorded in the Archdiocese sacramental records, with the mention that Pierre was a native of Bayonne, France. Nolan, *Sacramental Records*, 10:254. Also see Levet-Gerbel in *New Orleans Genesis*, 101–5, and Wilson, *The Architecture of Colonial Louisiana*, 49. William C. Davis's biography, *The Pirates Laffite*, indicates Pauillac as their birthplace. The first chapter of the book (and corresponding endnotes) displays more hypotheses than evidence. It does link Pierre Laffite to Saint-Domingue, mentioning at least two stays on the island: 1793 through 1794 and 1800 (or 1801) through 1803. This connection is also based on assumptions rather than documentary evidence.

90. Wittler-Ross, *Jean Lafitte*, 5, 11; Remini, *Battle of New Orleans*, 28; Saxon, *Lafitte the Pirate*, 44, 207. Only Ramsay says that Renato Beluche was born in New Orleans in 1780. *Jean Laffite*, Prince of Pirates, 14.

91. Cable, *Creoles of Louisiana*, 164, 170.

92. Saxon, *Lafitte the Pirate*, 264.

93. Cable, *Creoles of Louisiana*, 169.

94. Saxon, *Lafitte the Pirate*, 76–77, 267.

95. Gayarré, 2:7–8.

96. Saxon, *Lafitte the Pirate*, 47, 78.

97. Ibid., 207.

98. Ramsay, *Jean Laffite, Prince of Pirates*, 87.

99. Ibid., 145.

100. For more information on their role during the Battle of New Orleans, see, e.g., Remini, *Battle of New Orleans*, 34–36, or Ramsay, *Jean Laffite, Prince of Pirates*, 33–34.

101. Stanley Clisby Arthur, *Jean Lafitte, Gentleman Rover*, quoted in Wittler Ross, *Jean Lafitte*, 12. On the legendary quality of Jean Lafitte, also see Saxon, *Lafitte the Pirate*, 207.

102. Ramsay, *Jean Laffite, Prince of Pirates*, ix.

103. See Sainte-Gême Papers, folder 152; Babb, "French Refugees," 178; Debien and Le Gardeur, "Refugees in Louisiana," 172, 230; Marriage Contract, files of Marc Lafitte, December 5, 1810, 1:110; Debien and Le Gardeur, "Refugees in Louisiana," 230.

104. Debien and Le Gardeur, "Refugees in Louisiana," 215.

105. Hunt, *Haiti's Influence*, 65.

106. Babb, "French Refugees," 177; Debien and Le Gardeur, "Domingue Refugees in Louisiana," 230.

107. Debien and Le Gardeur, "Refugees in Louisiana," 210.

108. This chapter focuses on the economic influences. The cultural implications of the development of these new fields will be examined in chapter 7.

109. Debien and Le Gardeur, "Refugees in Louisiana," 219.

110. Ibid., 231.

111. With his wife, a local actress, the manager of the French Theater, Alexandre Placide, later took on the management of the American Charleston Theater. Hunt, *Haiti's Influence*, 71.

112. Le Gardeur to Debien, MS 561, Louisiana Collection, Tulane University, 60, 68.

113. Debien and Le Gardeur, "Refugees in Louisiana," 159, 160, 207, 223, and 228.

114. See Sullivan-Holleman and Hillery Cobb, 457; Marino, "Early French Newspapers in New Orleans," 310.

115. In Charleston, they founded and ran *Le Patriote Français* (for less than a year starting in 1795), *L'Echo du Sud, Moniteur Français* (from late April to mid-July 1801), and *L'Oracle, Français-Américain* (from January 1 to December 8, 1807). These contributions were short-lived, and most of the refugees involved in them later went to other refuges to launch new journalistic ventures (Claude Beleurgey, Jean Dacqueny, Alexandre Bourgeois, J. J. Negrin). For more information on the Charleston refugee press, see Haggy and Van Ruymbeke, 140–44. In New York or Philadelphia, Tanguy founded *Le Journal des Révolutions de la Partie Française de Saint-Domingue* before becoming the editor of another publication, *Etoile Américaine*, and the publisher of the *Niveau de l'Europe et de l'Amérique*, edited by another refugee, a certain Egron, a former jurist. After the interruption of his Charleston *Oracle*, Negrin moved north and took over the *Daily Advertiser* in New York. He renamed it *L'Oracle* and issued it from January 1 to September 10, 1808. He then moved to Philadelphia, where he published a bilingual newspaper, *L'Hemisphère*, from October 1809 to September 1811. The highly developed refugee press also contained the very famous *Courrier Français*, known for its republican trends, Gatereau's *Courrier Politique*, as well as his daily *Courrier de la France et des Colonies*, displaying clear royalist positions, published at Moreau de Saint-Méry's press in Philadelphia from October 15, 1795, until March 14, 1796. On the refugee press in the northern United States, see Sergeant Childs, *French Refugee Life*, 138–40. Gareschè Holland mentions Pierre and Francis Tesson, who, after being newspapermen in Boston and Charleston, came to St. Louis to conduct the same activities. "Saint-Louis Families from the French West Indies," 44.

116. In Charleston, as elsewhere, they had opened schools and become teachers. Although teachers were not numerous in the town, thirteen were refugees from Saint-Domingue. Among them, "Madame Anne-Marie Talvande, a St. Domingan, [who] established an academy that soon gained a reputation throughout the South for offering 'ladies of dignity' [a] liberal education of the old sort." Hunt, *Haiti's Influence*, 54.

117. Lachance, "The 1809 migration," 131.

118. *Memoirs of Eliza Williams (Chotard Gould)*, Marshall Papers #3256, Louisiana State University, Louisiana Collection.

119. For further details on the educational field in general, see Hunt, *Haiti's Influence*, 54–58; Babb, "French Refugees," 180; Debien and Le Gardeur, "Refugees in Louisiana," 158, 205–6; and Sullivan-Holleman and Hillery Cobb, 458.

120. See René Nicaud, "French Colonists from St. Domingue," 1.

121. Dubourg also founded three elementary and high schools in St. Louis, as well as the Maryville College and St. Louis College for boys (which later became the St. Louis University). Garesché Holland, "Saint-Louis Families from the French West Indies," 43.

122. See King, *Creole Families of New Orleans*, 399, Debien and Le Gardeur, "Refugees in Louisiana," 217, 222, and Sainte-Gême Papers, folder 230.

123. For a detailed narration of the Battle of New Orleans, see Remini, *Battle of New Orleans*, 100, or Gehman, *Free People of Color of New Orleans*, 59. Also see Cossé Bell's *Revolution*, 51–60, a well done study of the participation of the free refugees of color.

124. Debien and Le Gardeur, "Refugees in Louisiana," 227. Also see Beulah de Vérière Smith Watts and Nancy Jane Lucas de Grummond, *Solitude*, 11.

125. Sterkx, *Free Negro in Ante-Bellum Louisiana*, 184. In his PhD dissertation, Everett comments on the monthly $30 granted to Savary, comparing this amount to the usual sum of $8 given to veterans or their survivors. "Free Persons of Color in New Orleans, 1803–1865," 83. The difference is a good indicator of the gratitude of the American authorities.

126. Lachance, "The 1809 Migration," 125.

127. Remini, *Battle of New Orleans*, 100; Bernard Marigny, "Reflections on the Campaign of General Andrew Jackson in Louisiana in 1814 and 1815," 74. Also see Dunbar-Nelson, "People of Color in Louisiana," 24–25.

128. Lachance citing Ronald Morazan's research in "The 1809 Migration," 138.

129. Remini, *Battle of New Orleans*, 108.

## Chapter 5

1. To take one example, the collection of articles edited by James H. Dormon, *Creoles of Color of the Gulf South*, aimed at filling a historiographical gap by dealing with this often neglected group, creates a new gap by not mentioning the arrival of the Saint-Domingue refugees. Only 4 pages out of 190 allude to them in an article on the Creole language by Valdman, "The Place of the Louisiana Creole." The same phenomenon is found in Brasseaux et al., *Creoles of Color in the Bayou Country*, which makes but a short allusion to the refugees of color, also in connection with the Creole language (xi).

2. Lachance, "The 1809 Immigration," 278, 268. Lachance writes: "The racial mix of the 1809 migration meshed with that of the host society. In this respect, Saint-Domingue refugees differed from the uniquely white German and Irish immigrants who had the opposite effect: it reinforced the existing racial structure" (267–68). In "Repercussions of the Haitian Revolution," Lachance's opinion goes one step forward,

thus confirming the impact of the migration. He writes that it "substantially increased the proportion of free persons of color to the total population" (213).

3. Domínguez, *White by Definition*, 110.

4. Report of the mayor of New Orleans to Governor Claiborne on January 18, 1810, published in the *Moniteur de la Louisiane*, January 27, 1810.

5. Lachance, "The Formation of a Three-Caste Society," 227.

6. Berlin, *Many Thousands Gone*, 224.

7. Ibid., 334.

8. Augier et al., *Making of the West Indies*, 115.

9. Berlin, *Many Thousands Gone*, 350.

10. Fiehrer, "The African Presence," 20.

11. In his article "Were Saint-Domingue Refugees a Distinctive Cultural Group in Antebellum New Orleans?" Lachance shows that the free refugee women of color had more wealth than the Louisiana free Creole women. See his study of the marriage contracts, 191.

12. For Desdunes, the group cohesion is unquestionable. Mentioning the Creoles of color of Louisiana and the free people of color coming from Saint-Domingue and even Martinique, he writes that "having been subjected to the same conditions in life, they experienced among themselves a strong bond of unity." In *Our People and Our History*, trans. McCants, 3.

13. For a detailed comparative study of the Anglo-American South and the French and Spanish West Indian colonies, see Dessens, *Myths of the Plantation Society*, esp. 65–71.

14. Gehman, *Free People of Color of New Orleans*, 51. Also see Schafer, *Becoming Free*, as well as Hanger, *Bounded Lives*, 163.

15. Hanger, *Bounded Lives*, 143.

16. Foner, "The Free People of Color in Louisiana and St. Domingue," 427–28.

17. For more details, see Hanger, *Bounded Lives*, 163.

18. Gehman, *Free People of Color of New Orleans*, 53.

19. See Lachance, "Were Saint-Domingue Refugees," 191. He even shows that "displacement first by the revolution and then by events in Cuba appears to have narrowed racial differences in property owned by the Saint-Domingue refugees," which comparatively conferred more weight to the free refugees of color in New Orleans.

20. See marriage contracts (Marc Lafitte files) and the New Orleans Books of Wills (New Orleans Public Library), for evidence of their possession of property in chattel, including slaves. In vol. 4 of the Books of Wills (1824–33), see, e.g., 69, 71, 86, and 223. The last example, that of Marie-Madeleine, born in Petite Rivière, in the Artibonite, who knows neither her age nor the identity of her father, but who was born of a free woman of color, shows the extent of their possessions. She bequeaths to her natural children two lots of land in Faubourg La Course, the buildings on them, and four slaves.

21. Gehman cites the figure of $2.5 million in property in New Orleans by the mid-1830s. *Free People of Color*, 53. Berlin gives a total of $2,628,200 in real estate detained

by the free people of color in 1860. *Slaves without Masters*, 197. For precise examples, see marriage contracts and wills.

22. Cossé Bell, "Haitian Immigration," 5.

23. Gehman, *Free People of Color*, 74.

24. For more details on these petitions, see Hanger, *Bounded Lives*, 55–57, 127, 132–34. Although Hanger deals essentially with the colonial period, she cannot help but mention those Saint-Domingue free people of color, evoking the "dramatic increase and cultural influence" they brought to the Creole of color class (163).

25. See Hall, *Africans*, 237–74.

26. See, e.g., Debien and Le Gardeur, "Refugees in Louisiana," 173.

27. This was true in all the refugees' asylums. Daniel Schafer quotes the example of Francis Richard, a refugee in Florida, who made a will "providing for his large 'colored' family, as well as for his white son." He gives details about the property he bequeathed to each of them. Schafer, "A Class of People Neither Freemen Nor Slaves," 595. There are numerous such bequests in the New Orleans Books of Wills. See, e.g., Pierre Grégoire Allais, June 1827, vol. 4 (1824–33), 142, or Henry Ely, August 1830, 4:291.

28. Their political vitality will be discussed in chapter 6, and their cultural abilities and influences in chapter 7.

29. Gehman, *Free People of Color of New Orleans*, 54.

30. Cable, *Creoles of Louisiana*, 172.

31. Martin, "Plaçage and the Louisiana Gens de Couleur Libre," 68, 69.

32. It is very difficult to assess scientifically the comparative degree of tolerance in matters of race relations. What is certain is that although there was fluidity in Louisiana, especially in the rural areas, it seems to have been still truer in Saint-Domingue. Even if this had not been the case, the common experience of flight, migration, and successive relocations undoubtedly strengthened the ties between the white and black free refugees and prevented racial segregation in their relocation. On racial fluidity in Louisiana before the migration, see Usner, *Indians*, and Hall, *Africans*, among others.

33. This was true in all the refuges, although it was more visible in the non-Catholic asylums. In Jamaica or in Charleston, the arrival of the refugee community was followed by the development of an organized Catholic Church. In Charleston, e.g., their arrival favored the expansion of St. Mary of the Annunciation. On the development of the Catholic Church in Jamaica, see Cauna, "La diaspora," 351–55.

34. Melville, *DuBourg*, 42.

35. Debien and Le Gardeur, "Refugees in Louisiana," 162.

36. Melville, *DuBourg*, 1.

37. To give but a single instance of this, Pedro Barrère, who died in August 1809, is not identified in the entry as connected with Saint-Domingue, but there is a marginal note indicating "family from Santo Domingo." Nolan, *Sacramental Records*, 9:20.

38. Deggs, *No Cross, No Crown*, 18.

39. See Clark and Gould, "The Feminine Face of Afro-Catholicism."

40. Fiehrer, e.g., grants Delille Saint-Domingue ancestry in his article "Saint-Domingue/Haiti," 433. Cossé-Bell also writes: "The congregation of the Sisters of the

Holy Family was founded in 1842 by Henriette Delille, yet another prominent Afro-Creole of Haitian ancestry" ("Haitian Immigration," 14). She links her to the Oblate Sisters of Providence, founded in Baltimore in 1829, in which the role of the Saint-Domingue refugees was indeed essential.

41. Gould and Nolan, preface to Deggs, *No Cross, No Crown*, xxvi–xxvii. Virginia Gould, who is in the process of completing an exhaustive biography of Delille, shows that her ancestry can be traced back many generations in Louisiana. See Gould and Nolan, as well as Clark and Gould, "Feminine Face."

42. For a detailed account of Dubourg's early life, see Melville, *DuBourg*, 10–40. She gives much information about his family in Saint-Domingue, their flight, their various asylums (Baltimore, Philadelphia, Jamaica). From page 40 onwards, she gives details about his various appointments on the American continent.

43. Ibid., 5.

44. Ibid., 2. Melville's introduction really gives the impression of a series of close connections with the refugee diaspora, wherever Dubourg went in the Americas, including, of course, Louisiana.

45. Ibid., 42.

46. See, e.g., Gould and Nolan, preface, xxix–xxx.

47. Quoted in Melville, *DuBourg*, 2:282.

48. Gould and Nolan, preface, xxviii.

49. Cable, *Creoles of Louisiana*, 157, 167.

50. Ibid., 170, 172.

51. Ibid., 218.

52. They had the same kind of influence on all the asylums in which they settled, even temporarily. In Santo Domingo, Cuba, and Jamaica, they opened cafés and gambling places and stimulated socialization. For more details, see Demorizi, Deive, Debien, and Cauna's publications.

53. Babb, "French Refugees," 159.

54. Joan Martin, quoting "popular historian" Eleanor Early, confirms this reinforcement. "Plaçage," 62.

55. Ibid., 62–68; Gehman, *Free People of Color of New Orleans*, 14.

56. Marino, "Early French Newspapers in New Orleans," 317.

57. See, e.g., Debien, "Refugees in Cuba," 104.

58. See, e.g., Garesché Holland, "Saint-Louis Families from the French West Indies," 51. She also quotes historian J. Thomas Scharf in his *History of St. Louis City and County*, 2 vols. (Philadelphia: Everts, 1883), 1:308–9. Details on the other asylums may be found in Cauna or Debien, among others.

59. Babb, "French Refugees," 158.

60. More details will be given on this point in chapter 7.

61. Originally, King in *New Orleans: The Place, the People* (1895), 171–72, then quoted by many subsequent historians, e.g., John Smith Kendall in his 1922 *History of New Orleans*, 86, or René Nicaud, "French Colonists from St. Domingue," 4.

62. King, *New Orleans*, 171.

63. Even though the different waves that brought refugees to Louisiana were spread over a period of twenty years, the transfer of the territory that occurred exactly in the middle of the 1791–1810 time frame makes the migration and the transfer to the United States contemporaneous in the larger frame of Louisiana history.

64. Babb, "French Refugees," 158.

65. King, *New Orleans*, 172.

66. See, e.g., Saxon, *Lafitte the Pirate*, 124–28, where he quotes King extensively. The legend goes that, having to spend a night at a friend's on his way from New Orleans to Barataria, at a time when the authorities were attempting to dismantle Barataria, had imprisoned the leading privateers and were actively looking for Laffite, he encountered Mrs. Claiborne, concealed his identity from her, and it was reported that she had been absolutely charmed by him.

67. Lachance, "The 1809 Migration," 139.

68. Cable, *Creoles of Louisiana*, 160.

69. Debien and Le Gardeur, "Refugees in Louisiana," 114.

70. Lachance develops this thesis of a cosmopolitan Creole culture in his article entitled "Were Saint-Domingue Refugees." According to him, migration and intermarriage favored the development of a Creole culture which, in turn, favored further intermarriages and further creolization, concluding "it may be better to abandon the paradigm of a society stratified into culturally distinct and competitive groups for the alternative paradigm of a cosmopolitan city in which individuals from various parts of the world collected, interacted, intermarried, and produced a new generation that would in its turn interact, and intermarry with the next cohort of immigrants" (192).

71. Sullivan-Holleman and Hillery Cobb, 459.

72. Ibid.

## Chapter 6

1. This type of reaction was widespread in all the various asylums. In "'Hé St Domingo, songé St Domingo,'" Bridget Brereton shows that the free group of color probably suffered most from the political reaction to the settlement of the refugees in Trinidad.

2. See Hunt, *Haiti's Influence*, 108–9, 120.

3. See, e.g., Ingersoll, *Mammon and Manon*, 180, 186, 208, 239. Hanger gives an interesting interpretation of the exclusion of a Saint-Domingue free black tailor from Louisiana and comments on the Bailly trial. *Bounded Lives*, 152–53. Also see Dunbar-Nelson, "People of Color in Louisiana," 16, and Berlin, *Many Thousands Gone*, 340.

4. Berlin, *Many Thousands Gone*, 351.

5. For more details about this, see ibid., 356, and Cossé Bell, *Revolution*, 75–77.

6. See Hall on Cuba in *Social Control*, 126.

7. In a letter to James Madison, Claiborne explained in July 1804 that "the events which had spread blood and desolation in St. Domingo originated in a dispute between the white and mulatto inhabitants, and that the too rigid treatment of the for-

mer induced the latter to seek support and assistance of the Negroes." Rowland, ed., *Official Letter Books*, 2:234–45.

8. This was true in Cuba and in Jamaica, but also in Trinidad, as suggested by Bridget Brereton, "'Hé St Domingo, songé St Domingo.'"

9. See Babb, "French Refugees," 288–93.

10. Hunt, *Haiti's Influence*, 122, and Babb, "French Refugees," 247.

11. Cossé Bell concludes that "Colonel Savary and his soldiers nourished a republican revolutionary tradition within the New Orleans Afro-Creole community." "Haitian Immigration," 8.

12. This was true in Cuba but also in Trinidad, where a total ban on the importation of slaves followed arrival of the refugees on the island.

13. Yacou in Martin and Yacou, eds., *De la revolution*, 37–38.

14. Ott, *Haitian Revolution*, 194. Also see Cauna, *Haiti, l'éternelle révolution*, 288, and Alderson, "Charleston's Rumored Slave Revolt of 1793."

15. Rapport de V. Hugues and Lebas, Ventôse an 9 (1801), Archives Nationales des Colonies C7–A49. Also see José Marcial Ramos Guedez, "L'insurrection nègre."

16. Gardner, *History of Jamaica*, 239. Burton also studies this phenomenon in Jamaica, linking the organization of the Christmas uprising to Saint-Domingue slaves (*Afro-Creole*, 84) and speaking of the "knowledge of events in Saint-Domingue often diffused by slaves from the former colony," even if he says there is no proof it was the case of the Christmas uprising (85).

17. See Wall, *Louisiana: A History*, 101. There are also complaints addressed to Claiborne in 1804 concerning the visit of twelve black Haitians from a passing vessel who "used many insulting and menacing expressions" and "spoke of eating human flesh, and in general demonstrated great savageness of character, boasting of what they had seen and done in the horrors of Saint Domingue." Cossé Bell, *Revolution*, 33.

18. Letter to Claiborne, November 9, 1804, quoted in Debien and Le Gardeur, "Refugees in Louisiana," 186.

19. See Cauna, *Haiti, l'éternelle révolution*, 291; Ott, *Haitian Revolution*, 196. Dolores Hernandez Guerrero writes, "Es indubitable que la lucha de los esclavos de Saint Domingue repercutió en los levantamientos de esclavos en Charleston, Virginia y Pointe Coupée, Luisiana, especialmente a raíz de la migración de colonos franceses y sus esclavos a la Luisiana." [It is doubtless that the fight of the Saint Domingue slaves had repercussions on the slave uprisings of Charleston, Virginia, and Pointe Coupée, Louisiana, especially because of the migration of French colonists and their slaves to Louisiana.] *La revolución haitiana y el fin de un sueño colonial (1791–1801)*, 71. On Charleston, see Geggus, "The Caradeux," in Geggus ed., 231–46 and Matt D. Childs, "'A Black French General Arrived to Conquer the Island,'" in Geggus ed., 135–56.

20. Babb even speaks of "hysteria" and quotes an article published in a New York newspaper referring to the Saint-Domingue slaves' insolence. "French Refugees," 224.

21. Ibid., 227. This is confirmed by Hunt, who declares that Prosser had been inspired and advised by people connected with Saint-Domingue. *Haiti's Influence*, 118.

22. Egerton, "Denmark Vesey: The Buried History," 155.

23. For more details on this, see Egerton's article on Vesey's revolutionary theology, "Why They Did Not Preach Up This Thing."*

24. See Babb, "French Refugees," 227, and Hunt, *Haiti's Influence*, 119. Original trial documents, as compiled by Pearson, indicate that "as soon as they could get the money from the Banks," Vesey's army planned to "hoist sail for Saint Domingo in hopes of obtaining asylum from Haitian president Jean-Pierre Boyer." Pearson, *Designs against Charleston*, 187.

25. For a fuller of treatment of this issue as well as examples of contemporaries establishing connections with Haiti, see Hunt, *Haiti's Influence*, 121.

26. Cited in Debien and Le Gardeur, "Refugees in Louisiana," 176.

27. Address of Mayor John Watkin, September 28, 1805, cited in Babb, "French Refugees," 237.

28. Cited in Robertson, ed., *Louisiana under the Rule of Spain, France, and the United States*, 117–18.

29. Letter of Carrondelet to Las Casas, June 18, 1795, in Holmes, "The Abortive Slave Revolt at Pointe Coupée," 345.

30. See, e.g., Hall on the slave conspiracy in Pointe Coupée, *Africans*, 343–74.

31. Debien and Le Gardeur, "Refugees in Louisiana," 172. According to Debien and Le Gardeur, there are indications that this accusation may have been caused by jealousy or by a wish to rid the territory of the presence of Alliot, who may have been excessively politically involved and thus dangerous for some factions of Louisiana politics.

32. The introduction to Brasseaux and Conrad's *Road to Louisiana* mentions "the participation of Saint-Domingue refugees in the Pointe Coupée's abortive 1795 slave insurrection" (viii).

33. Debien and Le Gardeur write that Poydras had been "a soldier of fortune" there before establishing himself in Pointe Coupée around 1769. "Refugees in Louisiana," 127.

34. Berquin Duvallon cited in Robertson, ed., *Louisiana under the Rule of Spain*, France, and the United States, 179.

35. See, e.g., *Encyclopedia of Louisiana*, 93; Hall, *Africans*, 343–74. Berlin makes it clear that the conspiracies and rebellions of 1791, 1795, 1804, 1805, and 1811 are attributable to the influences exerted on the slaves by the stories told by the Saint-Domingue slaves. Mentioning Bailly, he writes that he was "proud that his people—the free people of color—had confronted their white tormentors in Saint-Domingue." *Many Thousands Gone*, 355.

36. Hall, *Africans*, 350–51.

37. Ibid., 371–72.

38. Littlefield, "Slavery in French Louisiana," 92; Dormon, "The Persistent Specter," 392.

39. Cossé Bell, *Revolution*, 47; Babb, "French Refugees," 239.

40. Ingersoll, *Mammon and Manon*, 192.

41. Letter from "A Gentleman at New Orleans" to "A Member of Congress," January 11, 1811, published in the *New York Evening Post* on February 19, 1811.

42. Dormon, "The Persistent Specter, 391.

43. This was true in all their asylums. In "'Hé St Domingo, songé St Domingo,'" Brereton mentioned individuals who became politically active in Trinidad, including Charles Joseph, comte de Loppinot, and Jean Charles, baron de Montalembert.

44. Such names as Alix, Gautreau, Duvergé, Montas, Richiez, Donastorg, Robiou, Coiscou, Fondeur, Capril, Civadier, Corporan, or Grateraux came recurrently in the political life of the Dominican Republic. Deive, *Los refugiados*, 107–8.

45. Tregle, "Creoles and Americans," 151, 153.

46. Sullivan-Holleman and Hillery Cobb, *Saint-Domingue Epic*, 458; Babb, "French Refugees," 175.

47. On Preval and Canonge, see, e.g., Sullivan-Holleman and Hillery Cobb, *Saint-Domingue Epic*, 457, and Lachance, "The Foreign French," 108; on Augustin, see Lachance, "The Foreign French," 108; on Bailly, see Debien and Le Gardeur, "Refugees in Louisiana," 208; on Dormenon, see Hunt, *Haiti's Influence*, 62.

48. On Davezac, see Sullivan-Holleman and Hillery Cobb, *Saint-Domingue Epic*, 457; Debien and Le Gardeur, "Refugees in Louisiana," 216; also see Augustin-Wogan-Labranche Family Papers, folders 4 and 8; Lachance, "The Foreign French," 108; Debien and Le Gardeur, "Refugees in Louisiana," 217.

49. On Pitot, see, e.g., Sullivan-Holleman and Hillery Cobb, *Saint-Domingue Epic*, 453. Etienne de Boré was technically the first mayor of American New Orleans, since he was maintained in his position at the time of the American takeover, following the terms of the Proclamation of 20 December 1803. He resigned in May 1804 and was replaced by Pitot, who became the first appointed mayor of American Louisiana.

50. Sullivan-Holleman and Hillery Cobb, *Saint-Domingue Epic*, 457.

51. Sainte-Gême Papers, folder 235. Also see Babb, "French Refugees," quoting the *Dictionary of American Biography*, 5:248–49; Hunt, *Haiti's Influence*, 62; Lachance, "The Foreign French," 112.

52. Sullivan-Holleman and Hillery Cobb, *Saint-Domingue Epic*, 457; Babb, "French Refugees," 175; Hunt, *Haiti's Influence*, 62.

53. Babb, "French Refugees," 171, quoting the *Dictionary of American Biography*, 5:89.

54. See Tregle, "Creoles and Americans," 153; Debien and Le Gardeur, "Refugees in Louisiana," 205; Sullivan-Holleman and Hillery Cobb, *Saint-Domingue Epic*, 451; Dargo, *Jefferson's Louisiana*, 151–52.

55. The present discussion will bear only on the cases of free people of color whose Saint-Domingue origins are certain. There are many other free blacks who may have had Saint-Domingue origins. Some historians have even stated that the persons mentioned did have refugee origins, but there is, for the moment, no definite proof that they had. Those persons are left out of the present discussion until their origins have been ascertained. What remains is that there were probably many more influential free blacks with Saint-Domingue connections than those cited in this chapter, especially among the second- or third-generation refugees, whose Saint-Domingue origins were

no longer stated in the sacramental records. A better assessment of the political influence of the Saint-Domingue free group of color will require a painstaking genealogical research. Many cases, such as that of Norbert Rillieux or Alexandre Pierre Thureaud, are still to be thoroughly researched. Nothing in the sacramental records indicates that Rillieux was connected with the refugee community. Several other Rillieux, however, were connected. J. C. Rillieux is mentioned as a free woman of color from Saint-Domingue in an 1820 marriage contract. V. E. Rillieux wrote a poem to the Desdunes when their mother died; the poem is joined to her obituary published in the September 10, 1895, issue of the *Crusader.* (See Desdunes Family Collection, Archives of Xavier University, New Orleans.)

56. Although these findings are contested by many historians of Louisiana, Ingersoll's findings indicate that the twenty-seven cases involving free blacks during the Spanish period show that "about two-thirds of the defendants were non-Louisiana free blacks who had been expelled from other colonies, especially from the West Indies." *Mammon and Manon*, 208.

57. Gehman, *Free People of Color of New Orleans*, 53.

58. Grandjean, a white refugee, plotted a slave rebellion, involving slaves and free blacks, in the aim of undermining the American authorities. One racially mixed man involved in the plot, Celestin, gave him away for an important sum of money, and Grandjean was arrested and convicted. For more details, see Gehman, *Free People of Color of New Orleans*, 53–55, or Ingersoll, *Mammon and Manon*, 291. One of the interests of this anecdote is to show that the white refugees were not hostile to group collusion in political action.

59. This petition was launched by the group of free men of color (among whom refugees were numerous) who later founded *L'Album Littéraire* and became star figures of the Louisiana literary world. Their works were gathered in *Les Cénelles* in 1845.

60. See, e.g., Hanger, *Bounded Lives*, 151; also see a more detailed discussion in Berlin, *Many Thousands Gone*, 337–38. Berlin writes that, "presenting slave ownership as evidence of their political reliability, the free people of color rested their case for enfranchisement and equality" (338).

61. This is a translated paraphrase of a quotation of Paul Lestrade in "José Marti et la Révolution Française," 208.

62. Logsdon and Cossé Bell, "Americanization," 205.

63. This expression was used by Sterkx as the title of one of his chapters in *The Free Negro in Ante-Bellum Louisiana.*

64. Sterkx, *Free Negro in Ante-Bellum Louisiana*, 170.

65. Gehman, *Free People of Color of New Orleans*, 70–71.

66. Sterkx, *Free Negro in Ante-Bellum Louisiana*, 165.

67. Gehman, *Free People of Color of New Orleans*, 71.

68. Assessing their republican idealism, Cossé Bell classifies them as "French Jacobins of the most radical stamp." *Revolution*, 47.

69. Ibid., 60.

70. For more details on these two societies, see ibid., 90, 125.

71. For a detailed discussion of *Les Cénelles*, as well as examples of poems contained in the 210-page volume, see Desdunes, *Our People*, ed. McCants, 10–47.

72. See Cossé Bell, *Revolution* and "Haitian Immigration," and Logsdon and Cossé Bell, "Americanization."

73. Cossé Bell, "Haitian Immigration," 10.

74. For the foundation and contents of *L'Union*, see ibid., 17–18.

75. See Cossé Bell's *Revolution*, 250–65, for a detailed presentation of the actions of the leaders of *La Tribune*. Also see Senter, "Creole Poets on the Verge of a Nation."

76. For all these activities, see Cossé Bell, *Revolution*, 268–82.

77. Logsdon and Cossé Bell, "Americanization," 254, 256.

78. For a detailed study of the *Crusader* and the intense activity of the free community of color, see ibid., 255–58.

79. Desdunes, *Our People*, ed. McCants, 148.

80. For a very detailed account of those actions, see chapter 12 of Desdunes, *Our People*, ed. McCants, 140–48. Also see Lester Sullivan's "The Unknown Rodolphe Desdunes: Writings in the New Orleans *Crusader*," which deals with *Abbott v. Hicks* of May 1892 in which the Supreme Court of Louisiana dismissed the charges against Daniel Desdunes. The A. P. Tureaud Papers (Amistadt Special Collections, Tulane University, New Orleans) contain documents of the Citizen's Committee on the action for the Annulment of Act 111. For a very good synthesis of these actions, see Scott's "Se battre pour ses droits," 199, 205. For a more general presentation, see Lofgren, *The Plessy Case*.

81. Regarding Du Bois, see Richardson in Sullivan-González and Wilson, eds., *The South and the Caribbean*, 17. The pamphlet can be found in the Tureaud Papers, Amistadt, Tulane University, New Orleans.

82. McCants, preface to Desdunes, *Our People*, Our History, xii, xxiii.

83. Nicaud, "French Colonists from St. Domingue," 6. For a detailed study of the Code, see Dargo, *Jefferson's Louisiana*, 156–64. For a comprehensive survey of the Common Law/Roman Law opposition, see Plauche Dart, "The Place of the Civil Law in Louisiana," esp. 168–70, and Kilbourne, *A History of the Louisiana Civil Code*.

84. Dargo, *Jefferson's Louisiana*, 151.

85. Ibid., 154.

86. Nicaud, "French Colonists from St. Domingue," 11.

87. Debien and Le Gardeur, "Refugees in Louisiana," 215.

88. Babb, "French Refugees," 172.

89. Hunt, *Haiti's Influence*, 60.

90. Debien and Le Gardeur, "Refugees in Louisiana," 213.

91. Nicaud, "French Colonists from St. Domingue," 6, 10.

92. Tregle, *Louisiana in the Age of Jackson*, 133.

93. Babb, "French Refugees," 304.

94. On the newspapers of Louisiana, see Marino, "Early French Newspapers in New Orleans."

95. Claiborne to Smith, November 18, 1809, in *Official Letter Books*, ed. Rowland, 5:14–15.

96. Claiborne, in ibid., 5:16.

97. The Batture controversy became one of the most disputed lawsuits of the early American period. It concerned ownership of the *Batture*—that is to say, piece of solid land left by the Mississippi alluvium—situated in front of the Faubourg St. Marie. On the Batture controversy, see Dargo, *Jefferson's Louisiana*, 100, and Dumas Malone, *The Sage of Monticello*, chap. 5.

98. See Dargo, *Jefferson's Louisiana*, 165, on this accusation. Thierry was accused of writing an anti-Jefferson article that he had not published, but of which all copies had not been destroyed. The article was then published by Colonel Bellechasse in 1808, so as to expose Thierry and reduce his influence in New Orleans.

99. Babb, "French Refugees," 301.

100. Cossé Bell, *Revolution*, 34.

101. For more details about this, see ibid., 258–61.

102. A closer study of these narratives would give interesting conclusions, but it would be too long to include here. For more details about this challenging thesis, see Fiehrer's "Saint-Domingue/Haiti," esp. 426, 434.

103. Ibid., 435.

104. Childs gives a detailed study of this question in *French Refugee Life*, 142–44.

105. There are several examples in De Bow, *The Industrial Resources, etc. of the Southern and Western States*, e.g., 342.

106. For instance, testimony of Captain Eggar, *Newport Mercury*, May 30, 1793, as well as an article published on February 14, 1792, in the *Maryland Journal* and *Baltimore Advertiser* or in the *Richmond Enquirer* on June 9, 1804. For other examples of such testimonies, see Ott, *Haitian Revolution*, 53–54; Babb, "French Refugees"; Hunt, *Haiti's Influence*, 115–16.

107. Ott, *Haitian Revolution*, 194.

108. Examples may be found in all the proslavery essays published in Faust, ed., *Ideology of Slavery*, and in Wish, ed., *Ante-Bellum*.

109. See, e.g., William J. Grayson's *The Hireling and the Slave* for examples of inclusion of references to Saint-Domingue in proslavery propaganda poetry. As Grayson does, many proslavery ideologues and fiction writers illustrated the necessity for the enslavement of blacks by the example of the economic fall of the richest Caribbean island once it had become Haiti. See, e.g., Grayson, "The bright Antilles, with each closing year. See harvests fail, and fortunes disappear. / See harvests fail, and fortunes disappear; / The cane no more its golden treasure yields; / Unsightly weeds deform the fertile fields; / The negro freeman, thrifty while a slave, / Loosed from restraint, becomes a drone or knave" (27).

110. See Hunt, *Haiti's Influence*, 107–46.

111. Ott, *Haitian Revolution*, 197.

112. Lee, *Memoir of Pierre Toussaint*, 7, 8.

113. After giving a slightly biased version of the revolution, Brown dwells at length

on its heroes, particularly Toussaint, of whom he makes a real panegyric, before imagining a similar revolution of the American slaves.

114. On this aspect of the question, see Hunt, *Haiti's Influence*, on abolitionist writers, 85–101, and on black leaders and the use they made of the Saint-Domingue revolution, 147–97.

115. Ibid., 190. See Hunt's discussion on the repercussions of the Haitian revolution on American abolitionism, 178–90.

116. Desdunes, *Our People*, ed. McCants, xviii, 109–48.

117. *L'Union*, September 27, 1862.

118. Cossé Bell, *Revolution*, 237.

119. C.R.L. James wrote *Black Jacobins* in 1938. Aimé Césaire *Toussaint Louverture: la Révolution Française et le problème colonial* in 1960.

120. For an exhaustive study of the importance of Saint-Domingue in the ideological developments in antebellum America, see Hunt, *Haiti's Influence*, 85–192.

## Chapter 7

1. See, e.g., articles by Marino, Neumann-Holzschuh, Homes, Johnson, and Le Gardeur in the bibliography.

2. In the concluding lines of *Haiti, l'éternelle révolution*, Cauna insists on this legacy, which he thinks should be studied in depth.

3. Ibid., 297 (integrally quoted in note 18 to the introduction).

4. See Tregle, "Early New Orleans Society," 26.

5. The press has been studied in previous chapters. For more details, see Marino, "Early French Newspapers in New Orleans."

6. Hunt, *Haiti's Influence*, 52, 54.

7. Childs, *French Refugee Life*, 66.

8. See Noble and Nurah, "Education in Colonial Louisiana."

9. Both figures are given in Desdunes, *Our People*, ed. McCants, 104n.

10. Quotations taken from Hunt, *Haiti's Influence*, 54, 56.

11. Quotations taken from Hunt, *Haiti's Influence*, 57, and Debien and Le Gardeur, "Refugees in Louisiana," 190.

12. Dunbar-Nelson, "People of Color in Louisiana," 27.

13. Crété, *La vie quotidienne en Louisiane*, 326.

14. On this controversy, see Le Gardeur's article of 1954. Until the publication of Le Gardeur's revised article, the creation of the first theater in New Orleans had always been attributed to Louis Tabary. It mostly still is (see, e.g., *Encyclopedia of Southern Culture*, ed. Wilson and Ferris, 92). For Le Gardeur—and several historians since his article—the foundation of the theater is now attributed to the Henry brothers from Paris in 1792. There is, however, a Henri highly involved in the theatrical world of Saint-Domingue, recorded by Fouchard (see *Le théâtre à Saint-Domingue*). Debien and Le Gardeur also indicate that Denis Richard Dechanet Dessassart, a refugee, was godfather to Jean-Marie Henry's son, and that Henry was witness for the will of free racially mixed refugee, Rosalie (157). Considering the habit the refugees had, especially

in the first waves, to ask some of their peers to be witnesses or godparents, the thesis of a Saint-Domingue connection still holds. Jean-Marie Henry might well be from Paris but by way of Saint-Domingue, or he might have indeed come from Saint-Domingue but via Paris. Documentary evidence still has to be found to confirm (or infirm) this thesis.

15. See Logan, *Diplomatic Relations*, 48; Hunt, *Haiti's Influence*, 68, 69; Debien and Le Gardeur, "Refugees in Louisiana," 159, 160, 206; Griolet, *Cadjins et Créoles en Louisiane*, 46; Kendall, *History of New Orleans*, 59; Smither, *A History of the English Theater in New Orleans*, 7; Babb, "French Refugees," 210–18. See also a typescript in Augustin-Wogan-Labranche Family Papers, Louisiana Collection, Tulane University. This typescript is a narration by an eyewitness of "the first theatrical performances by a dozen actors and actresses who had real talent, as they were attached to the theater 'Cap Français' in the Island of San Domingo," 22.

16. Hunt, *Haiti's Influence*, 70.

17. Babb, "French Refugees," 357.

18. Debien and Le Gardeur, "Refugees in Louisiana," 231.

19. Babb, "French Refugees," 2, 218. The reading of the only copy left of *Le Patriote Français* gives interesting hints as to the role of the refugees in the cultural life of Charleston. See Haggy and Van Ruymbeke, "The French Refugee Newspapers of Charleston," 140–41.

20. Beuze and Hayot, *Costumes Créoles*, 53; Moreau de Saint-Méry, *Voyage aux Etats-Unis*, 109.

21. Sainte-Gême Papers, folder 228. Dupuy, a Creole of Saint-Domingue (as Boze indicates), is said to have established a beautiful ballroom for the misses ("une très belle salle pour les mamzelles"), together with a gambling academy at the corner of Orleans and Bourbon.

22. The first Masonic lodges were founded in Cuba after their arrival. For more details, see Debien, "Refugees in Cuba," 105–6. In the northern United States, the phenomenon is also described. The lodge l'Aménité no. 73, e.g., was founded in 1797 by Claude-Corentin Tanguy de la Boissière. See Childs, *French Refugee Life*, 55.

23. There is a good list of the various lodges in Saint- Domingue in the archives of Louisiana State University. Some of those documents were translated by Earlene L. Zeringue and published under the title "Masonic Lodges of Ile Saint-Domingue 1808" in *New Orleans Genesis*. It lists sixty-eight persons, mostly born in France but resident in Saint-Domingue, together with their lodges, indicating those (the majority) which had been shut down by then. Among the remaining lodges, many were no longer in Saint-Domingue but in other asylums (in the United States and the Caribbean). The most often cited lodge is the Choix des Hommes, which had been the main Orient lodge of Port-au-Prince. At least three other lodges are mentioned in Port-au-Prince, three at Les Cayes, two at Le Cap, and one each in Petit Goave, Saint-Marc, and Jérémie. Zeringue, "Masonic Lodges," 473–79.

24. Among the sixty-eight persons cited, several are said to be affiliated with lodges in their new refuges, in Charle's town [*sic*] and Philadelphia, as well as in Jamaica.

25. For more details, see Cossé Bell, *Revolution*, 145–86.

26. Ibid., 70.

27. Hunt, *Haiti's Influence*, 66; Cable, *Creoles of Louisiana*, 207. Hunt cites Edwin Gayle's *History of Freemasonry of Louisiana* (New Orleans, 1932), 756–61.

28. Prevost Family Papers (U-232), Rare Book Collection, Louisiana State University, Baton Rouge; Lambert Family Papers and Augustin-Wogan-Labranche Family Papers, Louisiana Collection, Tulane University, New Orleans.

29. Debien and Le Gardeur, "Refugees in Louisiana," 219.

30. Babb, "French Refugees," 363.

31. King, *Creole Families of New Orleans*, 398.

32. *Louisiana Free Mason* 3, no. 3 (November 1951): 5; Sullivan-Holleman and Hillery Cobb, *Saint-Domingue Epic*, 451.

33. The Tureaud Papers (Amistad Library, Tulane University, New Orleans) contain a speech delivered by Desdunes before the brothers of the Loge de la Créole no. 1918 of the Grand Ordre Uni des Odd Fellows (Series X, Collected Historical Material).

34. Cossé Bell, *Revolution*, 182.

35. *Encyclopedia of Southern Culture*, ed. Wilson and Ferris, 405.

36. Vlach, "Plantation Landscapes of the Antebellum South," 40–41.

37. Gravette, *Architectural Heritage of the Caribbean*, 203.

38. M. B. Newton in *Encyclopedia of Southern Culture*, ed. Wilson and Ferris, 519–20.

39. This is an essential thesis developed at large by Vlach in his dissertation, "Sources of the Shotgun House." Also see Hunt, *Haiti's Influence*, 45.

40. Duncan, "The French Creole Style," 7.

41. In Saint-Domingue, the main houses were rarely luxurious. Most had only one floor and were surrounded with galleries to protect their inhabitants from the scorching sun. To favor air circulation, they were often built on promontories, to benefit from the cooling trade winds, had walls that did not reach the ceiling, and used windows with louvers (*jalousies*) instead of glass. Relatively poorly furnished, with local mahogany and rattan furniture, they were neither vast nor ostentatious, although according to inventories, most had bathrooms. Saint-Domingue legal inventories and wills are rich sources of information. For some examples, see monographs by Cauna (*Au temps des îles à sucre*) or Debien ("Une plantation de Saint-Domingue"). Also see Wimpffen, *Voyage à Saint-Domingue*, 113–15. Those features often recurred in Louisiana plantation houses. See Buisseret, *Histoire de l'architecture dans la Caraïbe;* Sternberg, *Along the River Road*; Rehder in *Encyclopedia of Southern Culture*, ed. Wilson and Ferris, 577; Lane, *Architecture of the Old South*, 83; Sexton, *New Orleans: Elegance and Decadence*, 15.

42. See "French Creole Architecture" in *Explore the History and Culture of Southeastern Louisiana*, http://www.cr.nps.gov/nr/travel/louisiana/architecture.htm. Sexton also concludes that there is much utility in those vernacular buildings, that they are "a more environmentally suitable way of building" brought by the "French West Indian Creoles when they came to Louisiana" (*New Orleans: Elegance and Decadence*, 15). Ed-

wards (in "The Origins of Creole Architecture," the *Winterthur Portfolio* 29, nos. 2/3)[**] juxtaposes a colonial presbytery in Port-of-Prince and the House of the Commandant in Baton Rouge to highlight obvious correspondences.

43. Estwick Evans's "A Pedestrious Tour, of Four Thousand Miles, Through the Western States and Territories, during the Winter and Spring of 1818," quoted in Babbs, "French Refugees," 367.[***]

44. The catalog of the 2003 Bicentennial of the Louisiana Purchase Exhibition at the Historic New Orleans Collection gives the example of the Palais du Préfet Colonial du Gouvernement Français, with a West Indian roofline and a two-story circular gallery, although the house was built in 1761 (Item 96).

45. Samuel Wilson, "Gulf Coast Architecture," 128.

46. See Duncan, "The French Creole Style," 8. Logan, citing Howard Munford Jones's *America and French Culture*, writes that in New Orleans as in Charleston, "many old buildings were constructed according to plans of the *émigrés* from Saint-Domingue." *Diplomatic Relations*, 47–48. The Historic New Orleans Collection exhibition of 2003 also displayed a picture of a house in New Orleans's Faubourg Marigny closely resembling a West Indian House (catalog, item 92).

47. Babb, "French Refugees," 366. Also see Logan, *Diplomatic Relations*, 47–48.

48. Lane, *Architecture of the Old South*, 169.

49. Sullivan-Holleman and Hillery Cobb credit Joseph Pilié with designing the Arc de Triomphe, the Doric Column, and the Obelisk of Jackson Square, as well as the gates and iron fence of the Place d'Armes. *Saint-Domingue Epic*, 455–57.

50. For precise definitions of this notion, see Relouzat, *Tradition orale et imaginaire créole*.

51. Hunt, *Haiti's Influence*, 53; Debien and Le Gardeur, "Refugees in Louisiana," 225.

52. King, *Creole Families of New Orleans*, 396.

53. Sullivan-Holleman and Hillery Cobb, *Saint-Domingue Epic*, 453.

54. Cossé Bell, "Haitian Immigration," 11. For more details, see Cossé Bell, *Revolution*, 89–136, and Desdunes, *Our People*, ed. McCants, 0–60.

55. This is the main thesis of Cossé Bell's *Revolution*.

56. Desdunes, *Our People*, ed. McCants, 81.

57. Chaudenson, *Des îles*, 250–51, 263–66; Relouzat, *Tradition orale et imaginaire creole*, 87, 192; Neumann-Holzschuh, "Textes anciens en Créole Louisianais."

58. "Joudoui pou ous, demain pou moin," in Haiti and "Jordi pou vou, demain pou moin," in Louisiana (Hearn, *"Gombo Zhèbes*," 21. [Today for you, tomorrow for me.]

59. Hearn, Proverb 282 and note (ibid., 32).

60. On Saint-Domingue, see Moreau de Saint-Méry, 63, 64, and 69; on Congo Square, see Cable's "Dance in Place Congo" in *Century Magazine* (February 1886). On similarities and derivations see Hunt, *Haiti's Influence*, 78.

61. Hunt, *Haiti's Influence*, 53; Crété, *La vie quotidienne en Louisiane*, 216; Fick, *The Making of Haiti*, 40; Cable, *Creoles and Cajuns*, 369.

62. Johnson, *Congo Square*, 40.

63. Ibid., 43.

64. Hunt, *Haiti's Influence* (citing Harold Courtlander, *Negro Folk Music*), 77.

65. Cable, "Creole Slave Songs," 401, 404.

66. Dunbar-Nelson, "People of Color in Louisiana," 26.

67. Hunt, *Haiti's Influence*, 72.

68. Ibid., 73.

69. Sullivan-Holleman and Hillery Cobb, *Saint-Domingue Epic*, 458.

70. Desdunes does not necessarily establish the connection with Saint-Domingue refugees. In some cases, their connection with the refugee community must be established by cross-checking. In other cases, more research is necessary before they can be classified among the refugees, if at all.

71. Sullivan, "Composers of Color," 75.

72. On free Creole composers, see Desdunes, *Our People*, ed. McCants, 80–84, and Sullivan, "Composers of Color," 75–77.

73. Hunt, *Haiti's Influence*, 73.

74. There were, e.g., several refugee sculptors in New Orleans: Daniel and Eugene Warburg, the marble sculptors, and Charles de Baligand, who in 1806 made a bust of Napoleon shown in Mr. Montegut's home. Debien and Le Gardeur, "Refugees in Louisiana," 219.

75. Chaudenson, *Des îles*, 285.

76. Debien, "Refugees in Cuba," 105–6.

77. Fiehrer, "African Presence," 28.

78. Chaudenson has very challenging pages on the process of creolization in the field of cooking. To him, cooking abolishes, from the start, any ethnic and social divide. The reason for this is that all the inhabitants of a new world have to change radically their food and modes of preparation on grounds of climate, available products, and material conditions. *Des îles*, 209; *Les Créoles*, 104–22.

79. Wimpffen, *Voyage à Saint-Domingue*, 115, 136.

80. Sybil Kein, "Louisiana Creole Food Culture," in *Creole*, ed. Kein, 244. For more details on the Louisiana Creole food culture, see 248–50.

81. Babb, "French Refugees," 2.

82. Logan, *Diplomatic Relations*, 48.

83. Hunt, *Haiti's Influence*, 70.

84. Burton, e.g., attributes the origin of Trinidadian Carnival to the French Caribbean planters who migrated to Trinidad in the early nineteenth century, adding that the Carnival was first a cultural specificity of the whites and free people of color. See *Afro-Creole*, 199.

85. Gill, *Lord of Misrule*, 30.

86. Nicholas R. Spitzer in *Encyclopedia of Southern Culture*, ed. Wilson and Ferris, 1231. Bettelheim, Bridges, and Yanker's *Caribbean Festival Art* also dwells on the pre-Lenten celebration called the Black Indians (or the Mardi Gras Indians) and shows that the call and response, the wide use of the tambourines, and the words of some songs are borrowed from the Afro-Caribbean traditions. The song "Xango Mongo Lo

Ha," e.g., refers to the Yoruba deiti, Shango, and uses "Haitian Vodun language." For more details, see the chapter 5 of their study, entitled "Festivals in Cuba, Haiti and New Orleans," 158–59.

87. Bettelheim et al., *Caribbean Festival Art*, 156.

88. Mitchell, *All on a Mardi Gras Day*, 26.

89. The conclusion of Bettleheim et al. is that "The Mardi Gras Indians exemplify the creolization at the heart of the pan-Caribbean aesthetic. African, Caribbean, and North American influences converging to create a fresh aesthetic is what occurred in the West Indies." *Caribbean Festival Art*, 163.

90. This fact was noted in all the other refuges, including Cuba. See Debien, "Refugees in Cuba," 105–6.

91. For descriptions of the very elegantly dressed free Creoles of color in Saint-Domingue, see Wimpffen, *Voyage à Saint-Domingue;* Labat, *Voyage aux Isles;* Girod de Chantrans, *Voyage d'un Suisse*, and Moreau de Saint-Méry, *Description topographique*, e.g., 76.

92. Babb, "French Refugees," 351.

93. Catalog of the Parisian exhibition "La Louisiane de la Colonie Française à l'Etat Américain" (Louisiana from a French Colony to an American State), organized by the Mona Bismark Foundation and the Historic New Orleans Collection (17 December 2003–February 28, 2004). It reads "celle-ci est coiffée à la mode des Caraïbes, ce qui signifie qu'elle est libre" [her hair is arranged in the Caribbean fashion, which means that she is free] (7).

94. To give but a single example, there is a shoefly on display at the Museum of the Olivier Plantation in the Evangeline Commemorative Area Park of St. Martinsville, and the explanation reads that it was called "Pankah" and that it is an "object that came from India through the West Indian colony of Saint-Domingue and is to be found only in the Lower Mississippi basin."

95. See Herskovits, *The New World Negro*; Pluchon, *Vaudou, sorciers, empoisonneurs*; Saint-Louis, *Le Vodou Haïtien;* and Tallant, *Voodoo in New Orleans*. A very good description is in Bastide, *Les Amériques noires*, 149; Crété, *La vie quotidienne en Louisiane*, 244; Deive, *Vodu y magia en Santo Domingo*, 221; Bodin, *Voodoo Past and Present*, 10. Some, like Herskovits, speak of "reinterpretation" instead of syncretism. Saint-Louis uses "hybridity."

96. Bastide, *Les Amériques noires*, 113, 149.

97. Ibid., 152; Gehman, *Free People of Color of New Orleans*, 239; Ferris in *Encyclopedia of Southern Culture*, ed. Wilson and Ferris, 492.

98. In "The Formation of Afro-Creole Culture," Hall writes that "slaves from the Bight of Benin *probably* account for the emergence of voodoo in Louisiana, which was reinforced by the massive immigration of Haitians in 1809" (85–86, my emphasis).

99. Basically, this is what Crété concludes in *La vie quotidienne en Louisiane*, 247. Also see Bodin, *Voodoo Past and Present*, 13; Tallant, *Voodoo in New Orleans*, 12. This does not run counter to Hall's argument, which traces the emergence of such words like *gri-gri* back to 1773, when it appeared in a court record.

100. Bodin, *Voodoo Past and Present*, 21; Crété, *La vie quotidienne en Louisiane*, 247.

101. See, e.g., Crété, *La vie quotidienne en Louisiane*, 251.

102. Laguerre, e.g., writes that "her parents were émigrés from Santo Domingo." In *Encyclopedia of Southern Culture*, ed. Wilson and Ferris, 433.

103. Tallant, *Voodoo in New Orleans*, 75.

104. Ibid., 52, citing the St. Louis Cathedral marriage records (August 4, 1819).

105. Ibid., 55, 114; Gehman, *Free People of Color of New Orleans*, 28; Hearn, *"Gombo Zhèbes,"* 71.

106. On Saint-Domingue, see Moreau de Saint-Méry, *Description topographique*, 65–70. Also see Descourtilz, Menfant, Gauban Joinville, and Drouin de Bercy, quoted in Pluchon, *Vaudou, sorciers, empoisonneurs*, 107–35.

107. See Malenfant in Pluchon, *Vaudou, sorciers, empoisonneurs*, 108, 133.

108. For Louisiana, see Crété, *La vie quotidienne en Louisiane*, 253. For Saint-Domingue, see Moreau de Saint-Méry, *Description topographique*, 63–69; Deive, *Vodu y Magica*, 149.

109. Chaudenson classifies music, language, and cooking among the transcommunity processes of creolization, stressing their strong "osmotic" capacity. To these fields, he opposes religions such as voodoo, which is, according to him, a process that involves a single community. He adds, however, that this is not true in Louisiana. *Des îles*, 285.

110. Hall, "The Formation of Afro-Creole Culture," 86–87.

111. Valdman, the famous linguist specialized in the study of Creole languages, asserts that Louisiana Creole language was undoubtedly imported from the Caribbean. *Le Créole*, 30. Hall, citing Neumann-Holzschuh, disproves this assumption in "The Formation of Afro-Creole Culture," 69, as does Holm in *Pidgins and Creoles*, 2:388.

112. Valdman, "The Place of Louisiana Creole," in Dormon, ed., *Creoles of Color*, 156.

113. The pioneering studies were Alfred Mercier's 1880 "Etude sur la langue créole en Louisiane," J. A. Harrison's "The Creole Patois of Louisiana" (1882), and Alcée Fortier's "The French Language in Louisiana and the Negro-French Dialect."

114. Cable, *Creoles of Louisiana*, 318.

115. In Dorman, ed., *Creoles of Color of the Gulf Coast*, although the focus is the Creoles of color of the Gulf South, the 190 pages mention the Saint-Domingue refugees only once, in Valdman's article, "The Place of Louisiana Creole." In the preface to Brasseaux, Fontenot, and Oubre, eds., *Creoles of Color of the Bayou Country*, there are exactly two lines on the refugees, acknowledging their leading role in the development of the Creole language, proclaiming that "many, if not most, Creole-speakers can point to ancestors who fled Saint-Domingue's black revolution in the late 1790s and early 1800s" (xi). Debien also notes the development of the use of the Creole language in the Spanish-speaking world of Cuba after the arrival of the refugees. "Refugees in Cuba," 105–6.

116. There are transcriptions of Saint-Domingue Creole in Moreau de Saint-Méry, *Description topographique* (80–83) and Girod de Chantrans, *Voyage d'un Suisse*. Vald-

man also studies proclamations by Sonthonax and Napoléon translated into Creole. Valdman, *Le creole*, 99–106.

117. For very detailed developments on Creole languages, see Chaudenson, *Des îles;* Holm, *Pidgins and Creoles;* Goodman, *A Comparative Study of Creole French Dialects*; Valdman, *Le créole;* Valdman, "The Place of Louisiana Creole"; Mosadomi, "Origin of Louisiana Creole"; Read, *Louisiana's French*; Neumann, "Le Créole des blancs en Louisiane";[**] and Griolet, *Cadjins et Créoles en Louisiane.*

118. See Holm, *Pidgins and Creoles*, I, 28;[***] Valdman, *Le créole*, 14, 216–18; Chaudenson, *Les Créoles*, 46; Valdman, "The Place of Louisiana Creole," 150; Goodman, *Comparative Study*, 56, 85.

119. Fortier, *Literature, Customs and Dialects*, 136. Also see Harrison, "The Creole Patois of Louisiana," and Goodman, *Comparative Study*, 53.

120. Valdman, *Le créole*, 284.

121. Neumann-Holzschuh, "Structures lexicale du Cajun," 62.

122. Ibid., 56; Mosadomi, "Origin of Louisiana Creole"; Reed, 118, 120, 123; Griolet, *Cadjins et Créoles en Louisiane*, 303; Chaudenson, *Les Créoles*, 92; Valdman, *Le créole*, 171. Even Gwendolyn Hall, who is the staunchest advocate of a direct African origin, concludes that "it is possible but far from certain that these terms were brought by slaves from Saint-Domingue, where they are also used," Hall, "The Formation of Afro-Creole Culture," 86.

123. This leads David Geggus to write that they "obviously did play a major role in shaping Louisiana's francophone cultures, which thrived until the Civil War." The use of the plural ("cultures") is here deeply interesting. Geggus, *Impact of the Haitian Revolution*, xiv. This judgment is not unlike what Debien writes about Cuba when tracing the long-term effects of the refugee movement. For him, the final amalgamation into the island's population of the refugees that had remained after the 1810 expulsions gave birth to a "Franco-Cuban blend." Debien, "Refugees in Cuba," 111.

124. This is an echo to Hunt's assertion that "Those responsible for introducing both the French opera and voodoo to the United States came to New Orleans . . . in the same refugee boats." *Haiti's Influence*, 4.

125. Chaudenson, *Des îles*, 17.

126. Bernabé, Chamoiseau, and Confiant, *Eloge de la Créolité/In Praise of Creoleness*, 92–93. Also see Chaudenson, *Des îles*, 186.

127. Hall, *Africans*, 158.

128. Wall, *Louisiana: A History*, 73.

129. Cable, *Creoles of Louisiana*, 260. Babb also says that their "language was more soft and liquid in its pronunciation." "French Refugees," 364.

130. Desdunes, *Our People*, ed. McCants, 113.

131. See, e.g., Cossé Bell, *Revolution*, 38; Hunt, *Haiti's Influence*, 4.

132. Fiehrer, "African Presence," 26. He refers to his article "From Quadrille to Stump." Widmer goes further, writing (with some reservations) the challenging statement that "Congo Square was ground zero for jazz." Widmer, "The Invention of a Memory," 70, 76.

133. Spitzer in *Encyclopedia of Southern Culture*, ed. Wilson and Ferris, 1037.

134. This is Wall's thesis, e.g., in *Louisiana: A History*, 73. On the maintenance of French culture, see Hunt, *Haiti's Influence*, 82–83, and Lachance "The 1809 Immigration," 281–83. This is perfectly confirmed by the already discussed tendency displayed by the refugees to continue to write their wills in French well into the nineteenth century, long after the Creoles and "foreign" French had ceased. It is also perfectly exemplified by the fact that Desdunes still wrote and published in French in the twentieth century.

## Conclusion

1. This quotation may be found, together with information on Ulrick Jean-Pierre, at http://www.tulane.edu/~isn/UlrickJP.htm.

2. On the Cable/Gayarré controversy, see Tregle's "Creoles and Americans," in *Creole New Orleans: Race and Americanization*, ed. Hirsh and Logsdon, 174–85.

3. See Dormon, ed., *Creoles of Color of the Gulf South*, and Brasseaux, Fontenot, and Oubre, eds., *Creoles of Color in the Bayou Country*.

4. See Hall, *Africans in Colonial Louisiana*, or Cossé Bell, *Revolution*.

5. Although Hall defends the thesis of direct African influences, the fact that she notes an occurrence of the word *gri-gri* in court proceedings in 1773 does not prove that the word had come directly from Africa. It may have, but it also could have come by way of the Caribbean through slave importations made during the colonial period. Neither position can be scientifically proved or disproved in the present state of research.

6. In Maryland, e.g., archeologists are unearthing the remains of large slave quarters in Frederick County. Those quarters, where some ninety slaves lived at certain times, were those of a 748–acre plantation founded in 1795 by a Saint-Domingue refugee, Payen Boisneuf. An article from the *Baltimore Sun* on October 29, 2003, indicates that the slave site "is of particular interest because it brings together an unexpected mix of cultural evidences." The article insists on obvious French influences (Catholicism, details of the plantation house) and concludes that "archeologists will also be looking for African or Haitian influences at the site, because Boisneuf is known to have brought at least 14 slaves from Haiti when he fled."

7. James Gill, e.g., shows that early nineteenth-century New Orleans was a cultural desert. He notes certain cultural advances: the town had "the only opera in the United States to warrant comparison with the European houses and had, in composer Louis Moreau Gottschalk and chess prodigy Paul Morphy, two sons of international renown." Gill, *Lord of Misrule*, 57. He says they were sons of New Orleans, but he does not note that they were grandsons of Saint-Domingue. The only steps forward he acknowledges in the Louisiana cultural life are obviously attributable to the refugees and their descendants, although he never acknowledges their role.

8. Both quotations from Fiehrer, "Saint-Domingue/Haiti," 437.

# Bibliography

## Primary Sources Archival Material

AMISTAD RESEARCH CENTER, TULANE UNIVERSITY, NEW ORLEANS

George Longe Papers, 1768–1971
Walter Morial Collection, 1797–1817
Alexandre Pierre Tureaud Papers

ARCHIVES OF THE ARCHDIOCESE OF NEW ORLEANS

Sacramental Records

ARCHIVO GENERAL DE LA NACION, SANTO DOMINGO, DOMINICAN REPUBLIC

Correspondencia de Godoy, García, Hedouville, Rigaud y otros, 1795–1802

LOUISIANA AND LOWER MISSISSIPPI VALLEY COLLECTIONS, HILL MEMORIAL LIBRARY, LOUISIANA STATE UNIVERSITY, BATON ROUGE

Marshall (Maria Chotard and Family) Papers
Pontalba's Memoir
Prevost Family Papers

THE HISTORIC NEW ORLEANS COLLECTION, WILLIAMS RESEARCH CENTER, NEW ORLEANS

Henry de Ste Gême Family Papers

LOUISIANA COLLECTION, HOWARD-TILTON MEMORIAL LIBRARY, TULANE UNIVERSITY, NEW ORLEANS

Augustin-Wogan-Labranche Family Papers, 1803–1936
Sabourin Papers, Charles Gayarré Collection
Folder History 1803–15 Territorial Saint-Domingue, 1992 NSG Conference in the States
Lambert Family Papers, 1798–1905
Manuscript letter from René Le Gardeur to Gabriel Debien, 2 November 1970 (Tulane University, New Orleans, Louisiana Collection, M 561)
Raynal Family Papers, 1807–37
Saint-Domingue Indemnities, 1828–33, MS 851

NEW ORLEANS PUBLIC LIBRARY

New Orleans City Council Proceedings
Books of Wills, New Orleans

NOTARIAL ARCHIVES OF NEW ORLEANS

Notarial Files of Christoval de Armas, Michel de Armas, Narcisse Broutin, Marc Lafitte, John Lind, Pedro (Pierre) Pedesclaux, Philippe Pedesclaux, Benedict Van Pradelles, and Stephen de Quinones

XAVIER UNIVERSITY SPECIAL COLLECTIONS

Desdunes Family Collection

## Printed Primary and Literary Sources

*A Calendar of the Rochambeau Papers at the University of Florida Libraries.* Comp. Laura V. Monti. Gainesville: University of Florida Libraries, 1972.

*A Guide to the Papers of Pierre Clément Laussat.* New Orleans: Historic New Orleans Collection, 1993.

Aquin Allain, Hélène d'. *Souvenirs d'Amérique par une Créole.* Paris: Périsses Frères, 1883.

Berquin Duvallon. *Vue de la colonie espagnole du Mississippi, ou des provinces de Louisiane et Floride Occidentale.* Paris: Imprimerie expéditive, 1803.

Brown, William Wells. *St. Domingo: Its Revolutions and Its Patriots. A Lecture Delivered before the Metropolitan Athenaeum, London, May 16, and at St Thomas' Church, Philadelphia, December 20, 1854.* Boston: Bela Marsh, 1855.

Buckley, Norman Roger, ed. *The Haitian Journal of Lieutenant Howard,* York Hussars, 1796–1798. Knoxville: University of Tennessee Press, 1985.

Cable, George W. *Creoles and Cajuns.* New York: Doubleday, 1959.

———. *Old Creole Days.* 1879. Gretna, La.: Pelican, 1991.

De Bow, J.D.B. *The Industrial Resources, etc. of the Southern and Western States.* 3 vols. New Orleans: Office of De Bow's Review, 1853.

Deggs, Sister Marie Bernard. *No Cross, No Crown: Black Nuns in Nineteenth-Century New Orleans.* Ed. Virginia Meacham Gould and Charles E. Nolan. Bloomington: Indiana University Press, 2001.

Descourtilz, Michel Etienne. *Voyage d'un naturaliste en Haïti, 1799–1803.* Paris: Plon, 1935.

Desdunes, Rodolphe Lucien. *Nos Hommes et Notre Histoire.* Montréal: Arbour & Dupont, 1911. Published in English as *Our People and Our History: Fifty Creole Portraits.* Trans. and ed. Sister Dorothea Olga McCants. Baton Rouge: Louisiana State University Press, 1971.

Faust, Drew Gilpin, ed. *The Ideology of Slavery: Proslavery Thought in the Antebellum South, 1830–1860.* Baton Rouge: Louisiana State University Press, 1981.

Girod de Chantrans, Justin. *Voyage d'un Suisse dans différentes colonies d'Amérique pendant la dernière guerre.* Paris: Poinçat, 1786.

Goguet, Antoine et Marie. *Lettres d'amour créoles.* Paris: Karthala, 1996.

Gottschalk, Louis Moreau. *Notes of a Pianist.* Philadelphia: J. B. Lippincott, 1881.

Grayson, William J. *The Hireling and the Slave.* 1856. Miami: Mnemosyne, 1969.

Hearn, Lafcadio. *"Gombo Zhèbes": Little Dictionary of Creole Proverbs*. New York: Will H. Coleman, 1885.

Kukla, Jon, ed. *A Guide to the Papers of Pierre Clément Laussat Napoléon's Prefect for the Colony of Louisiana and of General Claude Perrin Victor at the Historic New Orleans Collection*. New Orleans: The Historic New Orleans Collection, 1993.

Labat, Jean-Baptiste. *Voyage aux Isles: Chronique aventureuse des Caraïbes*, 1693–1705. 1720. Paris: Phébus, 1993.

Lacroix, Général Pamphile de. *Mémoires pour servir à l'histoire de la Révolution de Saint-Domingue*. Paris, 1819. Reprinted under the title *La Révolution de Haïti*. Paris: Karthala, 1995.

Lanusse, Armand. *Les Cénelles*. New Orleans: H. Lauve, 1845. Shreveport: Les Cahiers du Tintamarre, 2003.

Laussat, Pierre Clément de. *Memoirs of My Life to My Son during the Years 1803 and After*. Trans. Agnès J. Pastwa. Ed. Robert D. Bush. Baton Rouge: Louisiana State University Press, 1978.

Lee, Hannah Farnham Sawyer, ed. *Memoir of Pierre Toussaint, Born a Slave in St. Domingo*. Boston: Crosby, Nichols, 1854.

Maduell, Charles R. *Marriage Contracts, Wills, and Testaments of the Spanish Colonial Period in New Orleans, 1770–1804*. New Orleans: Privately published, 1969.

———. *New Orleans Marriage Contracts*, 1804–1820, Abstracted from the Notarial Archives of New Orleans. New Orleans: Polyanthos, 1977.

Malenfant, Colonel. *Des colonies et particulièrement de celle de Saint-Domingue*. Paris: Audibert, 1814.

McIntosh, M. E., and B. C. Weber, eds. "Une Correspondance familiale au temps des troubles de Saint-Domingue (1791–1796), lettres du marquis et de la marquise de Rouvray à leur fille." *Revue d'Histoire des Colonies* 45 (1958): 119–279.

Moreau de Saint-Méry. *Description topographique, physique, civile, politique et historique de la partie française de l'isle de Saint-Domingue*. 3 vols. Paris: Société de l'Histoire des Colonies Françaises et Librairie Larose, 1958.

———. *Voyage aux Etats-Unis de l'Amérique, 1793–1798*. New Haven: Yale University Press, 1913.

Nolan, Charles E., ed. *Sacramental Records of the Roman Catholic Church of the Archdiocese of New Orleans*. Vols. 5–16 (1791–1825). New Orleans: Archdiocese of New Orleans, 1990–2002.

Parham, Althéa de Puech, trans. *My Odyssey: Experiences of a Young Refugee from Two Revolutions, by a Creole of Saint Domingue*. Intro. Selden Rodman. Baton Rouge: Louisiana State University Press, 1959.

Pitot, James. *Observations on the Colony of Louisiana, from 1796 to 1802*. Trans. Henry C. Pitot. Ed. Robert D. Bush. Baton Rouge: Louisiana State University Press, 1979.

Robertson, James Alexander, ed. *Louisiana under the Rule of Spain, France, and the United States, 1785–1807: Social, Economic, and Political Conditions of the Territory Represented in the Louisiana Purchase as Portrayed in Hitherto Unpublished* Con-

*temporary Accounts by Dr. Paul Alliot and Various Spanish, French, English, and American Officials*. 2 vols. Cleveland: Arthur H. Clark, 1911.

Robin, C. C. *Voyages dans l'intérieur de la Louisiane, de la Floride Occidentale, et dans les isles de la Martinique et de Saint-Domingue pendant les années 1802, 1803, 1804, 1805 et 1806*. Paris: F. Buisson, 1807.

Rowland, Dunbar, ed. *Official Letter Books of W.C.C. Claiborne*, 1801–1816. 6 vols. Jackson, Miss.: State Department of Archives and History, 1917.

Saxon, Lyle. *Fabulous New Orleans*. 1928. Gretna, La.: Pelican, 1988.

Séligny, Michel, Homme de Couleur Libre de la Nouvelles Orléans. *Nouvelles et récits*. Comp. Frans C. Amelinckx. Québec: Presses de l'Université Laval, 1998.

*South Louisiana Records*. 12 vols. Baton Rouge: Claitor's, 1982.

Starr, S. Frederick, ed. *Inventing New Orleans: Writings of Lafcadio Hearn*. Jackson: University Press of Mississippi, 2001.

Wimpffen, Alexandre-Stanislas de. *Voyage à Saint-Domingue pendant les années 1788, 1789, 1790 par le Baron de Wimpffen*. Paris, 1797. Reprinted as *Haïti au XVIIIe siècle: Richesse et esclavage dans une colonie française*. Introduction and notes by Pierre Pluchon. Paris: Karthala, 1993.

Wish, Harvey, ed. *Ante-Bellum*. New York: Capricorn Books, 1960.

Yacou, Alain, ed. *Un esclave-poète à Cuba au temps du péril noir. Autobiographie de Juan Francisco Manzano (1797–1851)*. Paris: Karthala et CERC, 2004.

### Secondary Sources

Acosta Rodriguez, Antonio. *La población de la Luisiana española (1763–1803)*. Madrid: Ministerio de Asuntos Exteriores, 1979.

Adélaïde-Merlande, Jacques. *La Caraïbe et la Guyane au temps de la Révolution et de l'Empire*. Paris: Karthala, 1992.

———. *Histoire Générale des Antilles et des Guyanes des Précolombiens à nos jours*. Paris: L'Harmattan, 1994.

Adher, M. J. "Les colons réfugiés d'Amérique pendant la Révolution." *Société de Géographie de Toulouse* 34, no. 2 (1915): 152–68.

Alderson, Robert. "Charleston's Rumored Slave Revolt of 1793." In *The Impact of the Haitian Revolution in the Atlantic World*, ed. David P. Geggus, 93–111. Columbia: University of South Carolina Press, 2001.

Antoine, Régis. *La littérature franco-antillaise: Haïti, Guadeloupe, et Martinique*. Paris: Karthala, 1992.

Arigo, Joseph. *Louisiana's Plantation Homes: The Grace and the Grandeur*. Stillwater, Minn.: Voyageur Press, 1991.

Arthur, Stanley Clisby. *Old New Orleans*. 1936. Gretna, La.: Pelican, 1995.

Ashdown, Peter. *Caribbean History in Maps*. Trinidad and Jamaica: Longman Caribbean, 1979.

Augier, F. R., S. C. Gordon, D. G. Hall, and M. Reckord. *The Making of the West Indies*. Trinidad and Jamaica: Longman Caribbean, 1960.

Babb, Winston C. "French Refugees from Saint Domingue to the Southern United States, 1791–1810." PhD diss., University of Virginia, 1954.

Barbé-Marbois, François. *The History of Louisiana*. 1830. Baton Rouge: Louisiana State University Press, 1977.

Barthélémy, Gérard. *Créoles-Bossales: Conflit en Haiti.* Petit Bourg (Guadeloupe): Ibis Rouge, 2000.

Bastide, Roger. *Les Amériques noires*. 1967. Paris: L'Harmattan, 1993.

Baudier, Roger. *The Catholic Church in Louisiana*. New Orleans, 1939. Reprinted by the Louisiana Library Association Public Library Section, 1972.

———. *Historic Old New Orleans*. Compilation of his Thursday column in the *Catholic Action of the South*, 7 January 1943 to 28 December 1944.

Baur, John E. "International Repercussions of the Haitian Revolution." *Americas* 26, no. 4 (April 1970): 394–418.

Bellin, Jacques Nicholas. *Old Maps of the World.* Set III, Mexico, Central America and the West Indies. Featuring maps produced 1754–58 by Jacques Nicholas Bellin. Cleveland: Bloch, 1959.

Berlin, Ira. *Generations of Captivity: A History of African-American Slaves*. Cambridge: Belknap Press of Harvard University Press, 2003.

———. *Many Thousands Gone: The First Two Centuries of Slavery in North America.* Cambridge: Belknap Press of Harvard University Press, 1998.

———. *Slaves without Masters: The Free Negro in the Antebellum South*. New York: Pantheon Books, 1974.

Bernabé, Jean. *Grammaire Créole: Fondas kréyol-la*. Paris: L'Harmattan, 1987.

Bernabé, Jean, Patrick Chamoiseau, and Raphaël Confiant. *Eloge de la Créolité/In Praise of Creoleness*. 1989. Bilingual ed. Paris: Gallimard, 1993.

Bettelheim, Judith, Barbara Bridges, and Dolores Yanker. *Caribbean Festival Art: Each and Every Bit of Difference*. Seattle: University of Washington Press, 1988.

Beuze, Lyne-Rose and Loïs Hayot. *Costumes Créoles: Mode et Vêtements Traditionnels des Antilles Françaises de 1635 à 1948.* Fort-de-France: Editions Fabre Domergue, 1999.

Binder, Wolfgang, ed. *Creoles and Cajuns: French Louisiana = La Louisiane Française.* Frankfurt: Peter Lang, 1998.

Black, Alexandra. *Living in Cuba*. New York: St. Martin's Press, 1998. French version, Paris: Abbeville, 1998.

Bodin, Ron. *Voodoo Past and Present*. Lafayette: University of Southwestern Louisiana, 1990.

Boucher, Philip. *Les Nouvelles Frances: France in America, 1500–1815. An Imperial Perspective*. Providence: The John Carter Brown Library, 1989.

Brasseaux, Carl A. *French, Cajun, Creole, Houma: A Primer on Francophone Louisiana.* Baton Rouge: Louisiana State University Press, 2005.

———, ed. *A Refuge for All Ages: Immigration in Louisiana History*. Vol. 10 of the Louisiana Purchase Bicentennial Series in Louisiana History. Lafayette: University of Southwestern Louisiana Press, 1996.

Brasseaux, Carl A., and Glenn R. Conrad, eds. *The Road to Louisiana: The Saint-Domingue Refugees, 1792–1809*. Trans. David Cheramie. Lafayette: Center for Louisiana Studies, University of Southwestern Louisiana, 1992.

Brasseaux, Carl A., Keith P. Fontenot, and Claude F. Oubre, eds. *Creoles of Color in the Bayou Country*. Jackson: University Press of Mississippi, 1994.

Brathwaite, Edward. *Creole Society in Jamaica, 1770–1820*. New York: Oxford University Press, 1978.

Brereton, Bridget. "'Hé St Domingo, songé St Domingo': Haiti and the Haitian Revolution in the Political Discourse of Nineteenth-Century Trinidad." In *Reinterpreting the Haitian Revolution and Its Cultural Aftershocks*, ed. Martin Monroe and Elizabeth Walcott-Hackshaw. Vol. 1. Trinidad: University of West Indies Press, 2006.

Bruley, Georges. *Les Antilles pendant la Révolution Française*. 1890. Paris: Editions Caribéennes, 1988.

Bryan, Patrick. "Émigrés Conflict and Reconciliation: The French Émigrés in Nineteenth-Century Jamaica." *Jamaica Journal* 7 (September 1973): 13–19.

Buisseret, David. *Histoire de l'architecture dans la Caraïbe*. Paris: Editions Caribéennes, 1984. Translation with additions of 1980 English version.

Buisseret, David, and Steven G. Reinhardt, eds. *Creolization in the Americas*. Arlington: Texas A&M University Press, 2000.

Burton, Richard. *Afro-Creole: Power, Opposition, and Play in the Caribbean*. Ithaca: Cornell University Press, 1997.

Cable, George W. "Creole Slave Songs." *Century Magazine* 31 (April 1886). Reprinted in *Creole and Cajuns*, 394–432. New York: Doubleday, 1959.

———. *The Creoles of Louisiana*. 1884. Gretna, La: Pelican, 2000.

———. "The Dance in Place Congo." *Century Magazine* 31 (February 1886). Reprinted in *Creoles and Cajuns*, 366–93. New York: Doubleday, 1959.

Casey, Powell A. "Masonic Lodges in New Orleans." *New Orleans Genesis* 20 (January 1981): 1–20.

Cauna, Jacques de. *Au temps des isles à sucre: Histoire d'une plantation de Saint-Domingue au XVIIIe siècle*. Paris: Karthala, 1987.

———. "La diaspora des colons de Saint-Domingue et le monde créole: le cas de la Jamaïque." *Revue Française d'Histoire d'Outre-Mer* 304 (1994): 333–59.

———. *Haïti: l'éternelle révolution*. Port-au-Prince: Imprimerie Henri Deschamps, 1997.

———. "Les registres d'état civil anciens des Archives Nationales d'Haïti." *Revue de la Société d'Histoire et de Géographie* 162 (March 1989). Integrally reprinted without modifications at http://agh.qc.ca/dossier.htm

Chambers, Henry F. *A History of Louisiana*. Chicago: American Historical Society, 1925.

Chaudenson, Robert. *Les Créoles*. Paris: Presses Universitaires de France, 1995.

———. *Des îles, des hommes, des langues: Essai sur la créolisation linguistique et culturelle*. Paris: L'Harmattan, 1992.

Childs, Frances Sergeant. *French Refugee Life in the United States, 1790–1800: An*

*American Chapter of the French Revolution*. Baltimore: Johns Hopkins University Press, 1940.

Childs, Matt D. "'A Black French General Arrived to Conquer the Island': Images of the Haitian Revolution in Cuba's 1812 Aponte Rebellion." Geggus ed. *The Impact of the Haitian Revolution in the Atlantic World*. Columbia: University of South Carolina Press, 2001.

Cifre de Loubiel, Estela. *La inmigración a Puerto Rico durante el siglo XIX*. San Juan: Instituto de Cultura Puertorriqueña, 1964.

Clark, Emily, and Virginia Meacham Gould. "The Feminine Face of Afro-Catholicism in New Orleans, 1717–1852." *William and Mary Quarterly*, ser. 3, vol. 59, no. 2 (April 2002): 409–48.

Clark, John G. *New Orleans, 1718–1812: An Economic History*. Baton Rouge: Louisiana State University Press, 1970.

Conrad, Glenn R., and Ray F. Lucas. *White Gold: A Brief History of the Louisiana Sugar Industry, 1795–1995*. Lafayette: Center for Louisiana Studies, University of Southwestern Louisiana, 1995.

Cornevin, Robert. *Haïti*. Paris: Presses Universitaires de France, 1993.

Cossé Bell, Caryn. "Haitian Immigration to Louisiana in the Eighteenth and Nineteenth Centuries." Multi-Media *African American Migration Experience*. Schomburg Center for Research in Black Culture. New York Public Library Digital Gallery, 2005. http://www.inmotionaame.org/texts/index.cfm?migration=5&topic=99&type=text.

———. *Revolution, Romanticism, and the Afro-Creole Protest Tradition in Louisiana, 1718–1868*. Baton Rouge: Louisiana State University Press, 1997.

Courtlander, Harold. *Negro Folk Music USA*. New York: Columbia University Press, 1963; New York: Dover, 1992.

Crété, Liliane. *La vie quotidienne en Louisiane*, 1815–1830. Paris: Hachette, 1978.

Daigle, Msgr. Jules O. *A Dictionary of the Cajun Language*. Ann Arbor: Edwards Brothers, 1984.

Dargo, Georges. *Jefferson's Louisiana: Politics and the Clash of Legal Tradition*. Cambridge: Harvard University Press, 1975.

Daspit, Fred. *Louisiana Architecture, 1714–1830*. Lafayette: Center for Louisiana Studies University of Southwestern Louisiana, 1996.

Davis, William C. *The Pirates Laffite: The Treacherous World of the Corsairs of the Gulf*. New York: Harcourt, 2005.

Debien, Gabriel. *Les Colons de Saint-Domingue et la Révolution*. Paris: Armand Colin, 1953.

———. "De Saint-Domingue à Cuba avec une famille de réfugiés, les Tornézy (1800–1809)." *Notes d'Histoire Coloniale no. 74*, extrait de la *Revue de la Faculté d'Ethnologie* (de Port-au-Prince), no. 8 (1964): 7–31.

———. *Les esclaves aux Antilles françaises, XVIIe–XVIIIe*. Basse Terre and Fort-de-France: Sociétés d'Histoire de la Guadeloupe et de la Martinique, 1974.

———. *Esprit colon et esprit d'autonomie à Saint-Domingue au XVIIe siècle.* Paris: Larose, 1954.

———. *Etudes Antillaises XVIIIe siècle.* Paris: Association Marc Bloch, 1956.

———. "Une Nantaise à Saint-Domingue 1782–1786." *Revue du Bas-Poitou et des Provinces de l'Ouest* 6 (November/December 1972).

———. *Une plantation de Saint-Domingue: La sucrerie Galbaud du Fort (1690–1802).* Cairo: University of Cairo, 1941.

———. *Plantations et esclaves a Saint-Domingue.* Dakar: Publications de la Section d'Histoire no. 3, 1962.

———. "Réfugiés de Saint-Domingue aux Etats-Unis." *Notes d'Histoire Coloniale* 27 (1950): 2–138.

———. "Réfugiés de Saint-Domingue expulsés de la Havane en 1809." *Annuario de Estudios Americanos* 35 (1979): 555–610.

———. "The Saint-Domingue Refugees in Cuba, 1793–1815." In *The Road to Louisiana: The Saint-Domingue Refugees, 1792–1809*, ed. Carl A. Brasseaux and Glenn R. Conrad, 31–112. Trans. David Cheramie. Lafayette: Center for Louisiana Studies, University of Southwestern Louisiana, 1992.

———. "Vers la fin de l'expansion de Saint-Domingue." *Caribbean Studies* 2, no. 2 (July 1971).

———. "Les vivres sur une caféière de Saint-Domingue (1786–1791)." *Enquêtes et Documents* 1 (1971): 137–44.

Debien, Gabriel, and René J. Le Gardeur. "The Saint-Domingue Refugees in Louisiana, 1792–1804." In *The Road to Louisiana: The Saint-Domingue Refugees, 1792–1809*, ed. Carl A. Brasseaux and Glenn R. Conrad, 113–243. Trans. David Cheramie. Lafayette: University of Southwestern Louisiana Press, 1992.

Debien, Gabriel, and Philippe Wright. "Les colons de Saint-Domingue passés à la Jamaïque (1792–1835)." *Bulletin de la Société d'Histoire de la Guadeloupe* 26 (4[e] trimestre 1975): 3–217.

Deive, Carlos Esteban. *Las emigraciones Dominicanas a Cuba (1795–1808).* Santo Domingo: Fundación Cultural Dominicana, 1989.

———. *Los refugiados franceses en Santo Domingo.* Santo Domingo: Publicación de la Universidad Nacional Pedro Henriquez Ureña, 1984.

———. *Vodu y magia en Santo Domingo*. Santo Domingo: Ediciones Museo de Hombre Dominicano, 1979.

Demorizi, Emilio Rodríguez. *La era de Francia en Santo Domingo: Contribución a su estudio.* Ciudad Trujillo (Santo Domingo): Editora del Caribe, 1955.

Dessens, Nathalie. Contribution to "1803–1804: Re-Shaping the Atlantic World: Actors and Audiences." *The Louisiana Purchase Timeline.* Baton Rouge: Louisiana State University Press and Deep South Regional Humanities Center, 2003.

———. "From Plurality to Singularity: Otherness and Creolization in Nineteenth-Century Louisiana." In *Journey into Otherness*, ed. Ada Savin, 29–38. Amsterdam: VU University Press, 2005.

———. "From Saint-Domingue to Louisiana: West Indian Refugees in the Lower Mississippi Region." In *French Colonial Louisiana and the Atlantic World*, ed. Bradley Bond. Baton Rouge: Louisiana State University Press, 2005.

———. "Les migrants de Saint-Domingue en Louisiane avant la Guerre de Sécession: de l'intégration civique à l'influence politique. Immigration et citoyenneté aux Etats-Unis." *Revue Française d'Etudes Américaines* 75 (January 1998): 34–46.

———. *Myths of the Plantation Society: Slavery in the American South and the West Indies.* Gainesville: University Press of Florida, 2003.

———. "Saint-Domingue Refugees in New Orleans: Identity and Cultural Influences." In *Reinterpreting the Haitian Revolution and Its Cultural Aftershocks*, ed. Martin Munroe and Elizabeth Walcott-Hackshaw. Vol. 2. Trinidad, Jamaica, Barbados: University of West Indies Press, forthcoming.

Devèze, Michel. *Antilles, Guyanes, La Mer de Caraïbes de 1492 à 1789*. Paris: SEDES, 1977.

Dominguez, Virginia. *From Neighbor to Stranger: The Dilemma of Caribbean Peoples in the United States*. New Haven: Yale University Press, 1975.

———. *White by Definition: Social Classification in Creole Louisiana*. New Brunswick, N.J.: Rutgers University Press, 1986.

Dormon, James H. "The Persistent Specter: Slave Rebellion in Territorial Louisiana." *Louisiana History* 18, no. 4 (Fall 1977): 389–404.

———, ed. *Creoles of Color of the Gulf South*. Knoxville: University of Tennessee Press, 1996.

Dunbar-Nelson, Alice Moore. "People of Color in Louisiana." In *Creole*, ed. Sybil Kein, 3–41. Baton Rouge: Louisiana State University Press, 2000.

Duncan, Patricia L. "The French Creole Style." In *Louisiana Architecture: A Handbook on Styles*, ed. Jonathan Fricker, Donna Fricker, and Patricia L. Duncan, 1–9. Lafayette: Center for Louisiana Studies, 1998.

Eccles, William John. *The French in North America, 1500–1783*. East Lansing: Michigan State University Press, 1998.

Edwards, Jay D. *Louisiana's Remarkable French Vernacular Architecture, 1700–1900.* Baton Rouge: Louisiana State University Press, 1988.

———. "The Origins of Creole Architecture." *Winterthur Portfolio* 29, nos. 2/3 (1994): 155–99.

Egerton, Douglas R. *Gabriel's Rebellion: The Virginia Slave Conspiracies of 1800 and 1802*. Chapel Hill: University of North Carolina Press, 1993.

———. "'Why They Did Not Preach Up This Thing': Denmark Vesey and Revolutionary Theology." *South Carolina Historical Magazine* 100, no. 4 (October 1999): 298–318.

———. Review of David Robertson's *Denmark Vesey*. *South Carolina Historical Magazine* 101, no. 2 (April 2000): 155–56.

*Encyclopedia of Louisiana*. St. Clair Shores, Mich.: Somerset, 1999.

Everett, Donald Edward. "Free Persons of Color in Colonial Louisiana." *Louisiana History* 7, no. 1 (Winter 1966): 21–50.

———. "Free Persons of Color in New Orleans, 1803–1865." PhD diss., University of Tulane, 1952.

Fabre, Michel. "'Une émulation sans envie': la presse des Créoles de Couleur de la Nouvelle Orléans au 19è siècle." In *Creoles and Cajuns: French Louisiana = La Louisiane Française*, ed. Wolfgang Binder, 185–208. Frankfurt: Peter Lang, 1998.

Fattier, Dominique. *Le Créole haïtien de poche*. Paris: Assimil, 2001.

Faust, Drew Gilpin. "Slavery in the American Experience." In *Before Freedom Came: African-American Life in the Antebellum South*, ed. Edward D. C. Campbell Jr. Charlottesville: University Press of Virginia, 1991.

Fick, Carolyn E. *The Making of Haiti: The Saint-Domingue Revolution from Below*. Knoxville: University of Tennessee Press, 1990.

Fiehrer, Thomas. "The African Presence in Colonial Louisiana: An Essay on the Continuity of Caribbean Culture." In *Louisiana's Black Heritage*, ed. Robert R. Macdonald, John R. Kemp, and Edward F. Hass, 3–31. New Orleans: Louisiana State Museum, 1979.

———. "From La Tortue to La Louisiane: An Unfathomed Legacy." In *The Road to Louisiana*, ed. Carl A. Brasseaux and Glenn R. Conrad, 1–30. Lafayette: Center for Louisiana Studies, University of Southwestern Louisiana, 1992.

———. "Saint-Domingue/Haiti: Louisiana's Caribbean Connection." *Louisiana History* 30, no. 4 (Fall 1989): 419–37.

Foner, Laura. "The Free People of Color in Louisiana and St. Domingue: A Comparative Portrait of Two Three-Caste Slave Societies." *Journal of Social History* 30, no. 3 (1970): 423–30.

Forsyth, Alice D. "Santo Domingo Passports." *New Orleans Genesis* 20, no. 78 (March 1981): 235–40; no. 79 (June 1981): 349–54; no. 80 (September 1981): 409–16; 21, no. 81 (January 1982); no. 82 (March 1982): 144–47.

Fortier, Alcée. "The French Language in Louisiana and the Negro-French Dialect." *Transactions of the Modern Language Association of America 1884–85*, 2 (1886): 96–111.

———. *A History of Louisiana*. 1904. 5 vols. Baton Rouge: Claitor's Publishing Division, 1985.

———. *Literature, Customs and Dialects, History and Education*. New Orleans: F. F. Hansel, 1894.

Fossier, Albert E. *The New Orleans Glamour Period, 1800–1840: A History of the Conflicts of Nationalities, Languages, Religion, Morals, Culture, Laws, Politics, and Economics during the Formative Period of New Orleans*. New Orleans: Pelican, 1957.

Fouchard, Jean. *Artistes et répertoires des Scènes de Saint-Domingue*. Port-au-Prince: Henri Deschamps, 1988.

———. *Plaisirs de Saint-Domingue*. Port-au-Prince: Henri Deschamps, 1988.

———. *Le théâtre à Saint-Domingue*. Port-au-Prince: Henri Deschamps, 1988.

Gans, Herbert J. "Symbolic Ethnicity: The Future of Ethnic Groups and Cultures in America." In *On the Making of Americans: Essays in Honor of David Riesman*, ed.

Herbert J. Gans, Nathan Glazer, Joseph R. Gusfield, and Christopher Jencks. Philadelphia: University of Pennsylvania Press, 1979. Reprinted (with author's comments) in *Theories of Ethnicity: A Classical Reader*, ed. Werner Sollors, 425–59. New York: New York University Press, 1996.

Gardien, Kent. "The Domingan Kettle: Philadelphian-Émigré Planters in Alabama." *National Genealogical Society Quarterly* 76, no. 3 (September 1988): 173–87.

Gardner, W. J. *A History of Jamaica from Its Discovery by Christopher Columbus to the Year 1872*. London: T. Fisher Unwin Adelphi Terrace, 1909.

Garesché Holland, Dorothy. "Saint-Louis Families from the French West Indies." In *The French in the Mississippi Valley*, ed. John Francis McDermott, 41–58. Urbana: University of Illinois Press, 1965.

Gaspar, Barry, and David P. Geggus, eds. *A Turbulent Time: The French Revolution and the Greater Caribbean*. Bloomington: Indiana University Press, 1997.

Gayarré, Charles Etienne Arthur. *Historical Sketch of Pierre and Jean Laffite*. 1883. Austin: Pemberton Press, 1964.

———. *History of Louisiana*. 1903. New Orleans: Pelican, 1965.

Geggus, David P. "La céremonie du Bois Caïman." *Journal de L'Histoire Caribbénne* 25, nos. 1/2 (1991): 41–57.

———. "The French and Haitian Revolutions and Resistance to Slavery in the Americas: An Overview." *Revue Française d'Histoire d'Outre-Mer* 76, nos. 282–83 (1989): 107–24.

———. "Slave Society in the Sugar Plantation Zones of Saint-Domingue and the Revolution of 1791–93." *Slavery and Abolition* 20, no. 2 (August 1999): 31–46.

———. *Slavery, War, and Revolution: The British Occupation of Saint-Domingue, 1793–1798*. Oxford: Clarendon Press, 1982.

———, ed. *The Impact of the Haitian Revolution in the Atlantic World*. Columbia: University of South Carolina Press, 2001.

———. "The Caradeux and Colonial Memory." Geggus ed. *The Impact of the Haitian Revolution in the Atlantic World*. Columbia: University of South Carolina Press, 2001.

Gehman, Mary. *The Free People of Color of New Orleans: An Introduction*. New Orleans: Margaret Media, 1994.

Gehman, Mary, and Nancy Ries. *Women and New Orleans: A History*. New Orleans: Margaret Media, 1988.

Genovese, Eugene. *From Rebellion to Revolution: Afro-American Slave Revolts in the Making of the Modern World*. Baton Rouge: Louisiana State University Press, 1979.

Gill, James. *Lord of Misrule: Mardi Gras and the Politics of Race in New Orleans*. Jackson: University Press of Mississippi, 1997.

Girod, François. *Une fortune coloniale sous l'ancien régime: la famille Hécquet à Saint-Domingue, 1724–1794*. Paris: Les Belles Lettres, 1970.

———. *La vie quotidienne de la société créole: Saint-Domingue au XVIIIe siècle*. Paris: Hachette, 1972.

Goodman, Morris F. *A Comparative Study of Creole French Dialects*. London: Mouton, 1964.

Gould, Virginia Meacham. "In Defense of Their Creole Culture: The Free Creoles of Color of New Orleans, Mobile, and Pensacola." *Gulf Coast Historical Review* 9, no. 1 (Fall 1993): 26–46.

Grandière, Marcel. "Les réfugiés et les déportés des Antilles à Nantes sous la Révolution." *Bulletin de la Société d'Histoire de la Guadeloupe* 33–34 (3è–4è trimestre). Basse-Terre: Archives Départementales, 1977.

Gravette, Andrew. *Architectural Heritage of the Caribbean: An A–Z of Historic Buildings*. Kingston: Ian Randle, 2000.

Griolet, Patrick. *Cadjins et Créoles en Louisiane: Histoire et survivance d'une Francophonie*. Paris: Payot, 1986.

Guaita, Ovidio. *La Maison Coloniale*. Paris: Hazan, 1999.

Guerra y Sánchez, Ramiro. *Sugar and Society in the Caribbean: An Economic History of Cuban Agriculture*. New Haven: Yale University Press, 1964.

Guiberneau, Montserrat, and John Rex, eds. *The Ethnicity Reader: Nationalism, Multiculturalism, and Migration*. Cambridge: Polity Press, 1997.

Guicharnaud-Tollis, Michèle, ed. *Le sucre dans l'espace caraïbe hispanophone XIXe et XXe siècles*. Paris: L'Harmattan, 1998.

Haggy, James W., and Bertrand Van Ruymbeke. "The French Refugee Newspapers of Charleston." *South Carolina Historical Magazine* 97, no. 2 (April 1996): 139–48.

Hall, Gwendolyn Midlo. *Africans in Colonial Louisiana: The Development of Afro-Creole Culture in the Eighteenth Century*. Baton Rouge: Louisiana State University Press, 1992.

———. "The Formation of Afro-Creole Culture." In *Creole New Orleans: Race and Americanization*, ed. Arnold R. Hirsh and Joseph Logsdon, 58–90. Baton Rouge: Louisiana State University Press, 1992.

———. *Social Control in Slave Plantation Societies: A Comparison of St. Domingue and Cuba*. Baton Rouge: Louisiana State University Press, 1971.

Hanger, Kimberly. *Bounded Lives, Bounded Places: Free Black Society in Colonial New Orleans, 1769–1803*. Durham: Duke University Press, 1997.

———. "Patronage, Property, and Persistence: The Emergence of a Free Black Elite in Spanish New Orleans." *Slavery and Abolition* 17, no. 1 (April 1996): 44–64.

Harrison, J. A. "The Creole Patois of Louisiana." *American Journal of Philology* 3 (1882): 285–96.

Harvard, Gilles, and Cécile Vidal. *Histoire de l'Amérique Française*. Paris: Flammarion, 2003.

Hernández Guerrero, Dolores. *La revolución haitiana y el fin de un sueño colonial (1791–1801)*. México: Universidad Nacional Autónoma de México, 1997.

Herskovits, Melville J. *The Myth of the Negro Past*. Boston: Beacon Press, 1941.

———. *The New World Negro*. Bloomington: Indiana University Press, 1966.

Hirsh, Arnold R., and Joseph Logsdon, eds. *Creole New Orleans: Race and Americanization*. Baton Rouge: Louisiana State University Press, 1992.

Holm, John. *Pidgins and Creoles: Theory and Structure.* 2 vols. Cambridge: Cambridge University Press, 1988.

Holmes, Jack D. L. "The Abortive Slave Revolt at Pointe Coupée, Louisiana, 1795." *Louisiana History* 11, no. 4 (Fall 1970): 341–62.

Houdaille, Jacques. "French Refugees in the United States, 1790–1810." *National Genealogical Society* 51, no. 4 (December 1963): 209–13.

Hull, Alexander. "Evidence for the Original Unity of North American French Dialects." *Revue de Louisiane* 1 (1973): 59–70.

Hunt, Alfred. *Haiti's Influence on Antebellum America: Slumbering Volcano in the Caribbean.* Baton Rouge: Louisiana State University Press, 1988.

Hurbon, Laennec, ed. *L'insurrection des esclaves de Saint-Domingue.* Paris: Karthala, 2000.

Ingersoll, Thomas N. *Mammon and Manon in Early New Orleans: The First Slave Society in the Deep South, 1718–1819.* Knoxville: University of Tennessee Press, 1999.

Jackson, George C. "Some French Marriages (1780–1899) at Mayaguez, Puerto Rico." *New Orleans Genesis* 40 (October 2001): 301–10.

James, C.R.L. *The Black Jacobins: Toussaint L'Ouverture and the San Domingo Revolution.* 1963. New York: Vintage, 1989.

Jeanty, Edner A. *Speak Creole in No Time: And Get a Little Taste of Haitian Culture.* Port-au-Prince: Editions La Presse Evangélique, n.d.

Johnson, Jerah. "New Orleans's Congo Square: An Urban Setting for Early Afro-American Culture Formation." *Louisiana History* (Spring 1991): 117–57. Reprinted under the title *Congo Square in New Orleans.* New Orleans: Louisiana Landmarks Society, 1995.

Kein, Sybil, ed. *Creole: The History and Legacy of Louisiana's Free People of Color.* Baton Rouge: Louisiana State University Press, 2000.

Kendall, John Smith. "The Foreign Language Press in New Orleans." *Louisiana Historical Quarterly* 3 (1929): 363–380.

———. *History of New Orleans.* 3 vols. Chicago: Lewis, 1922.

Kilbourne, Richard Holcombe, Jr. *A History of the Louisiana Civil Code: The Formative Years, 1803–1839.* Baton Rouge: Paul M. Herbert Law Center Publication Institute of Louisiana State University, 1987.

King, Grace. *Creole Families of New Orleans.* New York: Macmillan, 1921.

———. *New Orleans: The Place and the People.* New York: Macmillan, 1895.

Klein, Rachel. *Unification of a Slave State: The Rise of the Planter Class in the South Carolina Backcountry, 1760–1808.* Chapel Hill: University of North Carolina Press, 1990.

Knight, Franklin W. *The Caribbean: The Genesis of a Fragmented Nationalism.* New York: Oxford University Press, 1990.

Lachance, Paul F. "The 1809 Immigration of Saint-Domingue Refugees to New Orleans: Reception, Integration, and Impact." In *The Road to Louisiana*, ed. Brasseaux and Conrad, 245–84. Lafayette: Center for Louisiana Studies, University of Southwestern Louisiana, 1992.

———. "The Foreign French." In *Creole New Orleans: Race and Americanization*, ed. Arnold Hirsh and Joseph Logsdon, 101–30. Baton Rouge: Louisiana State University Press, 1992.

———. "The Formation of a Three-Caste Society." *Social Science History* 18, no. 2 (Summer 1994): 211–42.

———. "Intermarriage and French Cultural Persistence in Late Spanish and Early American New Orleans." *Histoire Sociale/Social History* 15 (1982): 47–81.

———. "The Politics of Fear: French Louisiana and the Slave Trade, 1786–1809." *Political Science Quarterly* 1 (1979): 166–96. Available on Multi-Media *African American Migration Experience*. New York Public Library Digital Gallery. http://www.inmotionaame.org/texts/index.cfm?migration=5&topic=99&type=text.

———. "Repercussions of the Haitian Revolution in Louisiana." In *The Impact of the Haitian Revolution in the Atlantic World*, ed. David P. Geggus, 209–30. Columbia: University of South Carolina Press, 2001.

———. "La revolution haïtienne dans la mémoire des réfugiés de la Nouvelle Orléans." In *Mémoire collective dans l'Amérique pré-industrielle*, ed. Elise Marienstras and Marie-Jeanne Rossignol, 25–33. Paris: Berg International, 1994.

———. "Les vaincus de la révolution haïtienne en quête d'un refuge: de Saint-Domingue à Cuba (1803), de Cuba à la Nouvelle Orléans (1809)." *Revue de la Société Haïtienne d'Histoire*, de géographie et de géologie 37 (mars 1980): 15–30.

———. "Were Saint-Domingue Refugees a Distinctive Cultural Group in Antebellum New Orleans? Evidence from Patterns and Startegies of Property Holding." *Revista/Review Interamericana* 29, nos. 1–4 (1999): 171–92.

Laguerre, Michel S. *American Odyssey: Haitians in the United States*. Ithaca: Cornell University Press, 1984.

———. *Voodoo and Politics*. New York: St. Martin's Press, 1989.

———. *Voodoo Heritage*. London: Sage, 1980.

Lane, Mills. *Architecture of the Old South*. New York: Abbeville Press, 1993.

Laurent, Gérard M. *Contribution à l'histoire de Saint-Domingue*. Port-au-Prince: Imprimerie la Phalange, 1971.

Laurent-Ropa, Denis. *Haïti: Une colonie française, 1625–1802*. Paris: L'Harmattan, 1993.

Le Gardeur, René J. *The First New Orleans Theatre, 1792–1803*. New Orleans: Leeward Books, 1963.

———. "The Origins of the Sugar Industry in Louisiana." In *Green Fields: Two Hundred Years of Louisiana Sugar*, 1–28. Lafayette: Center for Louisiana Studies, University of Southwestern Louisiana, 1980.

———. "Les premières années du théâtre à la Nouvelle Orléans." *Comptes Rendus de l'Athénée Louisianais* (Mars 1954).

———. "The Refugees from Saint-Domingue." *New Orleans Genesis* 2, no. 6 (1963): 175–76.

Le Riverand, Julio. *Historia económica de Cuba*. Havana: Instituto Cubano del Libro, 1974.

Lestrade, Paul. "José Marti et la Révolution Française." In *De la Révolution française aux révolutions créoles et nègres*, ed. Michel Martin and Alain Yacou. Paris: Editions Caribéennes, 1989.

Levet Gerbel, Christine. "Information from the Family of Jean Lafitte, Buccaneer." *New Orleans Genesis* 40, no. 158 (April 2001): 101–5.

Littlefield, Daniel C. "Slavery in French Louisiana: From Gallic Colony to American Territory." In *Creoles and Cajuns: French Louisiana = La Louisiane Française*, ed. Wolfgang Binder, 91–114. Frankfurt: Peter Lang, 1998.

Lofgren, Charles A. *The Plessy Case: A Legal-Historical Interpretation*. New York: Oxford University Press, 1987.

Logan, Rayford W. *The Diplomatic Relations of the United States with Haiti, 1776–1891*. Chapel Hill: University of North Carolina Press, 1941.

Logsdon, Joseph, and Caryn Cossé Bell. "The Americanization of Black New Orleans, 1850–1900." In *Creole New Orleans: Race and Americanization*, ed. Arnold R. Hirsh and Joseph Logsdon, 201–61. Baton Rouge: Louisiana State University Press, 1992.

Logsdon, Joseph, and Lawrence Powell. "Rodolphe Lucien Desdunes: Forgotten Organizer of the *Plessy* Protest." In *Sunbelt Revolution: The Historical Progression of the Civil Rights Struggle in the Gulf South, 1866–2000*, ed. Samuel C. Hyde Jr., 42–70. Gainesville: University Press of Florida, 2003.

*Louisiana and the Deep South*. Hawthorn, Victoria, Australia: Lonely Planet, 2001.

Lubin, Maurice. "Les exiles antillais dans les cimetières St. Louis." *Revue de la Louisiane* 3 (1974): 83–88.

Lugue de Sanchez, Maria Dolores. "Les Français réfugiés à Porto Rico." In *De la Révolution française aux révolutions créoles et nègres*, ed. Michel Martin and Alain Yacou, 41–48. Paris: Editions Caribéennes, 1989.

Madiou, Thomas. *Histoire d'Haiti*. 1847. Port-au-Prince: Les Editions Fardin, 1981.

Malone, Dumas. *The Sage of Monticello*. Vol. 6 of *Jefferson and His Time*. New York: Little, Brown, 1981.

Marigny, Bernard. "Reflections on the Campaign of General Andrew Jackson in Louisiana in 1814 and 1815." *Louisiana Historical Quarterly* 6 (January 1923): 70–80.

Marino, Samuel J. "Early French Newspapers in New Orleans." *Louisiana History* 7, no. 4 (Fall 1966): 309–22.

Martin, François Xavier. *The History of Louisiana from the Earliest Period*. New Orleans: James A. Gresham, 1882.

Martin, Joan M. "*Plaçage* and the Louisiana *Gens de Couleur Libre*: How Race and Sex Defined the Lifestyles of Free Women of Color." In *Creole*, ed. Sybil Kein, 57–70. Baton Rouge: Louisiana State University Press, 2000.

Martin, Michel, and Alain Yacou, eds. *De la Révolution française aux révolutions créoles et nègres*. Paris: Editions Caribéennes, 1989.

Massio, Roger. "Les biens et le genre de vie d'une famille noble à Saint-Domingue et en Bigorre (1745–1836)." PhD diss., Université de Toulouse, 1950.

Maurel, Blanche. *Saint-Domingue et la Révolution Française: Les représentants des colonies en France de 1789 à 1795*. Paris: Presses Universitaires de France, 1943.

McConnell, Roland C. *Negro Troops of Antebellum Louisiana: A History of the Battalion of Free Men of Color*. Baton Rouge: Louisiana State University Press, 1968.

Melville, Annabelle M. *Louis William DuBourg, Bishop of Louisiana and the Floridas, Bishop of Montauban, and Archbishop of Besançon*. 2 vols. Chicago: Loyola University Press, 1986.

Mercier, Alfred. "Etude sur la langue créole en Louisiane." *Comptes rendus de l'Athénée Louisianais* 1 (1880): 378–83.

Métral, Antoine. *Histoire de l'expansion des Français à Saint-Domingue*. Paris: Khartala, 1985.

Métraux, Alfred. *Voodoo in Haiti*. New York: Oxford University Press, 1959.

Mills, Gary. *The Forgotten People: Cane River's Creoles of Color*. Baton Rouge: Louisiana State University Press, 1977.

Mitchell, Reid. *All on a Mardi Gras Day: Episodes in the History of New Orleans Carnival*. Cambridge: Harvard University Press, 1995.

Morazan, Ronald. *Biographical Sketches of the Veterans of the Battalion of New Orleans, 1814–1815*. Baton Rouge: Legacy, 1979.

Mosadomia, Fehintola. "The Origin of Louisiana Creole." In *Creole*, ed. Sybil Kein, 223–43. Baton Rouge: Louisiana State University Press, 2000.

Naudon, Paul. *La Franc-Maçonnerie*. Paris: Presses Universitaires de France, 1963.

Neumann, Ingrid. "Le Créole des blancs en Louisiane." *Etudes Créoles* 6, no. 2 (1984): 63–78.

Neumann-Holzschuh, Ingrid. "Structures lexicales du Cajun et du Créole louisianais." In *Creoles and Cajuns: French Louisiana = La Louisiane Française*, ed. Wolfgang Binder, 53–82. Frankfurt: Peter Lang, 1998.

———, ed. *Textes anciens en Créole Louisianais*. Hamburg: H. Buske, 1987.

Nicaud, René R. "The French Colonists from St. Domingue and, in particular, Louis Moreau Lislet." *New Orleans Genesis* 29 (January 1990): 1–11.

Noble, Stuart G., and Arthur G. Nuhrah. "Education in Colonial Louisiana." *Louisiana Historical Quarterly* 32 (1949): 759–76.

Osborne, Francis J. *History of the Catholic Church in Jamaica*. Chicago: Loyola University Press, 1988.

Ott, Thomas O. *The Haitian Revolution, 1789–1804*. Knoxville: University of Tennessee Press, 1973.

Pearson, Edward A., ed. *Designs against Charleston: The Trial Records of the Denmark Vesey Slave Conspiracy of 1822*. Chapel Hill: University of North Carolina Press, 1999.

Pérez, Francisco. *El Café: Historia de su Cultivo y Explotación en Cuba*. Havana: Jesús Montero Editor, 1944.

Perez, Luis M. "French Refugees to New Orleans in 1809 (with documents)." *Publications of the Southern History Association* 9 (1905): 293–310.

Pinalie, Pierre. *Dictionnaire élémentaire Français-Créole*. Paris: L'Harmattan, 1992.

Plauche Dart, Henry. "The Place of the Civil Law in Louisiana." *Tulane Law Review* 4, no. 2 (February 1930): 163–77.

Pluchon, Pierre. *Toussaint Louverture: De l'esclavage au pouvoir*. Paris: Fayard, 1989.

———. *Vaudou, sorciers, empoisonneurs: De Saint-Domingue à Haïti*. Paris: Karthala, 1987.

Porter, Betty. "The History of Negro Education in Louisiana." *Louisiana Historical Quarterly* 25 (July 1942): 728–821.

Ramos Guedez, José Marcial. "L'insurrection nègre de Coro en 1795 au Venezuela." In *De la Révolution française aux révolutions créoles et nègres*, ed. Michel Martin and Alain Yacou, 53–60. Paris: Editions Caribéennes, 1989.

Ramsay, Jack C., Jr. *Jean Laffite, Prince of Pirates*. Austin: Eakin Press, 1996.

Rankin, David. "The Politics of Caste: Free Colored Leadership in New Orleans during the Civil War." In *Louisiana's Black Heritage*, ed. Robert R. Macdonald et al., 107–46. New Orleans: Louisiana State Museum, 1979.

Read, William A. *Louisiana's French*. Rev. ed. Baton Rouge: Louisiana State University Press, 1963.

Rehder, John B. *Delta Sugar: Louisiana's Vanishing Plantation Landscape*. Baltimore: Johns Hopkins University Press, 1999.

———. "Sugar Plantation Settlements of Southern Louisiana: A Cultural Geography." PhD diss., Louisiana State University, 1971.

Relouzat, Raymond. *Tradition orale et imaginaire créole*. Fort-de-France: Ibis Rouge Editions, 1998.

Remini, Robert V. *The Battle of New Orleans*. New York: Penguin, 1999.

Rossignol, Marie-Jeanne. *Le ferment nationaliste: Aux origines de la politique extérieure des Etats-Unis, 1789–1812*. Paris: Belin, 1994.

Saint-Louis, Fridolin. *Le Vodou haïtien: Reflet d'une société bloquée*. Paris: L'Harmattan, 2000.

Saxon, Lyle. *Fabulous New Orleans*. 1928. Gretna, La.: Pelican, 1995.

———. *Lafitte the Pirate*. 1930. Gretna, La.: Pelican, 1989.

Schafer, Daniel L. "A Class of People Neither Freemen Nor Slaves: From Spanish to American Race Relations in Florida, 1821–1861." *Journal of Social History* 26, no. 3 (Spring 1993): 587–609.

Schafer, Judith Kelleher. *Becoming Free, Remaining Free: Manumission and Enslavement in New Orleans, 1846–1862*. Baton Rouge: Louisiana State University Press, 2003.

Scott, Rebecca J. "Defining the Boundaries of Freedom in the World of Cane: Cuba, Brazil, and Louisiana after Emancipation." *American Historical Review* 99, no. 1 (February 1994): 70–102.

———. "Fault Lines, Color Lines, and Party Lines: Race, Labor, and Collective Action in Louisiana and Cuba, 1862–1912." In *Beyond Slavery: Explorations of Race, Labor, and Citizenship in Postemancipation Societies*, ed. Frederick Cooper, Thomas C. Holt, and Rebecca J. Scott, 61–106. Chapel Hill: University of North Carolina Press, 2000.

———. "Se battre pour ses droits: Ecritures, litiges et discrimination raciale en Louisiane (1888–1899)." *Cahiers du Brésil Contemporain* 53/54 (2003): 175–210.

———. "Stubborn and Disposed to Stand Their Ground: Black Militia, Sugar Workers, and the Dynamics of Collective Action in the Louisiana Sugar Bowl, 1863–1887." *Slavery and Abolition* 20, no. 1 (April 1999): 103–26.

Senter, Caroline. "Creole Poets on the Verge of a Nation." In *Creole*, ed. Sybil Kein, 276–94. Baton Rouge: Louisiana State University Press, 2000.

Sexton, Richard. *New Orleans: Elegance and Decadence.* San Francisco: Chronicle Books, 1993.

Sitterson, J. Carlyle. *Sugar Country: The Cane Sugar Industry in the South*, 1753–1950. Lexington: University of Kentucky Press, 1953.

Slesin, Suzanne, Stafford Cliff, Jack Berthelot, Martine Gaumé, and Daniel Rozensztroch. *Caribbean Style*. New York: C. N. Potter, 1985.

Smith, J. Frazer. *White Pillars: Early Life and Architecture of the Lower Mississippi Valley Country*. New York: William Helburn, 1941.

Smither, Nelle. *A History of the English Theater in New Orleans*. New York: Benjamin Bloom, 1964.

Sollors, Werner, ed. *Theories of Ethnicity: A Classical Reader.* New York: New York University Press, 1996.

Stein, Robert Louis. *The French Sugar Business in the Eighteenth Century*. Baton Rouge: Louisiana State University Press, 1988.

Sterkx, H. E. *The Free Negro in Ante-Bellum Louisiana*. Rutherford: Fairleigh Dickinson University Press, 1972.

Sternberg, Mary Ann. *Along the River Road: Past and Present on Louisiana's Historic Byway*. Rev. ed. Baton Rouge: Louisiana State University Press, 2001.

Stoddard, Lothrop. *The French Revolution in San Domingo*. Boston: Houghton Mifflin, 1914.

Sullivan, Lester. "The Unknown Rodolphe Desdunes: Writings in the New Orleans *Crusader*." Centenary meeting of the Louisiana Historical Association, Baton Rouge, March 17, 1990. *Xavier Review* 10, nos. 1/2 (1990).

———. "Composers of Color of Nineteenth-Century New Orleans: The History behind the Music." In *Creole*, ed. Sybil Kein, 71–100. Baton Rouge: Louisiana State University Press, 2000.

Sullivan-González, Douglass, and Charles Reagan Wilson. *The South and the Caribbean*. Jackson: University Press of Mississippi, 2001.

Sullivan-Holleman, Elizabeth, and Isabel Hillery Cobb. *The Saint-Domingue Epic: The Rossignol des Dunes and Family Alliances*. Bay St. Louis, Miss.: Nightingale Press, 1995.

Tallant, Robert. *Mardi Gras as It Was*. 1947. Gretna: Pelican, 2000.

———. *The Pirate Lafitte and the Battle of New Orleans*. 1951. Gretna: Pelican, 1994.

———. *Voodoo in New Orleans*. 1946. Gretna, La.: Pelican, 1998.

Thibau, Jacques. *Le Temps de Saint-Domingue: l'esclavage et la revolution*. Paris: Lattès, 1989.

Thomas, J. J. *The Theory and Practice of Creole Grammar*. Port of Spain: Chronicle Publishing Office, 1869.

Todd, Loreto. *Pidgins and Creoles*. London: Routledge, 1974.

Toledano, Roulhac, and Mary Louise Christovich. *Faubourg Tremé and the Bayou Road: New Orleans Architecture.* Vol. 6. Gretna, La.: Pelican, 2003.

Transill, Charles G. *The United States and Santo Domingo, 1798–1873*. Baltimore: Johns Hopkins University Press, 1938.

Tregle, Joseph George, Jr. "Creoles and Americans." In *Creole New Orleans: Race and Americanization*, ed. Arnold R. Hirsh and Joseph Logsdon. Baton Rouge: Louisiana State University Press, 1992.

———. "Early New Orleans Society: A Reappraisal." *Journal of Southern History* 18 (February 1952): 20–36.

———. *Louisiana in the Age of Jackson: A Clash of Cultures and Personalities*. Baton Rouge: Louisiana State University Press, 1999.

———. "Political Reinforcement of Ethnic Dominance in Louisiana, 1812–1845." In *The Americanization of the Gulf Coast, 1803–1850*, ed. Lucius F. Ellsworth, 78–87. Mobile: University of Southern Alabama, 1972.

Usner, Daniel H., Jr. *Indians, Settlers, and Slaves in a Frontier Exchange Economy: The Lower Mississippi Valley before 1783*. Chapel Hill: University of North Carolina Press, 1992.

———. "Slave Society in the Sugar Plantation Zones of Saint-Domingue and the Revolution of 1791–93." *Slavery and Abolition* 20 (August 1999): 31–46.

Vaissière, Pierre de. *Saint-Domingue: la société et la vie créole sous l'ancien régime (1629–1789)*. Paris: Perrin, 1909.

Valdman, Albert. *Le créole: structure, statut et origine*. Paris: Editions Klincksieck, 1978.

———. "Le parler vernaculaire des isolats français en Amérique du Nord." *Revue de Louisiane/Louisiana Review* 1 (1973): 43–58.

———. "The Place of Louisiana Creole among New World French Creoles." In *Creoles of Color of the Gulf Coast*, ed. James H. Dormon, 144–65. Knoxville: University of Tenessee Press, 1996.

Villeré, Sidney L. "The Enterprising Career of Don Pablo Lanusse in Colonial New Orleans, and a Genealogy of His Descendants." *New Orleans Genesis* 2, no. 7 (June 1963): 243–47.

Vlach, John Michael. "Plantation Landscapes of the Antebellum South." In *Before Freedom Came: African-American Life in the Antebellum South*, ed. D. C. Campbell Jr., 21–50. Charlottesville: University Press of Virginia, 1991.

———. "Sources of the Shotgun House: African and Caribbean Antecedents for Afro-American Architecture." 2 vols. PhD diss., Indiana University, 1975.

Wall, Bennet H., ed. *Louisiana: A History*. Arlington Heights, Ill.: Forum Press, 1984.

Warne Price, Nelly. "Le Spectacle de la Rue Saint Pierre." *Louisiana Historical Quarterly* 1, no. 3 (January 1918): 215–23.

Watts, Beulah De Verière Smith, and Jane Lucas De Grummond. *Solitude: Life on a*

*Plantation in Louisiana, 1788–1968*. Baton Rouge: Claitor's Publishing Division, 1970.

West, Robert. *An Atlas of Louisiana Surnames of French and Spanish Origins*. Baton Rouge: Louisiana State University Press, 1986.

Widmer, Ted. "The Invention of a Memory: Congo Square and African Music in Nineteenth-Century New Orleans." *Revue Française d'Etudes Américaines* 98 (December 2003): 69–78.

Williams, Eric. *The Negro in the Caribbean*. 1942. New York: Negro Universities Press (Greenwood), 1969.

Wilson, Charles Reagan, and William Ferris, eds. *Encyclopedia of Southern Culture*. Chapel Hill: University of North Carolina Press, 1989.

Wilson, Samuel, Jr. *The Architecture of Colonial Louisiana*. Lafayette: Center for Louisiana Studies University of Southwestern Louisiana, 1987.

———. *Gulf Coast Architecture*. 82–130. Louisiana Collection, Tulane University, New Orleans.

Wilson, Samuel, Jr., Roulhac Toledano, Sally Kittredge Evans, and Marie Louise Christovich. *The Creole Faubourgs: New Orleans Architecture*. Vol. 4. Gretna, La.: Pelican, 1996.

Wittler Ross, Nola Mae. *Jean Lafitte, Louisiana Buccaneer*. Lake Charles, La: n.p., 1990.

Yacou, Alain. "L'émigration à Cuba des colons français de Saint-Domingue au cours de la révolution." PhD diss., Université de Bordeaux, 1975.

———, ed. *Créoles de la Caraïbe* Paris: Karthala, 1996.

Zeringue, Earlene L., ed. "Masonic Lodges of Ile Saint Domingue 1808." *New Orleans Genesis* 20 (September 1981): 473–79.

Zitomersky, Joseph. "Race, esclavage et émancipation: la Louisiane créole à l'intersection des mondes français, antillais et américain." In *Esclavages et abolitions: Mémoires et systèmes de représentation*, ed. Marie-Christine Rochman. Paris: Karthala, 2000.

## Web Sites

Amistad Research Center, Tulane University, New Orleans <http://www.amistadresearchcenter.org>

Archives of the Archdiocese of New Orleans <http://www.archdiocese-no.org/archives>

Association de Généalogie d'Haïti <http://www.agh.qc.ca>

Historic New Orleans Collection <http://www.hnoc.org>

Louisiana State University, Baton Rouge <http://www.lib.lsu.edu>

National Park Service <http://www.cr.nps.gov/nr/travel/louisiana/architecture.htm>

New Orleans Public Library <http://nutrias.org>

New Orleans Notarial Archives <http://www.notarialarchives.org>

New York Public Library Digital Library Collection. <http://www.digital.nypl.org/digital/>

Saint-Domingue Special Interest Group, New Orleans <http://freepages.genealogy.rootsweb.com/saintdomingue>

Special Collections, Tulane University, New Orleans <http://specialcollections.tulane.edu>

# Index

CPSIA information can be obtained
at www.ICGtesting.com
Printed in the USA
LVHW091054061218
599264LV00011B/2/P